EXOCONSCIOUS HUMANS

EXOCONSCIOUS HUMANS

Will Free Will Survive in an Increasingly Non-Human World?

REBECCA HARDCASTLE WRIGHT

Waterside Productions

Printed in the United States of America

First Printing, 2021

ISBN-13: 978-1-951805-60-9 print edition
ISBN-13: 978-1-951805-61-6 ebook edition

Waterside Productions
2055 Oxford Ave
Cardiff, CA 92007
www.waterside.com

"Clearly Silicon Valley wants the future human to be controlled by computers. They say that. The alternate to a technocratic "matrix" is an evolution in consciousness. Humanity rises – evolves – to a new level of personal awareness and capability. This book explains how that may well be happening with the help of others who have already made the evolutionary leap and are here to help. Very provocative reading."

—John L. Petersen, Founder and President,
The Arlington Institute

"A first of its kind and couldn't be more timely. This should be read by everyone on the globe right now as humanity moves towards sweeping change. Rebecca Hardcastle Wright gives the reader a truthful, experiential, intellectual and rare look deep inside what it means to experience "contact" and how this worldview exposes the reader to a limitless potential even beyond what transhumanism offers."

—Susan A. Manewich, President of New Energy Movement,
Director of The Nui Foundation for Moral Technology

"*Exoconscious Humans* is an intriguing exploration of human consciousness, mysticism, extraterrestrial contact, quantum physics, artificial intelligence, biology, neuroscience, psychology, and the future of humanity. Rebecca Hardcastle Wright presents a fascinating, well-researched, wide-ranging, and thought-provoking essay on the possibilities for humanity's exoconscious future."

—David Gunning, AI expert

"At this time in human history, there are no greater or awe-inspiring questions than those addressed in *Exoconscious Humans*. Rebecca Hardcastle Wright's message is timely, urgent, and thoughtful. She places in your hands the guidance required to navigate what is to come."

—William Henry, author, investigative mythologist, TV presenter

"Time will tell whether Hardcastle Wright's creative rearrangement and interpretation of historical and current narratives that shape the human understanding of consciousness will positively contribute to enacting transhuman communication. Courageously written and revealing."

—Helmut Wautischer, President, Karl Jaspers Society of North America, Philosophy, Sonoma State University

"Dr. Hardcastle Wright brilliantly explores the complexity and profound issues facing humanity as we become even more entrenched in this technological age. She explores what it means to be human and how our choices now will decide our future as a species. A fascinating and compelling read."

—Mary Rodwell, Principal, Australian Close Encounter Network ACERN, Author of *Awakening & The New Human*

"If one man stepping on the moon was a "giant leap for mankind", meeting our galactic neighbors will launch a magnificent new age for humanity to live together in peace while honoring Mother Earth and jumpstarting psychological and spiritual growth for all. Rebecca takes us on a visionary ride into the future and the enormous potential of meeting our neighbors in the stars."

—Ronald Peters, MD, MPH, Mind Body Medicine Center, Scottsdale, Arizona

"Rebecca Hardcastle Wright lays out a comprehensive and precise definition of exoconsciousness, the state of mind and psychic condition of those who experience the existence of and establish habitual communication with non-human forms of intelligence within the non-local quantic field. At the outset, she sets exoconsciousness apart from transhumanism and its scientific and technological notions and promises which threaten to reduce the human species to a subservient role in a new reality controlled by artificial organisms. She also shows exoconsciousness to be far ahead of the more empirical and investigative approach of ufology. Erudite, crisply written in an elegant and eloquent style, enlivened by personal recollections and luminous metaphors, supported by profuse scientific references, this work is a crucial signpost on the path towards a full understanding of consciousness and a harbinger of our future. The author reviews many of the modern theories in this domain and supplements them from a transcending perspective encompassing the full human dimension by unveiling its infinite scope."

—Come Carpentier, author, Convener of the Editorial Board, *World Affairs*, Associate IISES (Vienna, Austria), Consultant India Foundation, New Delhi India

"One of the hot new sub-fields in philosophy these days has to do with the impact of AI, the meta, and trans-human on philosophy. Rebecca Hardcastle Wright can be counted amongst the pioneers in this movement and I heartily endorse her work and her web work on exoconsciousness.com."

—Alan M. Olson, Professor Emeritus, Philosophy of Religion, Boston University

"Rebecca Hardcastle has done it again with her third book, breaking new ground in the exoconscious community and pointing out discoveries and developments in our society that impact every one of us at a time of monumental change. A must-read for everyone interested in the future of humanity."

—Mia Feroleto, Publisher of *New Observations Magazine*

"Rebecca shares a deep understanding of what it means to anchor the shared field of cosmic consciousness–exoconsciousness-and to connect our human consciousness with all of the multidimensional aspects of ourselves. The psychic intelligence and transhuman concepts that she shares leads the reader on a journey of thoughtful consideration and to a place of powerful, heartfelt pause."

—Sheila Seppi, Founder of SpiritWay Wellness, Conscious Awakening Series, author

"Language has always been the fundamental way the human family has communicated. Now there is more. In this work, Rebecca Hardcastle Wright has created a new epistemological and linguistic tool for humanity to express, re-define and transcend where we are headed as a cosmic species. Stunning, brave, and revolutionary. Do not – under any circumstances – miss this compelling read."

—Victor Viggiani, owner, news director, ZlandCommunications, international news service

"Rebecca is an excellent researcher in the area of consciousness and contact who also performs exceptional work with contactees. I highly recommend reading her new book where she explains the concept of Exoconsciousness while being up to date with new advances in technology."

—Gilda Moura, clinical psychologist, writer. Kairós Foundation, University of Illinois, a six-year study on Altered States of Consciousness and Brain Mapping

"A critically important book for this decade! Rebecca Hardcastle Wright frames the significance of Psychic Intelligence for our ever-evolving human species helping the reader recognize the value of their inner knowing. Staying grounded is paramount in our modern world as we interface with artificial intelligence more and more each year. As our species races into unfamiliar territory, new priorities must be established, that distinguish the real gift of being human. Understanding these consequences is more than important! Our survival depends on it."

—Jenifer W Stein, filmmaker

"When the world seems to be falling apart, this is a book that pulls it together as a map for a new level of consciousness. If we want to evolve the intelligence of the human race from endo (local mind) to exo-awareness (universal mind) Rebecca Hardcastle Wright lays out the way to activate a future civilization and wake ourselves to our true destiny as cosmic citizens."
— Alan Steinfeld, Producer of New Realities

"I compare Dr. Hardcastle's new book to an early ray of light presaging the end of the night. At the dawn of a new era, Dr. Hardcastle's work helps us recognize our spiritual and cosmic nature as to finally assume our presence in the universe."
—Rodolfo de Oliveira, Founder of academyfraternitatem.com

"Rebecca Hardcastle Wright is an expert in the field of Exoconsciousness and our human evolution. This book offers the possibility for us to consider where humanity is heading and what choices we have for our future. A must-read for all those who are still curious, courageous, and concerned. An "eye-opener" for sure."
—Darlene Van de Grift, Founder soul-union.com, Astrosociology, NYU

"Dr. Rebecca Hardcastle Wright was a dear friend of the late Dr. Edgar Mitchell, Apollo 14 astronaut and founder of the Institute of Noetic Sciences (IONS), the world's leading academic research institute on consciousness, PSI, and what is commonly called "the paranormal". Rebecca's new book, "Exoconscious Humans", continues the work of Dr. Mitchell and argues that human survival will depend on the continued development of human psychic abilities as we continue our growing interactions with multidimensional non-human intelligence. She argues that humanity needs to promote this symbiotic relationship which is essential for human survival. Her book is essential reading to properly understand the

relationship between human consciousness and our complex inter-
action with multidimensional intelligence."
—Reinerio Hernandez, JD, MCP, Ph.D. Candidate,
Director, Consciousness & Contact Research Institute

"Rebecca Hardcastle tackles and eloquently delves into an incredibly important topic and piece of work - artificial intelligence and
human consciousness as they define our evolution. A must-read for
anyone interested in expanding their consciousness to a whole new
level."
—Caroline Cory, film producer

"As long as I have known her Rebecca Hardcastle Wright does excellent research in an academic format. Her books are worth reading
and examining."
—Paola Leopizzi Harris, investigative journalist, author

"Exoconscious Humans is authored brilliantly by the preeminent
authority on the topic. Dr. Rebecca Hardcastle Wright creatively
and mindfully synthesizes science and culture, examining the poi-
gnant implications of transhumanism (the belief that the human
race can evolve beyond its current physical and mental limitations
through science and technology) and exoconsciousness (the study
of the origins, dimensions, and abilities of human consciousness
that link us directly to the cosmos and its inhabitants). With cred-
ible reports of technically advanced aerial and anomalous phenomena worldwide, combined with proposed visitations by intelligent
non-human entities, Dr. Hardcastle Wright broadens our knowledge and understanding, while providing a valuable vantage point
for humans to chart their future with conscious, thoughtful intent."
—Lynne D, Kitei, M.D., Global Health Educator,
Author, Filmmaker, CEO Phoenix Lights Network

TABLE OF CONTENTS

INTRODUCTION

A re your psychic abilities possible in a transhuman culture? Could artificial intelligence (AI) suppress or replace your natural human consciousness?

Let that sink in for a moment.

How much do you know about transhumanism and its effect on your everyday life? Do you identify with transhumanism and perceive AI as valuable? Do you view robots, AI, and social engineering dominant in your present and future?

Conversely, do you value your psychic intelligence and abilities? How aware are you of intuition, freedom of thought, enterprise, and creativity? Do you perceive these abilities as sourced in your consciousness and psychic intelligence? What about contact with non-physical beings? Do you appreciate your innate exoconscious ability to connect, communicate, and co-create with extraterrestrials (ETs) and multidimensionals? [1]

The purpose of this book is to guide you deeper into this reflection by comparing the present and possible future realities and distinctions between Exoconscious Humans and Transhumans.

For those who acknowledge and value their psychic intelligence, transhumanism may limit mental, spiritual, and physical health. Or not. The intent of this book is for you to decide. It presents the opportunity to clarify what it means to be either an Exoconscious

---

1 ETs refer to extraterrestrials, perceived as beings with a defined culture, timeline, and civilization. Multidimensionals refer to energetic beings such as angelic and dimensional.

Human or a Transhuman. I invite you to join me in an exploration of these two realities. Reading through referenced information, details, and life experiences will help assess how you fit into either culture—as an Exoconscious Human or a Transhuman.

The message from the community of the exoconscious—people who have ongoing contact, communication, and co-creation with ETs and multidimensionals—is that heightening their consciousness and psychic abilities is an exciting and valuable opportunity. They proclaim useful, proven, and reliable psychic abilities transfer into practical inventions and future innovations. They predict that split-second sharpened multidimensional intuition is better problem-solving. That may be your choice.

The message from Silicon Valley experts is that transhumanism is an exciting and invaluable opportunity for humans to integrate technology into our bodies and environment. They proclaim that life with robots, advanced data mining, and synthetic, digital biology create future innovations. They predict that factoring unsolvable equations with quantum computing is better problem-solving. That may be your choice.

And yet, neither choice needs to be mutually exclusive. Thoughtful consideration will be provided to creating, where appropriate, a common ground of interface and collaboration between Transhumans and Exoconscious Humans.

This introduction sounds carefree and effortless. Check a box. Choose a reality—Transhuman or Exoconscious Human. It is not. Instead, this detailed examination may be demanding of your focus and imagination. As you read this book, apply your reason and creativity to various scenarios and possibilities to create the future you choose.

I adopted a thoughtful approach to writing this book. The examination of transhumanism and psychic intelligence traveled with me from Washington, DC to Phoenix, Arizona.

Caught in a Closed Loop

Small spaces birth deep learning.

For two years, in a small apartment several miles off the congested Washington, DC, Capital Beltway, I struggled with studying the technology creation of transhumanism. Daily, like Persephone, a dystopian chasm of transhumanism swallowed me.

Like an addict, I digested technology's scientific research as well as its propaganda, its reality as well as its flimsy promises. When I shared my logical thought on the human ramifications of technology, others looked at me askance, as though I had a rogue mind, making faulty and outlandish connections and observations. Quickly, I learned to avoid the eye-glaze of the uninterested or "how dare you" stare. And yet, I was sure that I was on to something. I saw technology's transhuman achievements jumpstarting a redefining of human life.

At first, I was overwhelmed. I explored technology's labyrinth without Ariadne's red thread. I saw no way out of the transhuman destruction of our body, mind, spirit, and consciousness. I perceived dystopic transhuman reality as a societal Pacman devouring everything in sight: jobs, education, science, religion, health, arts, as well as everyday enjoyments like driving, reading, parenting, and even relationships and conversation. Transhuman culture would discard the leftover crumbs of human consciousness, taking hostage much that is human. Primarily, it was suppressing human consciousness.

Ironically, the deeper I read into transhumanism, the more frequent references emerged to ET and multidimensionals. These references included esoteric aspects like invisible craft navigated by consciousness and motherships as centralized systems, harboring scout craft. Other mentions included telepathically connected minds, downloaded and uploaded consciousness for data transmission, space travel via wormholes, and parallel and multiverse cosmologies. There was an allusion to science against the grain of materialism that included symbols transformed into the material, remote and hands-on energetic healing, and witness accounts of onboard craft replication, reproduction, and sustainability technology.

The power of these similarities magnified. What was going on? Were ET, multidimensional experiencers, and Transhumans conveying the same reality? If so, was there a difference in how they perceived reality? Or were they, in some way, related to one another? Specifically, was transhumanism deliberately linked to experiencer accounts broadcast through social and independent media for narrative marketing purposes? Were Transhumans using Hollywood and individual experiencer narratives to roll out a dominant culture of technology?

Conversely, was the cosmic consciousness of Exoconscious Humans dependent on the expansion of Transhuman science and technology? Were experiencers using science fiction, Transhuman language, and ideas to express their contact to a broader audience?

Were Exoconscious Humans and Transhumans cohabiting a closed-loop? As questions continued, a cybernetics double-bind situation grew apparent. Were experiencers intentionally complicit in transhumanism and vice versa? If so, how could Exoconscious Humans discern transhumanism, clarifying and addressing its consequences to human consciousness?

This book reveals radical differences between Exoconscious Humans and Transhumans. Each perspective promotes a preferred future. An in-depth examination of these preferences led to defining distinct differences. Yet, amid the differences, in some instances, a common ground emerged.

Future Exoconscious Humans

A central tenet is that Exoconscious Humans are essential for the survival and advancement of human consciousness. We have two choices. We can either recognize natural carbon-based human consciousness as a quantum field of possibility and potential. This field encompasses our bodies and beyond, where we transmit, receive, and create. It is the universal realm of conscious being—a nuanced and subtle reality—that births art, symbolism, ideas, philosophy, and science uniting humans and nature. Or we can default to Transhuman material science, which views the human brain function as a machine-like digital information system, void of spirituality, emotions, psychic abilities, and independent critical thinking. Strict material science maintains that all matter is unconscious and can be replicated through AI to create a linear uniform virtual reality.

Exoconsciousness is the innate human ability to contact, communicate, and co-create with ETs and multidimensionals. Consciousness as a quantum field phenomenon moves within and beyond our bodies. We experience it by connection, communication, and co-creation with beings that are both invisible and visible in our sensory reality. The survival and advancement of human consciousness validate knowing that we are not alone. It verifies that our consciousness participates with human as well as non-human, multidimensional beings.

Becoming an Exoconscious Humans is a birth push into a life of psychic knowing and abilities. Consciousness beyond the brain evolved in humans for eons. Ancients and indigenous also term it cosmic consciousness. But all too often, it was silenced by superstition, science, religion, and technology.

Exoconscious Humans are evolving out of necessity. We had to arrive—at this time.

Like the child born to save a faltering marriage, or family lineage, Exoconscious Humans emerge during the overwhelming threat of human survival unleashed by transhumanism. When a species smells the cadaverine scent of its demise—it fights back with birth.

Exoconscious Humans reorder the current playing field of reality. These humans are keenly aware that transhumanism narrows their ability and options to salvage their core being. Traditional salvation cards of science, technology, economics, politics, military, intelligence, pharmaceuticals, media, journalism, and religion are now face down, throwaway cards. All of these cards are complicit in transhumanism. All have either actively or passively colluded with the onslaught. Changing the primary sectors of society is no win. Exoconscious Humans are surrounded and dominated by Transhumans. Thus, all-out war against a Transhuman enemy is futile.

As awareness of the Transhuman directed demise of the human sets in—we are left with one choice—human consciousness, the ultimate wild card. Every individual possesses a wild card of consciousness and provides their own salvation. Playing the consciousness card involves stepping onto an individual inner path to access meaning, knowledge, information, and energy. It involves commitment to navigating the uncharted waters of our Transhuman world through intuition, psychic abilities, and accessing consciousness beyond the brain.

Humans revert to their consciousness—their innate ability to access, receive, communicate, and co-create within and beyond themselves through a field of consciousness. This field is second nature to humans—because it IS our Nature. We are energetic, conscious beings living in a field of intelligent beings. We are nature. And all of nature is alive.

Possibly no other human ability has been so controlled and denied than our innate consciousness. Four hundred years ago, the Enlightenment culture claimed materialism, handing over all academic knowledge to science, except for consciousness. The Church kept its stronghold on consciousness. And for 400 years, what did the church do with consciousness? Nothing.

By the early 90's, the church—hobbled by irrelevancy and corruption—lessened its grip on consciousness. During this critique of religion, universities recognized the possibilities and established departments of consciousness. Slowly. Meticulously. Unfortunately, these departments of consciousness predominantly honored science and technology, not spirituality or psychic abilities. These departments dissected brains. Overlaid metrics. Argued terminology. Accumulated databanks of information. And, when at a loss for a scientific explanation, turned to quantum science and proposed theories of particle physics.

To be fair, thirty years of academics and scientists claiming and researching consciousness achieved far and away more than the Church did by ignoring it for 400 years.

These corporate and government consciousness projects, often housed at universities, became the leading edge of transhumanism.

In so doing, they carved inroads into destroying what it means to be human, replacing it with a terrain of data mines, armies of neural implants, and artillery of computerized AI and synthetic biology.

Future Transhumans

Transhumanism promotes the development of technology for human enhancement. These technologies claim to advance human sensory, emotional, and cognitive abilities. They also claim to improve health and extend life spans. These technologies either temporarily or permanently integrate into the human body. Transhumanism promotes research in the fields of synthetic biology, brain science, robotics, AI, nanotechnology and geoengineering.

Julian Huxley first coined the term transhumanism in his 1957 essay of the same name.
The human species can, if it wishes, completely transcend itself—not only partially as with an individual here in one way, an individual there another way—but in its entirety, as humanity. We need a name for this new belief. Perhaps transhumanism will serve: man remaining man, but transcending himself, by realizing new possibilities of and for his human nature.[2]

Interestingly, like exoconsciousness, the inclinations and ideas of transhumanism are ancient. Its Transhuman concepts are related to the ancient practice of alchemy and its quest to modify matter. Early rudimentary alchemist lab experiments are now massive international projects funded by governments, corporations, and military—often housed in universities. The financial payoff for customizing humans rises with each success.

Over time, I observed mounting evidence of a developing transhumanist conquest over the human body and consciousness:

---

2   Huxley, *Transhumanism:: In New Bottles for New Wine* (London: Chatto & Windus, 1957), pp. 13–17.

- Humans, carbon-based flesh and blood, appear no match for the artificial network of sensors embedded in our bodies and connected to an Earth-space based system of linked satellites, HAARP, CERN, chemtrails, 5G, and nanotechnology in our food, clothing, and the air we breathe.
- The body's natural ability to heal appears no match for DNA bioweaponry and medicine.
- The comfort of cotton appears no match for offshore manufactured clothing laced with polymer nanotechnology.
- Disciplined learning and careful cognition appear no match for "genius" implants of brain technology, guaranteeing a top spot in university or career in an executive suite.
- The nurturing presence of a teacher or parent appears no match for technology-based, STEM gamified education beginning at birth, by a child fingering a tablet, whose first words spoken are, "Alexa," rather than mommy or daddy.
- A human's complicated emotional life appears no match for the emoji logo language of universalized feeling codes for communication.
- Human ingenuity appears no match for deep learning AI technology.
- Human hands appear no match for autonomous robotic devices.
- The religious and spiritual promise of the cord of eternal life into death appears no match for the immortality invitation to upload the contents of our consciousness and deep freeze our physical shell. Our mortal coil now a thing of the past.
- Millenniums of teachings on the spirit, the journey of the soul in the afterlife appear no match for immortal computer consciousness.
- The human community appears no match for disembodied consciousness communities and businesses staffed with smart contracts instead of employees.

As possibilities mounted, my one-sided perspective of transhumanism seized my mind, dampening my heart and closing off my rational mental circuits.

Healing Trauma = Trustworthy over Time

Studying transhumanism was an emotional slog. Digging into Transhuman topics engendered traumatic fear flashbacks. Again and again, I was hijacked by my analytic mind, wandering through circuitous routes of overwhelming information. Wise to my neural addiction as a trauma response, I admitted enjoyment of the mental freeze of "no way out" research. In many respects, analytical paralysis felt good—familiar to my neural system. My neural network, trained through decades of fear and trauma, liked the fear freeze. Ironically, it felt safe to be overwhelmed. I liked it. That is the irony of traumatized neural circuits—they love to run the rutted track of their familiar, no matter how harrowing. And my tracks ran deep like a field labyrinth tunneled into the earth where the devout pilgrim only sees the narrow trough ahead and behind. Carving a narrow gorge, my mind tunneled through transhumanism.

I burrowed in. Though mindful of my neural system's unhealthy desire for trauma and fear, I ignored all the warning signs. Aspects of my consciousness called for me to let go. Stop. Why I consciously chose to ignore the symptoms doesn't matter. The fact was—I did not stop researching.

Until gradually, scales fell from my eyes. I confronted my flawed, limited thinking, and emotion-based perceptions that provoked my fear response. Technology that once appeared as "no match for humans" was simply appearance. Much of transhumanism is cleverly designed appearance—propaganda aimed at human fear to generate more and more funding.

The same Washington, DC, environment where transhumanism coiled around me, also provided my way out of the labyrinth. I met people involved directly in technological transhumanism who shined the light of reality on the propaganda that lured me. They shook their heads, denying my conclusions, pointing out my flawed thinking. Slowly, my release began.

It took me two years, 730 days, to pull myself out of the depths of my transhuman underworld. I grasped hold of the lowered hands of Hermes, broke open the pomegranates of Hades, and seeds of knowledge led the way out.

Yet, even as I pulled myself over the ledge of fear to surface reality, able to separate my light from my darkness, my vision remained cloudy. For some time, I didn't recognize what I was seeing.

Like a brain-saturated alcoholic, it took me a year to think clearly. To feel safe enough to venture into the public realm with my ideas. To share how deeply I traversed the shadows of dystopian transhumanism and then reveal how my concept of Exoconscious Humans emerged as delicate, yet muscular—an able-bodied orchid.

My journey through transhumanism led to integrated ET, multidimensional contact, and communication. A new type of consciousness emerged in the form of Exoconscious Humans. Furthermore, I realized that Exoconscious Humans, as individuals and communities connected across the planet, would generate reasonable, pragmatic solutions to the challenges of an overarching dominance of transhumanism. Exoconscious Humans would restore our consciousness, creativity, soul, and spirit—what it means to be human.

A Proposed Path Forward

How do Exoconscious Humans live and advance in a dominant 21st Transhuman century?

To clear a path forward, I asked two clarifying questions: (1) how will we know if exoconsciousness is successful and (2) how will we know if transhumanism is successful. Examining one led to clarity in exploring the other.

How Will We Know if Exoconsciousness is Successful?

Exoconsciousness is a function of nonlocal consciousness, where our body and brain are free to interact in a field of ETs and multidimensionals. Interaction in this field includes contact, communication, and co-creation. We collaborate with beings, offering access to information and energies for new ideas and creations. These collaborative co-creations evolve all of the participants — the ET, multidimensional beings, and humans. This collaboration extends across our planet, ultimately our cosmos. We experience an open, collaborative system that creates peace, freedom, natural harmony, and health.

A fundamental principle of exoconsciousness is the basic right to free, limitless consciousness through all dimensions and across a universe of intelligent beings. It moves humans far beyond the computer, AI, synthetic biology, even the quantum computing limits of technological transhumanism.

Exoconsciousness is rooted in the belief that individual awareness and consciousness is beyond the brain, in a collective field of consciousness that spans multiple dimensions. This field and dimensions are accessible by all humans. As such, authoritarian control of consciousness is blocked because innate exoconsciousness knows no bounds, other than the voluntary awareness of what is conscious and unconscious, which can resolve and dissolve at any time. Information, desire, intention, and creativity break all barriers. The following chapter outline expands the details and preferences of exoconsciousness.

Conditions for a Successful Exoconscious Reality:

Chapter 1: Exoconscious Humans are preferred.
Chapter 2: Psychic Intelligence is preferred.
Chapter 3: Conscious Downloads and Co-creation are preferred.
Chapter 4: Exoconscious Co-Creative Self is preferred.
Chapter 5: Exoconscious Cosmic Connection is preferred.
Chapter 6: Exoconscious Moral Autonomy is preferred.
Chapter 7: Exoconscious Human Civilization is preferred.
Chapter 8: Conclusion: Institute for Exoconsciousness (I-EXO)
Appendix I: Exoconscious Human Bill of Rights

How Will We Know if Transhumanism is Successful?

Transhumanism is a social and philosophical belief or theory that humans can evolve beyond current physical and mental limitations by utilizing science and technology. It entails mind control via synthetic biology, robotics, nanotechnology, and technocracy. Its outcome is a computerized incursion into individual rights, consciousness, soul, and mortality. Its moral foundation based on engineered Transhumans providing equality for all, for the common good.

By asking how we will know if transhumanism is successful, it reveals many underlying assumptions, cultural and ideological.[3] Each chapter will expand on the conditions and aspects of this reality.

Conditions for a Successful Transhuman Reality

Chapter 1: Transhumans are preferred.
Chapter 2: AI is preferred.
Chapter 3: Socially engineered artificial reality is preferred.
Chapter 4: Biologically Engineered Synthetic Self is preferred.
Chapter 5: Controlled Earth-Space Infrastructure is preferred.
Chapter 6: Transhuman Morphological Freedom is preferred.
Chapter 7: Surveillance Empire is preferred.

Transhumanism and technocracy[4] are rooted in the belief that the human brain is the center of consciousness. Control this brain-centered consciousness, and you control the human.

---

3   Conditions for the success of transhumanism are based, in part, on Kyle Munkittrick. Kyle Munkittrick, " When will we be Transhuman: Seven Conditions for attaining Transhumanism", Discover Magazine, https://www.discovermagazine.com/mind/when-will-we-be-transhu-man-seven-conditions-for-attaining-transhumanism.

4   Technocracy is a technology-based global economic system managed by scientists and engineers for optimum efficiency, which includes monitoring, metering, and monetizing humans as a commodity similar to agricultural products and natural resources.

Capturing human consciousness is an ancient game, whether played by religion, propaganda, drugs, politics, memetics, or education. Convince humans that they are but a brain, and you have them. Transhumanists are confident that they can convince humans to forfeit control of their minds and bodies to technology and engineering. Using synthetic implants and hijacking neural systems, transhumanists confidently run an engineered society.

Fortunately, Exoconscious Humans, joined by scientists, are aware of transhumanism's weakness. These weaknesses include hackable computer systems, brain-exclusive orientation, intention to implement a global economic system through virtual reality (VR), and denial of the power and predominance of nature.

CHAPTER 1

EXOCONSCIOUS HUMANS ARE

PREFERRED

TRANSHUMANS ARE PREFERRED

Section 1

Who are Exoconscious Humans?
Distinguishing Exoconscious Human and Transhuman

I left Washington, DC, in 2016 and returned to Phoenix—shedding my transhuman addiction and my dreams of UFO ET Disclosure through political channels. I had moved to DC to work with Apollo 14 astronaut Dr. Edgar Mitchell's Quantrek organization researching zero-point energy, consciousness, and the extraterrestrial presence. Working with an international science team, I promoted the organization and lobbied for innovative energy technologies and UFO, ET disclosure. In March 2014, I arranged a meeting for Dr. Mitchell and myself with John Podesta, Counselor to the President in the Obama administration. We intended the meeting with Podesta to be the first step in arranging a meeting with President Obama.

While Podesta graciously agreed to meet with us the week of August 11, 2014, to discuss a follow-up meeting with President Obama, Dr. Mitchell's health prevented him from traveling to DC. Negotiations continued to arrange a skype but were futile.

Dr. Mitchell's health deteriorated, and he died on February 4, 2016. He died nearly 45 years after he deployed the US flag on the lunar surface during the early moments of the Apollo 14 mission's first spacewalk on February 5, 1971.

Disappointed and a bit discouraged, I dismantled my work with Quantrek along with my political expectations for change. Disclosure and alternative energies like zero-point appeared unattainable. Then, what I thought was complete, cycled back around.

The early morning of October 7, 2016, Victor Viggiani, a Canadian journalist and colleague in Exopolitics, awakened me with a phone call telling me to get out of bed and turn on my computer. "Wikileaks published John Podesta's emails, containing your emails arranging your meeting with Dr. Mitchell."

I went online and saw my emails that arranged Edgar and my visit with Podesta amid the more than 2,000 hacked emails published by WikiLeaks, exposing Podesta's private information as Hillary Clinton's campaign chairman.

The Podesta emails cited my message, email address, and phone number. So began weeks of random phone calls and interest in whether my emails were authentic. They were. Despite the chatter and sudden interest in my Disclosure work, I continued slowly releasing my work with Quantrek.

After my dystopic transhumanism deep dive, my disappointment with political reality, and unfulfilled expectations for high-level disclosure of the extraterrestrial presence—I retreated. As a close friend used to recommend, I lay fallow. Like an unplanted field, I let my mind, body, and spirit rest and recuperate.

During this time, I received a strange email from Kevin Briggs, a psychic medium in Florida. Through MUFON researcher Kathleen Marden, Kevin sent me a message from Dr. Mitchell.

Kevin was out walking his dogs one evening in Florida, not far from where Dr. Mitchell once lived. As is common in Florida, a rainbow appeared, and out of it came Dr. Mitchell's voice asking Kevin to send me his message. In Kevin's email, he relayed Dr. Mitchell's communication asking me to leave Washington, DC, for my health. My work there was complete, and others would carry on. Positive feelings flooded through me as I read Dr. Mitchell's message. My husband and I were planning to leave Washington, DC, and returning to Phoenix.

As our move became a reality, I began to regain healthy energy. I arrived full circle back to my Exoconscious roots. I returned to the precious resource of human consciousness and the wealth of information and connections of my ET and multidimensional awareness.

Before leaving DC, I reached out internationally to my community of colleagues who were ongoing integrated experiencers to establish a monthly mastermind. These colleagues lived with ET experience long enough to release their fear and trauma response that often accompanies contact. Gradually, they matured, integrating ET contact into their daily life. They had effortlessly shifted through multiple states of consciousness until they developed a stable, conscious relationship with ET. They communicated with ET from a place of human sovereignty and mutual respect.

For all of us, our ET knowledge became our work. We employed the information and energy of ET contact. Whether healers, artists, inventors, scientists, or spiritual teachers, each integrated ET information into their occupations. Our limitless field of consciousness opened as we accessed our self and ET in new ways that created possibilities for building a healthy human society.

Quickly I realized that our monthly Mastermind participants were Exoconscious Humans. You may identify with us. Here's a clue.

If you embarked on a journey as an ET multidimensional experiencer, then chances are, you may be drifting, trying to figure out where you are, who you are, and what's going on. If you explored and embraced your confusion and trauma aspects of your experience, the shadow side, then you may see yourself in a new light. Please, read on. Consider the possibility that you are an Exoconscious Human. It may be an identity that fits.

Defining Consciousness

Comprehending exoconsciousness requires a clear definition of consciousness. A description of consciousness contextualizes exoconsciousness. So, what is consciousness? Easy question. Hard answer. To date, there is no scientific, philosophical, or religious consensus on the definition of consciousness. Neuroscientist Ram Lakhan Pandey Vimal identified "40 meanings (or aspects) attributed to the term consciousness, extracted from the literature and recent online discussion." [5] Vimal opened a discussion of consciousness to reach some consensus between materialists, who define consciousness by function (Chalmers easy problem of discrimination, recognition, cognition) versus the subjective experience of consciousness (Chalmers' hard problem).[6]

Vimal, pursuing the varieties of the meaning of consciousness, collected online evidence that underlies a continuum of research, scholarship, and beliefs. Thus, he designed a consciousness continuum originating with brain scientists who define consciousness as primarily a materialistic biological brain, neurological function. The next sector included brain technology adherents who identify consciousness as a hybrid of brain and technology. Then Vimal moved to subjective consciousness adherents who bridge science-based brain research and metaphysics-based quantum consciousness research involving the observer effect. The next sector of qualia consciousness focused on subjective experiences separate from beliefs, those who regard consciousness as a fundamental principle. Ultimately Vimal's continuum arrived at researchers concentrating

---

5   Ram Lakhan Pandey Vimal, "Meanings attributed to the term 'consciousness': an overview", Journal of Consciousness Studies: Special Issue on Defining Consciousness, 16 (5), 9-27, https://goo.gl/4TVSym
6   Philosopher, David Chalmers introduced the terms "hard problem" and "easy problem to discriminate definitions of consciousness. He first cited the term "hard problem" in a paper he presented in Tucson, AZ "Toward a Scientific Basis of Consciousness". http://consc.net/papers/facing.pdf.

on consciousness defined as Rupert Sheldrake's morphic resonance and morphic fields where he proposes that memory is inherent and that "natural systems...inherit a collective memory from all previous things of their kind." [7] This field may align with information accessible in the field of consciousness, such as the akashic records, possibly first referred to as Akasha by Theosophist Colonel Olcott in his book, *The Buddhist Catechism*. Akasha is Sanskrit, referring to the sky, space, or Aether.

My research and ET multidimensional experience guided me to consciousness as a field. Exoconsciousness occupies the last segment of Vimal's consciousness continuum.

Consciousness is a field phenomenon. Our mind is a field of possibilities. As such, consciousness is beyond the brain. It encompasses the awareness and experience of a vast field of energies and information in which a human participates as both receiver, transmitter, and creator. Consciousness is a subjective experience beyond the brain that also involves the mind-body-spirit as a participant. This definition of consciousness as a field is like ancient discussions of akashic records and Edgar Mitchell's Quantum Hologram. [8] According to Mitchell, the Quantum Hologram is an energy phenomenon that links macro-scale matter with the quantum world. It applied quantum nonlocality principles to the macro-scale world, thereby making quantum information useable. Human consciousness and the energy of awareness, intention, and memory are directly involved in the Quantum Hologram.

---

7   Rupert Sheldrake, Morphic Resonance and Morphic Fields - an Introduction. https://www.sheldrake.org/research/morphic-resonance/introduction.

8   Edgar Mitchell, Sc.D., "Nature's Mind: The Quantum Hologram", http://www.experiencer.org/natures-mind-the-quantum-hologram-by-edgar-mitchell-sc-d/. According to Marilyn Schlitz, President Emeritus of Institute of Noetic Sciences, equating quantum holography with the ancient idea of Akashic Records, Mitchell argued, "nature doesn't lose its experience."

Significantly, Vimal emphasizes the current unsettled state of defining consciousness. Any definition of consciousness remains open to questions and controversy. Perhaps this reflects our human consciousness's inner state, preparing to create new meanings and opportunities, free of biases and past limitations. If this is the case, then humans may be preparing to meet ET, multidimensionals half-way. As such, Exoconscious Humans are open to redefining our extraterrestrial origins, dimensions, and abilities—seeded in consciousness.

Defining Exoconsciousness

Exoconsciousness is a profoundly transformative human experience of contact with ETs and multidimensionals. It represents a current ufology stage that notably redirects the focus of research from UFOs craft research and sightings in the sky— to humans.

Exoconsciousness is an organic, living word. Its meaning changes as individuals, communities, and cultures comprehend reality through their experience and relationship with an ET, multidimensional presence.

Consciousness is a primary pillar. Exoconsciousness proposes that we study the human aspect of ET, multidimensional contact experiences, primarily through conscious awareness. And yet it is more. Exoconsciousness is a holistic transformation of self and cultural identity. It is researched within the framework of quantum science, legitimizing subjectivity, and human experience. Its primary sources of information and wisdom about ETs, multidimensionals are direct experiencers—those who are the cultural vanguard, out in front, confirming the extraterrestrial presence via their personal experience as they contact, communicate, and co-create with ET.

Significant shifts of reality often transpire as slight movements. Imagine gently turning a camera lens to focus. A minute movement dramatically alters sight. The blurred, inadequate, and incomplete—shifts to clear, vibrant, and whole. From unconscious to conscious. Exoconsciousness is a gentle unfolding of what has always been within. Humans shining the light of knowledge on themselves changes the definition of ET and what it means to be Exoconscious. We hold a plumb line to determine our conscious reality.

Humans possess an ancient cosmic consciousness. Our connection to the stars was painted in caves, carved on stones in sacred places, and sung to the celestial ceiling's movements. Ancient mariners sighted a plumb line, a string with a lead weight, held to the heavens to determine course navigation by two stars, vertical in a straight line, using the Southern Cross, Pegasus, Orion. [9]

Exoconsciousness is ancient, but our contemporary context alters its definition. We now have 70 years of ufology and experiencer research as a context. It is a massive, measurable database of sightings and witness reports.

Exoconscious Humans emerge from this cultural database as a part of ufology, but distinct. We are modern and relevant. We bridge scientific and spiritual. This book discusses how ET, multidimensional contact results in the physical, emotional, and spiritual transformation of becoming an Exoconscious Human. It theorizes that individuals experiencing ongoing conscious contact come to identify themselves as Exoconscious Humans. Integration of their ET, multidimensional contact experience moves them out of the state of being unconscious and unaware. Through awareness of ongoing contact, Exoconscious Humans modify and integrate their self-identity through participation in the field of consciousness shared with ETs and multidimensionals. These individuals gradually identify with these beings. In these cases, their shared consciousness defines their self-identity and worldview.

How Do We Talk about Exoconsciousness?

Exoconscious anomalous experience beyond the confines of mainstream culture generates the need for a new language. The common vernacular, in this case, English, is unable to express the experience. Words often fail when describing an experience of

---

9   Tony Crowley, *Lo-tech Navigator* (Sea Farer Books, 2004), p. 134.

ETs, multidimensionals. Blank space, silence, indicates where a new expression could fill a void.

"Exoconsciousness" is such a word. The word "Exoconsciousness" developed over my lifetime of ET, multidimensional contact, beginning in early childhood. My first recall of ET contact started around the age of three and continues today. Dolores Cannon termed childhood contact experiencers, like myself and many others, who were born in the 50s and 60s as the "first wave."[10] She designated us as an initial wave of volunteers who pioneered the path for subsequent waves of contactees. Coming in as the first wave, we hacked dense debris and smoothed the way for the coming generations. In many instances, we helped create the language, organizations, and cultural framework to experience and share contact.

My contact experience progressed smoothly through childhood innocence, which was seamless contact and communication, free of critique or fear. Early adolescence marked a distinct disconnect between my reality and that of my friends and social group. With this awareness, for a time, I chose to keep my contact private and at arm's length.

Though my contact continued, it was not until adulthood, the mid-1990s, that I shifted into a more mature relationship with ET, multidimensional presence and communication. Moving to the small town of Fountain Hills, outside of Phoenix, introductions soon led me to meet Dr. Ruth Hover, who ran a monthly contactee

---

10 "The first wave of these souls, now in their late 40s to early 60s (the Baby Boomer generation), have had the hardest time adjusting to life on Earth. They are horrified by the rampant violence of our world and (continued) want to return "home" – even though they consciously have no idea where it is. Strong emotions like anger and hate deeply disturb them. Some rebelled against the status quo and even committed suicide to escape the chaos of Earth. They are the pioneers who paved the way for the second and third waves of volunteers." "The Three Waves of Volunteers and the New Earth: Three Generations of New Souls", https://dolorescannon.com/waves-volunteers-earth-generations-souls/.

group. For the first time, I was able to speak openly about my life-time of contact, share experiences, and receive validation from new-found friends. In 1993, Dr. Hover joined Leo Sprinkle and several other clinical psychologists in John Mack's Harvard-based Program for Extraordinary Experience Research (PEER).[11] With Dr. Hover's contactee group, my ET, multidimensional education began in earnest.

In 1997, Dr. Lynne Kitei [12] was the key witness to the Phoenix Lights. It was one of the most significant mass sightings in the nation. An estimated mile-wide craft traveled the state of Arizona on a night when a meteor shower led many local citizens out into their back yards for a star show.[13] Instead of a meteor shower, the wit-nesses encountered a massive craft that flew low and silently across their sky. Though I lived in Phoenix, I did not see the Phoenix lights UFO. No one phoned me. No intuition nudged me to go out-side and look at the night sky. I missed the event and was unable to express the same awe that my colleagues felt. I was left out. Yet, being left out did not come as a surprise.

During my years of studying ufology that intensified with Dr. Hover, I became aware that my contact experience, and that of many of my friends, was primarily a consciousness experience. Ours was not an isolated craft in the sky phenomenon. Ours was not a searching secret government files phenomenon. Ours was not a drug-induced experience. Instead, our contact was a profoundly personal encounter with many ETs and multidimensionals who

---

11 "Program for Extraordinary Experience Research", http://johnemack-institute.org/2003/01/program-for-extraordinary-experience-research-peer/.

12 Dr. Lynne Kitei was the key witness to the Phoenix Lights, http://www.thephoenixlights.net/Bio.htm.

13 Aldo Vasquez, "Did You See Strange Lights in the Sky Last Night? Here's Why", http://www.abc15.com/news/state/did-you-see-strange-lights-in-the-sky-last-night-here-s-why.

entered, exited, and in some cases, lingered across years. In my case, a lifetime.

Natural human consciousness was the lynchpin of my contact. And unfortunately, the least discussed aspect within the ufology community. Perhaps the issue was the lack of words to relay conscious contact experience. Yet, words to express an event should not be a stumbling block. After all, humans create words as they play with syllables, expressions, or sounds. However, the word exoconsciousness had a different creation.

I forgot the exact date, but the experience of the word exoconsciousness remains with me. A single mother of three children, I woke one morning to my clock radio alarm. I remember hitting the snooze button for a few precious moments of quiet before diving into my day of packing lunches, backpacks, and work paraphernalia to move everyone out the door and on their way to school and work. Parents know cherished silence. The alarm silenced, my head fell back on the pillow, and the word exoconsciousness entered my entire body. The word exoconsciousness embodied me as expressed in spiritual and religious writings. The word became flesh (John 1:14). But terms need definitions to elaborate on their meaning.

What is Exoconsciousness?
Exoconsciousness is a Function of
Nonlocal Consciousness

During the early years, I defined exoconsciousness as "Beyond the Brain." [14] That meaning remains relevant. Nonlocal consciousness refers to consciousness beyond the brain.

What does that mean?

Essentially, beyond the brain means that objects in the world cannot live independently from the rest of the world. On the quantum level, objects or particles, though separated, are entangled.

---

14 Rebecca Hardcastle Wright, "Exoconsciousness: Beyond the Brain A Second Chance", *Exopolitics Journal*, January 2006. https://exopolitics-journal.com/Journal-vol-1-2.htm.

Physicist Erwin Schrödinger first used the word entanglement to describe the connection between separated particles that persists regardless of distance. A nonlocal field unites.

An easy way to see nonlocal entangled consciousness is to imagine that you and your friend have lived together for many years. You know one another's energies, likes, and dislikes. You know one another's behavior information.

Then, through life changes, you are separated by hundreds of miles. You now live in separate geographical locations. Then, in one measurable moment, simultaneously, you are sitting on your geographically distant beds. Your partner raises his left hand, and you raise your right hand. You are exhibiting entanglement in a nonlocal field.

Quantum scientists claim that everything in our awareness is in the same area. A field of consciousness that is the continuous movement of wave and particle collapse—again and again.

Nonlocal also means that consciousness is not only located in space and time. In other words, throughout nature, something is going on under the surface. Life is communicating unseen under the surface. To an extent, these behaviors and communications can be scientifically measured, but science is just beginning to crack the code.

Migratory birds may also exhibit entanglement. They navigate from one place on the planet to another, for example, migrating from Michigan to Mexico. Scientists surmise that these birds possess a built-in compass connected to the angle between the earth's magnetic field and its surface. But when an experiment blindfolded the birds, they could not migrate, even though the magnetic field was present. Here is that nature code again. Were the migratory birds navigating via entanglement in a nonlocal field of consciousness that required visual participation? Or is something else communicating guidance under the surface?

Families also exhibit similar field behavior. In these systems, we locate and define within our family field. This family field stretches to accommodate family members who live long distances from one another. A telepathic connection may be related to this nonlocal field and provides a window into memory's importance.[15]

Einstein termed this nonlocal entangled reality "Spooky Action at a Distance." Its action surprised him. He identified the behavior but didn't crack the code.

Experiencers and scientists may heighten the need to crack the code through exoconscious information. As humans, we like to know one another's location and what is going on. When quantum scientists tell us that how we see reality is wrong, we do not like it. But they keep telling us anyway.

These scientists tell us that our world only appears separate. As humans, we want to declare our separateness. Then out of the blue, someone comes up, taps us on the shoulder, and tells us that we are not separate. We are entangled. At first, it is distressing.

When the founder of Starbucks, Howard Schultz, announced that he was running for President early in the 2020 election primary, he said, "I'm self-made." He flew the flag of independence for a few media minutes before critics clamored that, no, Howard was not a self-made man. He grew up in public housing. He attended a public university. And on and on went the Twitter clap-back for him to cease his chatter. Howard was shaken, stirred, and covered with entanglements. Howard was served-up as a steaming quantum cup of nonlocal consciousness.

ET, multidimensional experiencers frequently refer to being beyond the space-time continuum. We experience altered states where the rules of rational thought do not apply. We feel we can break out of the linear movement of time. We may lose time or gain time. We may travel to the past or the future. And yet we always arrive back to our present. Here, not there. Apologies to Jimmy Buffett.

---

15 Rupert Sheldrake describes the field phenomena of family and its use in Family Constellation therapy in his video, "Morphic Fields and Family Constellations", https://youtu.be/JydjryhEl5o.

Quantum scientists tell us that everything is in awareness. Everything participates in the same field of consciousness. Everything around us is a churning field of probability. We give it the appearance of linear objects because we are looking at a large surface and missing what is going on under the surface. We can't see the Spooky. But, exoconsciousness allows us to explore the Spooky.

Exoconsciousness as Biophoton Function: Light Beings

The hundred-year scientific study of biophotons offers insight and evidence into nature's secret code of communication, which may lead us into a deeper understanding of consciousness as a field. The study of biophotons at the cellular DNA level, advanced by Charles Sanders, now expands to animals and humans who may communicate with each other by electromagnetic waves called biophotons.[16]

Biophotons come from the Greek meaning life (bio) and light (photon). These are low visibility photons of light produced by a biological system. Researchers discovered that neurons in the mammalian brain could produce photons of light. Furthermore, these photons are on the visible spectrum of near-infrared through violet.

Simply stated, brain neurons communicate through light. Scientists are further speculating that the brain may have optical communication channels and that neurons use photonic communication. [17] What is the nature of these light transmission? This recent research examines the subjective nature of consciousness. Questions remain about biophoton communication— what, how, and where they communicate. However, this research strengthens the possibility of consciousness as a nonlocal field and the existence of multidimensions.

---

16 Charles L. Sanders, "Speculations about Bystander and Biophotons, Dose-Response," December 2014. https://www.ncbi.nlm.nih.gov/pmc/articles/PMC4267444/.

17 Jumar Karkeshian and Tuszynski and Simon Barclay, "Are there optical communication channels in the brain?" *Front Bioscience*, March 2018. https://www.ncbi.nlm.nih.gov/pubmed/29293442.

Biophoton studies indicate that quantum entanglement may be the link between consciousness and photons and the field of consciousness.

Given the nature of biophotons and scientific advancements, researchers can now measure these photons' effectiveness. They identify scales within life and propose hierarchies. For example, rats pass one biophoton per neuron per minute. In comparison, humans move one billion biophotons per neuron per second. This photon movement between species may be why we feel affinity and communicate with our animals. It's a biophoton based relationship.

It may be a relationship based on numbers. The more light produced, the more communication between neurons, the more conscious the being, or the life form. Higher consciousness may be an exercise of higher frequency in the production of biophotons. We are light generators, as spiritual teachings have long emphasized. A more appropriate reading of Genesis, "Let there be Light," may now be interpreted as "Let there be Consciousness." Further, the Exoconscious who relate to Light Beings or Light Language may exhibit a high generation of biophotons, communicating with the field of consciousness and the beings therein.

Plus, there are more implications. Biophoton research moves the research marker from the brain into the field of consciousness through entanglement. Two entangled photons react if one of the photons is affected—immediately, no matter where the other is in the universe.

What does this have to do with exoconsciousness? Applying the biophoton neuron activity in humans to describe consciousness: we may all live in a world of light, not localized in our brains. We may see ourselves amid a biophoton field of beings beyond our brains, living into and through channels or portals that lead to multiverses.

The experience of contact with ETs and multidimensionals may awaken humans such that they begin to produce more light. And as such, humans embody more of the function of consciousness as a field. With increased light movement, we simultaneously are more and can do more. This light movement logically leads to the Exoconscious Human's development of psychic abilities.

Pineal gland research related to transmission and optics of light is also relevant to biophotons and similar to Stuart Hameroff and Roger Penrose's work on the quantum properties of microtubules in the brain.

Biophoton research stretches into theories of multiverse, which experiencers often describe. The multiverse theory, initially developed by Everett, stated that there must be a "timeline" or "universe" actualizing that potential for every set of possible observations.[18] Though initially dismissed by scientists, many-world and multiverse theories may find new life through biophoton research.

Multiverses may reflect entangled biophotons in nonlocal consciousness, experienced as simultaneously present. Varying degrees of awareness and biophoton light production of neurons may be necessary to access these multiverses. Importantly, humans may experience these multiverses as dimensions with higher and lower frequencies of light.

Exoconsciousness as Consciousness Frequency: Do we Ascend or Expand?

Frequently people ask, "how do I reach higher consciousness?" They usually demonstrate with their arms reaching up or out to embrace what they are seeking. They indicate that they are looking for someone (teacher, guru, community) or something (idea, vision, energy) to bring them to a higher state. I feel and respect the desire and passion of their request.

Exoconsciousness describes consciousness as a field and a frequency. Imagine you are standing amid conscious energies. A human, in a living field, who is also alive with the powers of consciousness. Who are you in this state?

---

18 Bruce DeWitt and Neill Graham, *The Many-Worlds Interpretation of Quantum Mechanics* (Princeton Series in Physics, 1973).

Physicists might describe you as a human complex waveform—a series of sine wave frequencies known as harmonics. As a complex waveform, you can be divided into individual components called fundamental frequency or into groups of waves called harmonic frequencies. These are sound healing principles.

As you become self-aware of functioning as a waveform, you also become aware of the vast waveform field you can access. But how do you access areas of information that you have not accessed before?

Do you ascend into it? Or do you stretch out into it?

My practical experience as an Exoconscious Human is that my consciousness and my consciousness body expanded. Some may call that ascension, but it was a tactile, physical feeling of expansion for me. The boundaries of my perceived reality dissolve. I perceive an expanded field. As I move into this field of consciousness, I know more. My consciousness "holds more." It stretches to accommodate this expansion of information.

As I stretch into the field of information, something else happens—my frequency changes. The field changes my frequency. It is a co-creative process. As I expand my consciousness and add information, I develop wisdom and knowledge, altering my energetic frequency. New information changes beliefs, ideas, and perspectives in an organic, natural process.

Exoconscious expansion opens windows of space in your frequency field as further information is sought by you and comes into you. As this happens, you release information from old programming that no longer belongs in your field of awareness. As you release and let go, your consciousness loosens up and lights up.

This expansion process begins with learning emotional detachment. Each frequency you possess makes up your composition. Subjective experiences of good or bad, right or wrong, compose your frequency. Learning to discriminate your emotions and learning to read your frequency field often means turning your emotional read on the frequency upside down. Topsy-turvy feels uncomfortable. You feel like the tarot hanged man, dangling by one foot. A hug or a kind gesture might be manipulative. A stern command or a verbal shove in another direction might be the best advice you received. Learning to discriminate involves detachment, suspension of judgment.

Like millions of people, I stumbled blindly into learning emotional detachment. My doorway opened by admitting that I was co-dependent. I walked into Al-Anon meetings, and my world capsized. What I assumed, no, was convinced, were my best choices, were not. I needed to learn the value of new decisions. To survive marriage to an alcoholic, as a co-dependent, I had to learn to let go and trust the process. I was so scared. I clung to the flotsam and jetsam of my life. My fear wanted to resume old behaviors, even if just a shard. But that was not to be. It all had to go. Gradually, over time, I found that I could detach, and I would not shatter into a million pieces. It was a challenging lesson.

Emotional detachment or learning to be the "observer self" is mandatory in expanding exoconsciousness. There are many tools, such as hypnotherapy, journaling, breathing, meditation, yoga, prayer. Many tools teach loving detachment.

For a time, you need to put on "blinders" to culture, especially the online entertainment culture, that emotionally pulls you into their sound tirades, electrifying images, and righteous judgments. Instead, you need a culture of quiet and self-trust to learn the ways of detachment.

The payoffs and benefits of developing your observer self are immeasurable. One primary advantage of detachment is that you begin to move with ease into your inner self and the field of consciousness frequencies. There you start to tap into psychic information as well as beings who communicate this information.

Scientific Relevance of Exoconsciousness

As quantum science wrestles with subjectivity and why we experience meaning, exoconsciousness advances. Exoconscious Humans join the ranks of those recognized by quantum science for their abilities and information. Consciousness researchers formally study those who have past lives memory, near-death experiences, psychic adepts, and the siddhis of meditation and yoga. Add to that list Exoconscious Humans. One goal of exoconsciousness is to scientifically mainstream research into the abilities of Exoconscious Humans. Research institutes throughout the world study the paranormal. In the future, these groups may look to Exoconscious Humans for information and research studies. Then the work of opening exoconsciousness to scientific research begins.

The Evolution of Exoconsciousness within Ufology

Initially, exoconsciousness was the academic study of the extraterrestrial origins, dimensions, and abilities of human consciousness. [19] This working definition laid out research areas that became the book, *Exoconsciousness: Your 21st Century Mind.*[20]

The Institute for Exoconsciousness,[21] an international community of experiencers, included inventors, scientists, and researchers.[22] Formally organized as a 501c3 nonprofit led to a deepening and broadening of the definition. Exoconsciousness is the innate human ability to connect, communicate, and co-create with ETs and multidimensionals.

In the context of ufology research, exoconsciousness references a different source. It sources information about human-extraterrestrial contact directly from individuals. Its approach to source material differs dramatically from mainstream ufology. Instead of individual experiencer reports, ufology primarily references official whistleblowers, FOIA documents, and UFO sightings.

Over 70 years, progressively, through research-based on government, military, intelligence, corporate, and religion—ufologists

---

19 Rebecca Hardcastle, "Exoconsciousness: Beyond the Brain a Second Chance" *Exopolitics Journal,* January 2006, http://www.exopoliticsjournal.com/Journal-vol-1-2-Hardcastle.pdf.

20 Rebecca Hardcastle, *Exoconsciousness: Your 21st Century Mind* (Authorhouse, 2008).

21 http://www.exoconsciousness.com/.

22 https://exoconsciousness.org/.

have aligned with their sources. Despite claims of objectivity, they adopted the reality or worldview of these authorities.[23] Ufologists climbed the ladder of expertise as rungs of information transferred to them. Through this process, they became identical to their sources. Consciousness works like this. What we read, research, run after—we adopt their point of view. Until now, the government and some ufology sectors live together in what has become a closed information loop.

In contrast, UFO-related and personal ET, multidimensional experience source exoconsciousness. Exoconsciousness is post-disclosure, having no academic or personal need to prove the ET, multidimensional presence. Exoconsciousness is not an archeological or diagnostic expedition to discover hidden secrets from government X files or the Vatican Library or dig beneath cavernous military intelligence underground bunkers.

The conscious human experience is a primary source for exoconscious information. Exoconsciousness focuses on how ET, multidimensional experience influences humans. How we respond, develop, and transform as humans who have conscious ongoing contact. Humans are the primary focus. Humans are the source—as sovereign beings who possess critical thinking, creativity, and control of their experience with ET.

Extended Exoconscious Influencers:
John Mack, Phoenix Traumatology
Community, Edgar Mitchell

The word, exoconsciousness, was given to me and developed academically and experientially over time. It also evolved through the influence of others. It stands within a legacy. Ruth Hover and her contactee group was my initial influence. Ruth led me to study

---

23 For a deeper discussion of Ufologists becoming their sources, please refer to Rebecca Hardcastle Wright, "An Exoconscious Proposal: The Common Ground of Consciousness Science and Psychic Intelligence", https://goo.gl/MqBIMn (2015).

John Mack, the Harvard psychiatrist. Mack, with the assistance of Budd Hopkins, opened academic, spiritual, and mainstream doors to the ET experiencer phenomenon. Using the term abduction, Mack brought public and academic recognition to ET experiencers. Initially, he carefully diagnosed experiencers regarding their mental health, using psychiatric metrics, which led him to declare them sane, rational, and mentally healthy. Later, Mack consulted with spiritual leaders and linked ET contact to the ancient history of visionary experiences that continues with spiritual practitioners in our modern era. He perceived ET contact as transformative[24] and spiritual as well as physical. He even went so far as to propose that the phenomenon required new science. [25]

---

24 John Mack Institute, "Human Transformation and Alien Encounters", http://johnemackinstitute.org/category/human-transformation-and-alien-encounters/.

25 "There is a—I believe, a gradation of experiences and that go from the most literal physical kinds of hurts, wounds, person removed, spacecraft that can be photographed, to experiences which are more psychological, spiritual, involve the extension of consciousness. The difficulty for our society and for our mentality is, we have a kind of either/or mentality. It's either, literally physical; or it's in the spiritual other realm, the unseen realm. What we seem to have no place for— or we have lost the place for—are phenomena that can begin in the unseen realm, and cross over and manifest and show up in our literal physical world.

So, the simple answer would be: Yes, it is both. It is both literally, physically happening to a degree; and it's also some kind of psychological, spiritual experience occurring and originating perhaps in another dimension. And so the phenomenon stretches us, or it asks us to stretch to open to realities that are not simply the literal physical world, but to extend to the possibility that there are other unseen realities from which our consciousness, our, if you will, learning processes over the past several hundred years have closed us off. "Interview with John Mack Psychiatrist, Harvard University", *Nova Online*, 1996, http://www.pbs.org/wgbh/nova/aliens/johnmack.html.

My perspective of exoconsciousness deepened further through members of a trauma research community in Phoenix, Arizona. In 1980, the American Psychiatric Association (APA) added PTSD to the third edition of its Diagnostic and Statistical Manual of Mental Disorders (DSM-III). This addition was significant because, for the first time, it identified that the source of the trauma mental disorder was literally outside the individual (as in a traumatic event, for example, during a war of violent encounter or emotional trauma of neglect and abandonment). This trauma identification removed its stigma as a disorder caused by human weakness inherent in a person's character.[26]

The reordering of trauma, replacing it as a flawed character or weakness and in its place defining it as sourced outside of the individual, was significant. Though few academics discuss this reordering, it primarily moved the standard psychiatric Freudian-based therapy and chemical-based drug treatment approaches from their dominant position in trauma research and clinical practice. Yet, even today, with increased emphasis on PTSD and categories of treatment, such as attachment therapy, few therapists practice as trauma specialists. As a mind-body therapist specializing in trauma, my treatment approach is radically different from a classically trained therapist.

Recent developments in the field of trauma research dovetailed my research into traumatic effects experienced by ET contactees.

My introduction to trauma came with an introduction to Lee Gerdes. In 2007, I met Lee, founder of Brain State Technologies. [27] Lee came to Phoenix from Silicon Valley, where he designed some of the first algorithms to enhance Amazon purchases. (If you buy that, you might be interested in this.) Lee suffered a significant head trauma injury, which led him to apply technology to brain

---

26 Matthew J. Friedman, MD, PhD, "PTSD History and Overview", Last updated February 23, 2016, https://www.ptsd.va.gov/professional/ptsd-overview/ptsd-overview.asp.

27 https://brainstatetech.com/

waves to heal traumatized neural pathways. On the healer's journey, Lee set out first to heal himself.

Brain States uses technology to rebalance the brain with personalized sound so that the client relaxes as their brain resets. Through its technology, on a quantum level, the brain watches itself and heals. "Brainwave Optimization harnesses the power of advanced computing technology to create a high-definition Acoustic Brain Mirror™. This real-time reflection of brainwave activity generates a pattern of music-like tones, which supports and accelerates the brain's ability to achieve deep states of relaxation where it can fully let go and reset itself. Trauma and chronic stress can overwhelm the brain – when the brain resets itself, it will self-optimize to improve well-being and return to a more highly capable state." [28]

Meeting Lee led to introductions to other experts active in the field of neural and technological trauma treatments. Lee introduced me to David Berceli, whose sense of service and adventure led him on a 15-year worldwide journey to study how cultures heal trauma. His research culminated in developing a TRE protocol—Tension, Stress, and Trauma Release Exercises that focused on releasing deep muscular patterns. [29] According to Berceli's method, when you physically shake or tremble, your neural system releases and resets. You heal. His TRE protocols use yoga-like postures to release trauma from the body.

Dr. Scaer's scientific research, which focused on the body-brain role, also emphasized the role of shaking in releasing trauma. Scaer's research into animal trauma led him to identify the necessity of shaking to relieve the body's shock and the need for a safe community to heal.[30] He discovered that when a polar bear was trapped or unable to move, their trauma scars deepened. When

---

28 https://brainstatetech.com/overview/.

29 https://traumaprevention.com/.

30 "Dr. Robert Scaer on Trauma", *Thriving Now*, February 2010, http://www.thrivingnow.com/scaer-trauma/.

allowed to shake and move after trauma, the polar bear broke up the trauma scars naturally.

The research of Scaer and Berceli reminded me of the number of times, as a child, many of us endured demands to be quiet when we needed to cry and release trauma. Unfortunately, it reminded me that as a well-meaning parent, the number of times that I used the same discipline with my children. I now know differently.

The Phoenix trauma research community also included Stanford physicist William Tiller, who invented the machine that holds and dispenses human intention. Tiller's work demonstrates that human intent as an ability of consciousness is measurable. Tiller's radical experiments included raising and lowering the PH of water through intention. [31]

Working with the trauma community led to developing insights and tools for healing my trauma scars. Many experiencers identify trauma wounds, as they feel scarred through silence, demeaning, disenfranchisement, and alienation.

Fresh off my travels through traumatology and the publication of *Exoconsciousness: Your 21ˢᵗ Century Mind*, I was invited to join Apollo Astronaut's Dr. Edgar Mitchell's, Quantrek organization for the research and application of zero-point energy. This group of scientists and ET experiencers worked from the hypothesis that the UFO, ET phenomenon was fundamental in developing new forms of energy. Our Quantrek community held that much of the secrecy surrounding the public admission of ET was due to their connection to the radical energy systems that would upset the petroleum-based dollar and world economic systems. We envisioned new energies lighting up the world for a fraction of the cost—small portable systems.

---

31 "The Spirit of MAAT, How the Power of Intention Alters Matter with Dr. William A. Tiller: Scientific proof that human intention raises local symmetry in the substratum of space", *Spirit of Maat*, Vol 2, No 8, http://www.spiritofmaat.com/archive/mar2/tiller.htm.

Notably, Mitchell's team consisted of 3 ET contactees, me being one. Primarily a rational scientific thinker, Mitchell integrated metaphysical and spiritual perspectives. He admired psychic knowledge and abilities—what a courageous thinker.

Writing my book *Exoconsciousness: Your 21st Century Mind* strengthened my belief that consciousness was an integral component of contact and that quantum science offered the best scientific research option.

Mitchell informed his zero-point energy research with quantum science and consciousness studies. In 2011, Mitchell received the Leonardo Da Vinci Society for the Study of Thinking[32] award. In his presentation, he emphasized the need for science and metaphysics to dialogue. Mitchell's paper on the Quantum Hologram, developed with German mathematician Walter Schemmp integrated quantum effects measurable in the macro world. [33]

Furthermore, Mitchell held a firm belief that extraterrestrial information, or as he termed it, the Extraterrestrial Presence, was available to human consciousness and was necessary to access to develop zero point and alternative energies.

Who is an Exoconscious Human?

If exoconsciousness describes the innate human ability to connect, communicate, and co-create with ETs and multidimensionals, who are Exoconscious Humans?

Exoconscious Humans are persons who experience ongoing ET, multidimensional contact, and communication. They possess three primary aspects:

---

32 https://en.wikipedia.org/wiki/The_Leonardo_da_Vinci_Society_for_the_Study_of_Thinking.

33 Larry Lowe, "Dr. Edgar Mitchell, The Unexpected Benefit of Apollo 14", *Journal of Anomalous Science*, 2012, https://www.paradigmresearchgroup.org/graphics/Unexpected%20Benefit%20of%20Apollo%2014.pdf.

1) They integrate their ET experiences into who they are as humans. They develop an exoconscious self-identity, experiencing this in varied ways. They regard themselves as grounded in a cosmic consciousness with access to ET, multidimensional beings. Some beings similar to humans. Some different. As their exoconscious self-identity strengthens, they develop mature relationships with ET, based on mutual respect.

2) They possess high psychic intelligence. Psychic abilities are their primary orientation in life. It influences their worldview as well as their problem-solving and everyday decision making. They regard themselves as psychic, empathic, creative, curious, galactic, time travelers, healers, spiritual, multidimensional, and above all, ET, multidimensional-sourced.

3) Through their relationship with ET, multidimensionals, they co-create. It is a multi-layered process. As personal integration of ongoing contact develops, eventually, they apply the information and energy to their psychological transformation and professional work. Throughout this process, they utilize their ET, multidimensional relationship to co-create—bring innovative ideas into material reality. They become Exoconscious artists, healers, scientists, inventors, engineers, teachers, and spiritual adepts. They do this by co-creation with ET, multidimensionals.

Exoconscious Humans as CE6

One means of defining Exoconscious Humans is to contextualize them in the history of classifying contactees. How are they classified within accepted categories of ET contact experience? Astronomer and Ufologist J. Allen Hynek proposed the first three close encounter categories to describe various UFO sightings: CE1 as nocturnal, CE2 as daylight, and CE3 as radar.

Later, astronomer and computer scientist Jacques Vallee developed the category CE4 to describe UFO encounters, emphasizing the contactee's sense of reality. How did the participant's awareness of reality shift during what he described as abduction? Vallee examined the encounter via various states of contact: abduction, hallucinatory, out-of-body, dream-like events, and even its similarity to folktales.

Physician and Ufologist Steven Greer developed the category CE5 to describe the UFO encounter characterized by mutual, bilateral communication rather than unilateral contact. He noted respectful exchange between humans and ET. Greer's popular CE5 events focus the participants outward into the sky. Skywatching for ET. Lookup and ET will appear. CE5 emphasizes ET as above and outside of humans.

Instead of looking up, waiting, and hoping for contact, I propose a CE6 category—the Exoconscious Human. Ongoing ET conscious contact, communication, and co-creation characterize this encounter. This category expresses an intentional human decision to shift their relationship with ET, multidimensionals from unconscious to conscious. From lights above to human participants. A CE6 encounter is human-oriented. Human sourced. In this encounter, the human participants self-identity psychic abilities, intelligence, and creativity through a relationship with ET, multidimensionals via consciousness. This change in self-identity arises from an awareness of the power and abilities of mind and body.

Exoconscious are aware that humans and ETs, multidimensionals share a conscious reality. Importantly, humans have the freedom to relate or not in this shared reality. They have the freedom to act on their knowledge that some ETs, multidimensionals are like us, and some are not. Primary CE6 emphasis is on abilities of human consciousness, secondarily on ET shared consciousness.

Exoconscious Human CE6 is an empowering shift from former categories of abduction, hallucinations, altered states of consciousness (CE4), and waiting for ET to fly out of the sky in a UFO (CE5). It implies an examination of who we are as humans and the nature and abilities of our consciousness. But let us note—this is no trivial undertaking. As explained earlier, our historical reality is that for the past 400 years, the study of consciousness was placed in solitary lockdown, separated from science. For centuries, religion, secret societies, and mystery schools tightly controlled the primary research and consciousness application. These groups had a high price for admission as well as an elite vetting. Primarily family and occasionally fate were the admission ticket to membership. Schools, rituals, robes, and cultural advantages were the formula. This secrecy is operative today but gradually breaking open.

I cannot put my finger on the historical date when doors of secret school consciousness opened to the public, but one indication was when the Eastern and Western mystery schools merged. This merger was orchestrated in the late 1800s by Theosophy schools. A century later, by the early 1990s, universities opened departments for the scientific study of consciousness. In particular, Princeton and Duke pioneered this process, as did Edgar Mitchell's Institute for Noetic Sciences and Stanford Research Institute.

Mystery school archives opened, and ufologists like Hynek, Greer, and Vallee furthered exoconsciousness. Continuing this lineage, the Institute for Exoconsciousness provides a collaborative network for exoconsciousness as a serious subject.

The Seriousness of Exoconsciousness

As part of the scientific legacy of paranormal, psychic, and consciousness research, exoconsciousness is serious. It overflows with potential for science, art, technology, space, health, religion, and the life of our planet.

More importantly, it is a shared, innate ability that all humans possess. What is this ability?

Exoconsciousness is the innate human ability to contact, communicate, and co-create with ETs and multidimensionals.

Throughout this book, I will elaborate on contact, communication, and co-creation. What do these abilities mean for humans? How we can use them effectively. Why our relationship with ET multidimensionals matters.

Humans are an evolving space-faring civilization. With each new space technology, travel, and habitation—exoconsciousness exponentially increases in importance. Who better to consult about time travel, out of body experiences, manipulating matter with consciousness, energy innovations, the spiritual dimension, and the ethics and diplomacy of space culture than Exoconscious Humans? Who better to provide information about ETs, multidimensionals, and the multiverse than humans who have ongoing contact and communication?

Exoconsciousness is a Serious Post Disclosure Community

While those in Exopolitics and ufology debate about their viability and political platforms, we engage with ET, multidimensionals through first-hand subjective experience. Like early explorers who entered isolated communities, we lived with, learned from them, and reported back their findings to skeptical audiences who never step foot outside their labs or university positions. Engaging in conversation without context is often futile. Engaging in debate without first-hand experience is usually purely theoretical and often ineffective. Exoconscious Humans bring a unique and valuable perspective to ufology discussions.

As a post-disclosure community, we source our experience and information differently than ufologists who sourced their information about UFOs and ETs from government, intelligence, and military. Thus, they fit their data into a mainstream material dominated, reductionist science, charted with the mission of defense and militarization. If the government, intelligence, or military sources claimed that it was true—to them, it was so.

Yet, years of ufology and Exopolitics research and relationships with government, intelligence, and military yielded scant progress. Ufology remains mired in seeking out secrets. Exopolitics remains mired in political theater. Both approaches expose an Achilles heel—intelligence agencies that frequently position them as fertile ground to launch narratives and psyop programs. If you look to counterintelligence as your source, then you can expect to be regularly lied to and cleverly deceived. If you look to counterintelligence as your source, you can expect to be used to lure others into the public eye to be identified and surveilled. If you look to counterintelligence as your source, you can expect whistleblower information from those receiving government pensions less than forthcoming. As intelligence knows—once you are in, you never leave. Intelligence work is a permanent contract.

Affirming ET, multidimensional experiencers as experts involves another contract. It consists of acceptance of the reality of human-extraterrestrial consciousness. This path of integrating Exoconscious sources includes experiencers, along with consciousness science experts. Our experience is experientially validated.

Exoconscious Humans become Experts. As we Exoconscious take ourselves seriously, we become our source. We speak for ourselves. We self-authenticate.

For decades, psychiatry, psychology, medicine, and hypnotherapy collated and classified ET, multidimensional experiencers. It was helpful in some cases, detrimental in others. Though researchers were well-meaning, many had no contact experience. Their blind spot only expanded as they populated ufology with their studies. They filtered our information through their lack of knowledge and personal biases. They told us what we meant. Others guided us in the wrong direction. Others questioned and judged what we said. And yes, others often kept us disenfranchised through incorrect diagnoses.

Exoconsciousness is transformative—a holistic spiritual, emotional, mental, and physical experience. Each individual travels their awakening path alone, at their own pace, gathering their personal information. It is like a mystic's spiritual journey compared to a religious experience.

Religious travel in supportive communities. They travel bound by allegiance to a divine source translated into sacred texts, dogma, doctrine, and rituals. These religious communities move in lockstep. The faithful marked excommunicated if stepping forward too far, too fast. But, according to tradition, safety is assured—in this life and the next.

In comparison, Exoconscious Humans travel alone. They risk confusion, missteps, and challenges of the independent journey. They choose a path and speed to travel. They recognize when they reach various levels of learning and knowledge. Exoconscious wisdom is endowed individual by individual.

As such, the Exoconscious realize that their narrative is primarily meaningful only to them. Secondarily, it may be useful to others. While a formal group narrative is critical to religion, it is less significant to the Exoconscious because they quickly learn that their account has echoes of many others' reports and also may differ.

Initially, we experiencers behave like the alcoholic at their first AA meeting. When we experience our first contact, we want to tell others—convinced that certainly, others will acknowledge our reality and be moved and perhaps awed as we were. Then gradually, we settle down and listen. At that moment, we hear echoes of our own story in others reverberating through the exoconscious community. And at that moment, we experience our subjective transformation and value its seriousness in our lives.

We speak for ourselves. Frequently we speak a few words that transmit volumes of information. Often, we communicate through the silence that holds our wisdom. Gradually, over time we settle and integrate. We allow our knowledge to become active. We allow our actions to become co-creation. We transmit our being into collaborative human-ET-multidimensional doing. We speak for ourselves—in words and actions.

What is Exoconsciousness NOT?

Defining what exoconsciousness is <u>not</u> avoids confusion and elicits clarity.

Exoconsciousness is <u>not</u> a new method of contacting ETs, multidimensionals. Exoconsciousness is beyond contact. We Exoconscious make contact, but that is not our end game. The first event of ET contact is an initiation. This contact initiation may shock our view of reality, our body, and our emotions. The new facts we encounter may jar us, overshadowing what is known and familiar. But, the first event of exoconsciousness is just the beginning. What follows is continuous conscious contact.

Exoconsciousness is <u>not</u> a shortcut for knowing ETs, multidimensionals. Instead, it is a gradual unfolding of many experiences, one after the other—an accumulation of knowledge. Exoconsciousness is known and experienced through ongoing, continual contact. Our emphasis is on personal integration, growth, and development as we learn to relate to ourselves and ETs, multidimensionals. Over time, it becomes a grounded, centered experience that heals trauma and fear.

Exoconsciousness is <u>not </u>an altered state like a drug-induced, out of body journey. On the contrary, exoconsciousness emphasizes ongoing conscious contact. For some people, initial forays into contact may involve drugs or ceremonies or mind exercises to feel and explore altered states, but continuous exoconscious contact is primarily conscious. We exoconscious are Conscious. We are awake and aware as we choose to participate in relationships with ET, multidimensionals.

Exoconsciousness is <u>not</u> abduction, kidnapping, or a violent encounter. While researchers have validated cases of extreme and traumatizing contact, this is not exoconsciousness. Some of us were initially awed or fearful of the reality shift that occurred in our first connections. Early contactees, those whom Dolores Cannon defined as the First Wave, were significantly threatened by what was happening to them without guidance from literature available today. Then, over time, experiencers settled down as their contact felt healthy and safe, even familiar.

Exoconsciousness is <u>not</u> against our free will, or a trick, or imprisonment. As we develop through our contact, we begin to exercise our free will. We learn to create healthy boundaries— when we want to say yes to contact and when we want to say no. We feel empowered and able to guide our contact.

Exoconsciousness is <u>not </u>about an alien project to take over the Earth. It is not about a Gray or Reptilian plan to take over our planet. Certainly, Grays and Reptilians are experienced by the exoconscious. But these are but two races among many. As exoconsciousness develops, we become aware of many other races of beings and our ability to contact and communicate with them.

Exoconsciousness does not indicate that humans are inferior to ETs, multidimensionals. It is not an experience of human inferiority, stupidity, overwhelm, or shame that we are human. Instead, it is about empowerment. As we begin to guide and direct our contact relationships, we discover innate human consciousness abilities that we can use and learn to appreciate.

Exoconsciousness is not religion. It does not espouse dogmas and doctrines or promote sacred laws or texts. Instead, we experience an entangled, nonlocal consciousness with ETs, multidimensionals. And in doing so, we may use familiar language in world religions and spiritual teachings that describe our experience.

Exoconsciousness is not evil or good. It is a field of many emotions that we may quickly label to find our footing and feel safe. Humans prefer labels to the unknown and unnamed. So, we point fingers of judgment, and create hierarchies, and tell stories. We want to feel secure in this new reality, so we overlay it with our former ideas and categories—it's all good, it's all evil. Our labels work for a time. But eventually, we begin to see a plethora of races and beings with whom we participate and co-create as Exoconscious Humans. We begin to communicate. Over time, we feel the strength of our ability to pick and choose our relationships.

Exoconsciousness is not a Hollywood movie. It is authentic, owned by the experiencer. A scriptwriter, actor, producer, or special effects creator does not own exoconsciousness. Hollywood films are a mishmash of contact experiences and ideas, often with the requisite dark dystopian backdrop and war messages. Hollywood scripts showcase winners and losers, but rarely Exoconscious Humans as collaborators and co-creators.

Exoconsciousness is not a psyop. It is not part of an intelligence operation such as a Military Abductions (MILABS) or a False Flag

UFO invasion as predicted by Werner Von Braun via Carol Rosin, according to Linda Moulton Howe.[34] Indeed, some tricked experiencers may relay a message for an intelligence operation or push inaccurate information to mislead the public. Intelligence calls itself covert for a reason. It knows how to mislead, confuse, and deceive. In contrast, ongoing Exoconscious experience is authentic. We are careful with our words and descriptions, especially when it involves the public and the media.

Exoconsciousness does not indicate a person is gifted or superior. The entangled nonlocal field is open for all humans to experience. The abilities we describe in exoconsciousness belong to all humans. No one is below or above. To reiterate, we all can move with exoconsciousness beyond the brain in the field of consciousness.

Exoconsciousness is not superhuman. It does not signify that Exoconscious Humans can skip our 3-D development. We live through everyday commonplace learning. We take our health seriously. And we heal and resolve physical, emotional, and mental challenges just like all humans. We don't get a cosmic pass. We sometimes accumulate more than our share of issues because we are so sensitive, and the integration of contact can be challenging.

Exoconsciousness focus is not ETs, multidimensionals. Our focus is on humans. We figure out what is going on through our ET multidimensional contact and relationships, just as many are doing. But through analysis, we always bring our focus back to humans. We examine what exoconsciousness brings to human self-understanding. We deem it more important to know ourselves more deeply through the contact rather than to argue or rattle off details about ETs: what they eat, where they live, what they wore, their Earth

---

34 According to Carol Rosin, Wernher von Braun continuously repeated that government/military composed an enemy list that included Russia, terrorists, Third World countries, asteroids, and ET. Linda Moulton Howe, "Eye-Opening Interview with Carol Rosin about the Late Wernher von Braun," Ventura California, 2004. https://www.bibliotecapleyades.net/exopolitica/esp_exopolitics_zcb.htm.

agenda. Mostly, we flip upside down the usual ufology study. We turn our focus first to humans, then to ETs, multidimensionals.

As exoconsciousness focuses on humans and the effect of ET, multidimensional contact, transhumanism examines the influence and impact of technology on humans. Why exoconsciousness and transhumanism matter to humans.

Section 2

Who is Transhuman?
Defining Transhumanism

Transhumanism is a social and philosophical belief or theory that humans can evolve beyond current physical and mental limitations, especially utilizing science and technology. It explores connecting consciousness and mind control technology via synthetic biology, robotics, computerized invasion of privacy, surveillance, nanotechnology, and technocratic systems.

Transhumanism is expressed in AI that replaces humans, whether delivery drivers with autonomous vehicles, or blue-collar assembly line workers, or white-collar workers who crunch numbers, analyze intelligence data, or medical professionals who treat disease. Its foundational premise is Singularity, developed by Ray Kurzweil (among others). Technological singularity posits that evolved technology will become super intelligent as computers become conscious. Singularity is when a computer or machine learning technology surpasses human intelligence. Everything shifts to a new reality at that tipping point—an augmented reality, which is an interactive experience of one's environment. Computer-generated perceptual information, including artificial visual, auditory, olfactory, and somatic, enhances human sensory perception.[35]

---

35 https://en.wikipedia.org/wiki/Augmented_reality.

According to Kurzweil, this tipping point of singularity is just around the corner. At the SXSW Conference in Austin, Texas, in 2017, he predicted it would happen in 2045. He predicted that by 2029, computers would have human-level intelligence. He also indicated that placing computer chips inside our brains and connecting them to the cloud would expand who we are.

2029 is the consistent date I have predicted for when an AI will pass a valid Turing test and achieve human levels of intelligence. I have set the date 2045 for the 'Singularity,' which is when we will multiply our effective intelligence a billion fold by merging with the intelligence we have created.[36]

Economics of Technocratic Transhumanism

The history of singularity links to globalism and reaches back into the early decades of the 20th century. Patrick Wood, author of *Technocracy Rising: The Trojan Horse of Global Transformation*, is a historian. He notes that in the heat of the Great Depression during the 1930s, prominent scientists and engineers proposed a utopian energy-based economic system called Technocracy that would be run by those same scientists and engineers instead of elected politicians. Wood emphasizes that technocracy is an economic system, not a political system.

Technocracy is a technology-based global economic system managed by scientists and engineers for optimum efficiency, including monitoring, metering, and monetizing humans as commodities similar to agricultural products and natural resources.

Technocracy was designed by elite intellectuals, scientists, and engineers to seed the beginnings of a global economy taking

---

36 Christianna Reedy, "Kurzweil Claims That the Singularity Will Happen by 2045: Get ready for Humanity 2.0," Futurism https://futurism.com/kurzweil-claims-that-the-singularity-will-happen-by-2045.

root today. We see this technocratic system in major international movements like UN Agenda 21, Sustainable Development, Green Economy, Councils of Governments, Smart Growth, Smart Grid, Smart Cities, Total Awareness surveillance, and many other technology-based programs. An elite group of scientists and engineers lead technocracy.

Science, especially computer science, is foundational in developing a technocratic economy. In this economy, every human act is monitored and monetized from the amount of water used in your morning shower, to electricity flowing into your home, to your shopping habits and relaxation, to your online interests and research. Fans of the inventor, Nikola Tesla, were upset by the mainstream elimination of his alternating current electricity, replacing it with Edison metered direct current electricity. Imagine your entire life being measured and monitored in an extremely data-driven, data-defined world. This data-driven economy is your future in technocracy.

The climate change political plan is the primary driver of technocracy. They intend to move the economy from a human-based economic system to an energy, resource-based financial system. Technocracy replaces traditional money exchange with energy, resource exchange. It replaces humans as determining supply and demand, deciding the confidence index in monetary policies with metered and monetized energy resources.

Megalithic energy, resource-based AI computer economy would be comparable to a "company store" model providing all of your needs—housing, food, medical, social. Your monetary allotment apportioned according to your allegiance and behavior monitored through 24-7 surveillance of your every thought, word, and deed. Physical coin and currency are no longer available. Instead, it replaces sovereign financial systems with a planetary network of cryptocurrencies. It is data-driven, not human-driven. This ultimate technocratic oligarchy promises transhuman technocratic equality and protection from climate catastrophe.

The initial forays into climate change monetization were driven by Al Gore, David Blood, and Mikhail Gorbachev in 2009. Their attempt to move the market toward cap and trade may have initially failed. Still, attempts to push the adoption of energy, resource-based economic system, meter, and metric, did not disappear.

In the summer of 2019, Representative Alexandria Ocasio-Cortez's chief of staff, Saikat Chakrabarti, admitted that the real motivation behind introducing the Green New Deal was to overhaul the entire economy. According to a Washington Post reporter who attended a meeting with Chakrabarti and Inslee's climate director, Sam Ricketts, Chakrabarti said, "The interesting thing about the Green New Deal is it wasn't originally a climate thing at all. Do you guys think of it as a climate thing? Because we think of it as a how-do-you-change-the-entire-economy thing," he added.[37] Chakrabarti confirmed climate change as the economic driver of technocracy.

Tentacles of Transhumanism

Listing how we will know if transhumanism is successful, you will see the emerging tentacles of technocracy. Kyle Munkittrick offers a comprehensive summation of how we will know if transhumanism is successful. He outlines the preferences of Transhumans.

- Prosthetics Preferred: Medical technology modifications preferred over the human body. We choose prosthetics and implants as we believe they are superior to our bodies. A stroll through any sports store features massive banners by Nike and Under Armour featuring athletes with prosthetics. Hollywood digitalized beings with superpowers familiarize us with computerized robotic implants.

---

37 Jack Crowe, "AOC's Chief of Staff Admits the Green New Deal Is Not about Climate Change," *National Review*, https://www.nationalreview.com/news/aocs-chief-of-staff-admits-the-green-new-deal-is-not-about-climate-change/

- Cyber Intelligence Preferred: Medical smart drug daily use enhances cognitive function in cooperation with cyber brain implants. University competition that flows into corporate career competition favors those at the top of the intelligence ladder. What better way to climb to the top, but with neural implants and drugs?

- Artificial Sensory Abilities Favored: A combination of AI analyzes sensory data for relevance and designs artificial reality (AR) projected on optic implants to help humans maneuver through life. Transhumanism augments and eventually controls our sensory reality and thereby, our minds and consciousness.

- Amazing Average Age: Aging, identified as a disease, is modified by nanotechnology and geoengineering to slow the process. The propagandized promise of immortality is ancient. Transhumanism uses the same ploy, presenting itself as the new fountain of youth.

- My Body, My Right: A Somatic Rights legal structure protects individual freedom to experiment and enhance one's physical body. When you convince people that they are entitled to do whatever they like with their bodies, you have free reign to offer them products and programs, many with lifelong effects. Your body becomes an art palette with tattoos, a cosmetic perfection with treatments, and a sexual expression with surgical enhancements. The main cultural message is that your body is flawed and fluid, so you have the right to improve upon it. It is imperative to enhance your physical appearance, especially in a social media reality. None of us is exempt from this appearance-based culture.

- Persons not People: Personhood determines traits rather than common humanity. This modification places animals, plants, and humans on a personhood continuum that includes artificial forms of intelligence, such as robots. Transhumanism flattens, discredits, and destroys natural human reality to impose an artificial reproduction of reality. Thus, demeaning humans by continually analyzing and critiquing their culture: who we are racially, ethnically, sexually, or in community and who are we spiritually and through religion. Confusion, inversions, and chaos create openings to design a transhuman reality.

Transhumanism and technocracy are rooted in the belief that the human brain is the center of consciousness. Confuse and fracture this brain-centered consciousness, and you control the human.

Who is a Transhuman?

Transhumans are biologically and psychologically engineered by science and technology to participate in a technocratic artificial reality. They control consumers as a surveilled resource in an AI metric economic system. Transhumanism's primary goal is to monitor and regulate human consciousness such that it becomes synonymous with and eventually identical to digital computer intelligence. Thus, all social transactions and interactions become monetized through given metrics. All energy and resources, including humans, translate as metrics to be monitored and economically controlled. With the human component of economics removed, human supply and demand are artificially determined.

Engineered responses to artificial reality program the transhuman. In other words, humans self-program using AI. The gradual integration of augmented sensory reality replaces natural human sensory perception. The Transhuman identifies as a machine. The following cultural milestones accomplish the human to Transhuman transition.

Transhuman Distanced from Nature

Human consciousness responds to and participates with sensory information experienced in nature. The recorded history of humans on earth connects intimately with nature. In turn, the natural world communicates and engages with human consciousness. As described earlier, this may be a natural biophoton exchange.

In transhumanism, humans are "taught" through augmented reality to respond to and participate with machines. Man, as a machine, replaces man as nature.

Thus, Transhumans develop through separation from involvement with the dynamic complex of nature. There is no longer "human nature." This replacement of human nature disconnects traditional markers for biological, spiritual, mental, and emotional connections to life.

Before you scoff, listen to this. In the mid-'80s, my Dayton, Ohio neighbors created the Missing Children's Network. They produced public service announcements on missing children for television stations. Their smart marketing highlighted missing children's images on milk cartons. Remember either seeing these milk cartons or reading about them? Their home phone became a report center for missing children's calls. Media across the country broadcast their stories of abducted children reunited with parents.[38]

The missing children meme began with a 1983 Department of Health and Human Services statistic that cited 1.5 million children missing EACH year. Fright skyrocketed across the nation and landed on milk cartons. Despite the flawed government study, culture remained damaged.[39] Today, something as innocent as a milk carton image transfers onto a massive national highway sign program alerting for "missing children." This orchestrated fear eventually steered a generation of parents from knowing neighbors and letting their children play freely, exploring nature. Separation from nature—mission accomplished. Generations onward would be alienated from nature through fear as coordinated transhumanism unfolded

---

38 Barbara Mahany and Jack Houston, "Mom, 2 Kids Reunited," *Chicago Tribune,* May 1, 1985, https://www.chicagotribune.com/news/ct-xpm-1985-05-01-8501260604-story.html.

39 Albert Scardino, "Experts Question Data about Missing Children," *New York Times,* August 18,1985, https://www.nytimes.com/1985/08/18/us/experts-question-data-about-missing-children.html.

Children, removed from nature and free play, are now to be ushered into corporatized, expensive sports and teams. Imagination and discovery of the natural world is no longer part of their development. A child's parietal lobe develops around five years old when they begin to develop independence and explore their world. When denied an orientation in nature, a child's parietal lobe does not develop fully, and they will not use the sensory world of life to understand what is real. The parietal lobe helps us orient in space, recognize landmarks, and, importantly, use all senses to begin to compose reality. Transhumans, alienated from nature, form reality through two primary mediums—television and computers. Suppressed development of the parietal lobe ushers in transhumanism.

Transhuman Mentally Engineered Insecurity

Human consciousness, especially in childhood, is seamlessly integrated and unified. A happy child who is loved, nourished, and cared for in a safe home may cry or express wants and desires, but they are primarily in a state of peaceful, harmonious play or sleep—even when rambunctious and energetic.

A calm child with an integrated mind is a secure child. According to John Bowlby's book, *A Secure Base: Parent-Child Attachment and Healthy Human Development* (1988, Reprint), there are four types of attachment: one secure and three insecure – 1) avoidant/dismissive, 2) anxious/preoccupied, and 3)disorganized (fearful-avoidant). We tend to favor and use one primary type of four attachment. Our choice is especially apparent when we are coping with high stress. At these times, we become aware that we are not functioning optimally. We are dysfunctional and emotionally disintegrate.

These dysfunctional emotional reactions are frequently sourced in early childhood when there was a lack of secure attachment, primarily with the mother—this lack of attachment results in insecurity, fear, and anxiety.

As a mother, initially, I took the possible lack of attachment during my children's early years to heart. Was I a present and reliable, loving parent? At times, I lost my temper, worried about organizing our home, and checked out preoccupied with work.

Gradually, I learned to let go of self-criticism and love myself through my imperfections. I try to be present with my adult children instead of shadowing our time together with my guilt and self-criticism.

In his book, *Wired for Love* (2011), Stan Tatkin explores how understanding your partner's attachment styles can help build a secure, happy relationship. He refers to our attachment style as our "social wiring." According to attachment theory, our social wiring establishes in the first three years of our life. In my therapy work, I refer to our attachment style as our imprint.

Human neural wiring is set early in life and leaves a lasting imprint of reactions and behaviors that often-become unconscious beliefs. Our imprint locks us into who we are. That is why our adult work to let go of "acting like our parents." is so challenging. These childhood imprinted reactions and behaviors are unconscious. We do not know we are reacting or behaving. As unconscious, our responses to stimulations and habitual behaviors are automatic.

Unfortunately, if your childhood was challenging, your imprinted reactions and behavior are deeply embedded in your neural system. Your attachment style and social wiring are insecure if you lived in an emotionally or physically abusive home or felt abandoned.

Who is a securely attached person?

If you grew up in a home where your parent valued you and spent more face-to-face time (or skin-to-skin) time with you, especially from birth to three years old, then you probably developed a secure attachment. If your parent put a high priority on raising you, attending to you and your needs, and expressed interest in your development, then you probably developed a secure attachment. Even with challenges, your parent quickly reestablished a safe relationship.

In a secure parent-child relationship, the home is lively, fun, curious, and playful. Good feelings predominate.

Tatkin categorizes those with secure attachments as Anchors. This attachment means that you place a high value on your intimate relationships. You form close, stable relationships and have healthy boundaries that maintain and enhance your positive energy.

While Anchors benefit from healthy, loving parenting, the good news is that each of us, as we mature, can work to become Anchors. We do this by "reparenting" ourselves in a healthy way. Reparenting requires self-knowledge. Examine what your parents did not give you. Identify those needs, find ways to prioritize how you answer those needs, and you are on your way to the process of reparenting.

What's This Got to Do with Defining Transhumans?

When comparing transhumanism to secure attachment theory, the issues of separation and dissociation stand out. For example, tablets and televisions separate parents and children. In place of a loving conversation with a parent, children detach to delightful ever-changing screen images. The neglected child easily connects to a virtual world. In this virtual world, a child's sense of self dissociates from his or her natural family identity

According to Dr. Fran Walfish, a Los Angeles-based child and family psychotherapist, "We have a lot of 2-year-olds using tablets now, and I see 3- and 4-year-olds that are already addicted. It's mind-blowing and a little scary." [40]

The proliferation of tablets as preferred child entertainment led to car manufacturers removing the drop-down DVD players from cars. Today, every child has their private customized videos on their tablet. Perfect for extended trips or events. Perfect for the inevitable, "are we there yet?"

Bowlby explained that a child's secure attachment formed from birth to three. As a mother cradles a child, their brain develops with the release of hormones. The hormones oxytocin and dopamine

---

40 Elyse Wanshel, "10 Reasons why you shouldn't give your child a smart phone or tablet," https://www.littlethings.com/reasons-not-to-give-children-technology/.

play a critical role in the infant's brain and overall physical development. When a child is left alone and cradles a tablet, the lack of tactile stimulation weakens the body's health, especially during birth to three years.

This attachment discussion is essential. Notably, the major challenge of forming healthy attachments in an era of Transhuman technological parenting is obvious. The removal of human interaction harms the emotional, mental, and physical health of the child. They are pulled from the natural sensory attachment to a parent and pushed to less desirable artificial devices.

Why does this matter? Because a child's secure attachment, primarily to mother, determines how safe and secure they feel in the world. A confident child moves with ease out into the world as they mature and develop. An insecure child either withdraws (to their tablet) or experiences waves of anxiety and fear. These overwhelming feeling of dread and fear become their common neural system reaction. Insecure children either isolate and become invisible or overdramatize and act-out. In comparison, an integrated child feels safe and secure in the world. Life is manageable.

Transhuman Brain Separated from the Field of Consciousness

In the early 90s, universities began offering courses and opening departments to study consciousness. These first departments opened at the University of Arizona, Tucson; University of Southern California, Santa Cruz; Princeton; University of Michigan; and New York University. Despite a few academic departments, the subject of consciousness began to dominate scientific discussions. The advent of courses on Eastern Religion also complimented consciousness studies, as East met West in studies of the mind. While Eastern religion emphasized consciousness as a field phenomenon, Western science moved closer to biological brain research. These Western scientists began to correlate brain function with computers.

As computer science opened venues to scientific research, the US government saw the need for brain research. By categorizing the brain's neural network, computer scientists could eventually build a brain, or at least create a conscious computer, via AI or machine learning. Money, intellect, and energy poured into studying the Brain.

In 1990, President George H W Bush declared the "Decade of the Brain." It was a collaborative effort of the Library of Congress, the National Institute of Mental Health, and the National Institutes of Health and psychological, medical, and neurological associations. Though off to an impressive start, the Decade of the Brain was mostly successful as a marketing project that inspired interest in brain research that encompassed consciousness studies.

The 90s Decade of the Brain introduced several research applications, including fMRI, bold neural imagining that is used today in consciousness science research. The discovery of neural plasticity and identifying significant phases of human neural development also came during this time. Next-generation anti-depressants and anti-psychotic pharmaceuticals also were pioneered.[41]

But when compared to the government's Human Genome Project (HGP), also launched in 1990, the Decade of the Brain failed to produce noteworthy results. HGP, an international scientific research project to map the human genome, ended in 2003 to acclaim. "The Human Genome Project (HGP) was one of the great feats of exploration in history... the HGP gave us the ability, for the first time, to read nature's complete genetic blueprint for building a human being."[42]

And yet, as government brain research lagged genome research, computers and their potential to connect to the human mind increased. In 1990, the same year that the Brain Initiative and the HGP were launched, quietly at CERN, outside Geneva, Switzerland, World Wide Web software was first tested by Tim Berners-Lee. Six years later, Google began indexing the World Wide Web. In 1990, Macintosh and Microsoft launched updated systems, along with the

---

41 https://en.wikipedia.org/wiki/Decade_of_the_Brain.
42 https://www.genome.gov/human-genome-project.

release of Microsoft Office. Bill Gates declared, "DOS is Dead." In 1994 major PC games were first released. In 1995 Global Positioning System (GPS) was launched. What a decade.

But, the Bush BRAIN initiative, while weak, was not dead...yet. In 2013, Obama began the BRAIN Initiative (Brain Research through Advancing Innovative Neurotechnologies), led by the White House Office of Science and Technology Policy. Following the HGP's successful structure, the BRAIN initiative developed a brain activity map to research 10s of billions of neurons. This time the government met with success. Like the HGP, the BRAIN initiative endeavored to provide the brain's organization, structure, and function, especially concerning human behavior.

As cultural evidence accumulates on humans' gradual alienation from nature, the evolution of humans into machines appears inevitable. But is it? One calls to mind the saying-"it's not nice to fool with mother nature" from the 1950s Chiffon margarine commercial. Nature pushes back as cultural pendulums swing and cycles repeat. Eventually, a common ground materializes.

Section 3

Common Ground:
Transhuman Brain Research and
Exoconscious Humans

As Exoconscious experiencers move through integration and utilization of their contact, communication, and co-creation with ETs, multidimensionals, they provide a rich archive of information about how the human mind relates to the field of consciousness. Experiencers provide the subjective component to the scientifically objective brain initiatives.

Transhuman scientific advancements complement Exoconscious Human experience. In particular, computer analysis, algorithms, and brain research are fertile common ground. This common ground includes:

Brain Balancing/Sound Healing: The Brain States Technology's Brainwave Optimization, founded by Lee Gerdes in Scottsdale, Arizona, [43]influenced my journey into balancing, relaxing, and integrating my physical neural system. Their system improves upon many bio-feedback programs using advanced biometrics and bio-logical signals (collected in an extensive database of clients) with customized sound. Brain technology prompts healing on a quantum level, as your brain watches your brain and heals itself. Using real-time reflection, you participate as you watch your brainwaves calm in response to sound. Algorithms and computer imaging, along with data analysis and storage, improve treatment in the field of trauma that once fell stagnant, failing to produce new forms of healing.

Neural Plasticity: Neural plasticity introduced the powerful ability of the brain to change and heal. In early 2001 several of my children received developmental eye therapy or vision therapy. This therapy is a series of visual exercises and protocols. I recall asking the eye physician how eye therapy worked. His response was, "we are going to change the pathways of your child's brain, how she sees."[44] Initially taken aback by these new methods, my children moved through the process. I witnessed the reality of neural plasticity, the body's ability to change. Neural plasticity became mainstream medicine and healing via Bush's brain decade research.

Trauma/PTSD Treatment: Brain scans, though not currently used to diagnose trauma responses and PTSD, indicate areas of the

---

43 https://brainstatetech.com/.

44 Neural plasticity is the foundation of vision therapy. Neuroplasticity refers to the ability of neurons and neural networks in the brain to change their connections and actual behavior in response to new information and sensory stimulation. Neural networks carry out specific functions, yet they retain the capacity to deviate from their usual functions and to reorganize themselves. https://www.optometrystudents. com/vision-therapy-neuroplasticity-optometry-student-perspective/.

brain generating responses. My professional opinion is that trauma responses are multifaceted.

The holistic treatment of trauma works with the complexity of human biology and nature. I adopt a layered approach.

1) Emotional work to identify the unconscious pattern of trauma response to certain situations. The client becomes aware of how they promote the continuation of suffering and trauma because their neural system has been wired for years to respond in this manner.

2) Mental work prepares and strengthens new patterns of response that gradually leads to a rewiring of one's brain and neural system via neural plasticity.

3) Physical work involves harnessing the movement of the body to heal. For example, if a client has a primary freeze trauma response, their physical body must be disciplined to move, not freeze. Movement breaks the freeze.

4) Spiritual work unifies the emotions, body, and mind by opening perspectives of creating a healthy life. Spiritual work often involves releasing outgrown religious beliefs of shame and self-punishment, replacing them with a spirit of forgiveness and self-love. The human spirit moves out into the field of consciousness for information, wisdom, and guidance.

In special situations, self-monitoring and thoughtful response diagnostics work effectively through phone apps that a client can use daily to access their progress. Daily progress creates new neural networks. Diet and nutrition apps such as Weight Watchers or Fitness Pal have tested and proven that algorithms and AI complement the human desire to lose weight, stop smoking, or learn to calm through prayer or meditation. All of these apps rewire the user's nervous system.

Would these health advancements be available without transhumanism and their accompanying science and technology? I doubt it. While scientists remain skeptical of subjective experience, they witness how their technology influences health. While Exoconscious Humans remain skeptical of objective science without the balance of subjectivity, they observe scientific discoveries enriching self-knowledge. Science and massive databases may not thoroughly examine the soul, spirit, emotions, and mind. Still, together we move forward to shape an understanding of humans and our brain/neural system.

Chapter 2

Psychic Intelligence is Preferred

Artificial Intelligence is Preferred

Section 1

Psychically Intelligent Exoconscious Humans

In May of 2019, the nation's media headlines broadcast a college admissions scandal. Reports revealed parents paying $6.5 million to get their kids into top tier universities, using faked athletic scholarships and test scores. Hollywood entertainers and Wall Street high rollers ducked behind their posse of attorneys into a courtroom; some departed under a cloud of verdicts including prison, fines, and probation.

What if this news story is a precursor to future academic admission manipulation that we are only now imagining? Transhumanism is quietly seeding a new form of educational privilege that can be applied early-on by wealthy, competitive parents of young children through a carefully dosed regime of smart drugs and neural implants. Could this implanted and supplemented next college-age generation become the baseline for a Transhuman quantitative intelligence necessary for academic success? As elementary and secondary online education removes human teachers from providing input on intelligence and achievement testing, Transhuman students regurgitating AI information—data in, data out—would become the baseline for measuring all students from all socio-economic groups. Take a minute and let this sink in.

If this happens—and all indications are that it is—then we are witnessing a reverse of what the Transhumans told us. They claim that computers are being engineered to one day achieve and surpass human intelligence (Synchronicity). What if this is not true? **What if the hidden strategy of transhumanism is to cultivate humans to have computer intelligence? Humans, who think like, identify as computers.** Online education's use of tablets and computers through centralized networks combined with implants and smart drugs accomplish this covert strategy. If this speculation is correct, it is brilliant marketing, challenging to dislodge in our mass consumer minds.

Humans brought to the level of AI, not vice versa. We may be witnessing a marketing sleight of hand—suppressing psychic intelligence and creativity for computer compliance and conformity.

Let us consider what's at stake with the loss of human psychic intelligence, limited by computerized education, implants, and smart drugs.

Contrasting Psychic Intelligence and AI

One of the first manifestations of ET, multidimensional experience in an Exoconscious Human, is an increase in psychic intelligence. An experiencer "senses" differently. They perceive a broad spectrum that includes beings, energies, and information. In turn, psychic abilities heighten precognition, astral projection, psychokinesis, remote viewing, telepathy, and mediumship. An Exoconscious Human develops psychic intelligence.

Note the use of intelligence, as opposed to intellect. Intellect is an individual's ability to acquire and use knowledge and skills. It refers to cognitive abilities such as memory, analysis, identification, and categorization. As an ability to acquire knowledge, collect data, it is subjective and developmental, integrating environment and exposure. In other words, intellect develops over time. Intellect prefers facts and abstract rational thinking.

In contrast, intelligence is inborn, innate—a function of consciousness. It goes beyond facts and moves into the ability to determine meaning and purpose. It is objective in that it refers to the individual's ability to use reason to, for example, choose a course of action. These intelligence abilities apply to transhumanism with the goal of machines developing artificial intelligence—a higher function of consciousness than data collection.

In this chapter, I propose that Exoconscious Humans activate psychic intelligence through ET, multidimensional contact. Before contact, some may have a propensity to use their intuition and possess a knowing, but most fall in the normal range.

Many experiencers claim that before contact, they had a below-average to average psychic ability. The FREE scientific survey of over 4,200 participants who had contact experience experienced a change in psychic abilities.[45] A majority (58%) of experiencers surveyed stated that they became more psychic than before due to their contact experience. Their contact seeded and, in some cases, enhanced their psychic development.

Gardner's Multiple Intelligences: Psychic Intelligence as Ninth Intelligence

In the 1980s, I read Howard Gardner's book, *Frames of Mind: Theory of Multiple Intelligences.*[46] Like Gardner, I found intelligence based

---

45 FREE is The Edgar Mitchell Foundation for Research into Extraterrestrial and Extraordinary Experiences headed by Rey Hernandez. Their book, *Beyond UFOs: The Science of Consciousness and Contact with Non Human Intelligence, Volume 1,* (2018) compiled over 5 years, surveyed over 4,200 participants with Non Human Intelligence Contact in 100 countries. I wrote a chapter in Beyond UFOs entitled "The Psychological Transformation of the Experiencer After Contact: An Exoconsciousness Analysis of the FREE Research Data".

46 Howard E. Gardner, *Frames of Mind: The Theory of Multiple Intelligences* (New York: Basic Books, 1983).

on standard IQ testing narrow and incomplete. Teaching child development and vocational education, I saw that many bright students did not fit into linguistic, logical, mathematical intelligence. They skillfully applied their knowledge outside the bounds of traditional IQ testing. Reading Gardner's book affirmed what I was observing as both a teacher and a parent.

Gardner's theory now proposes eight categories of intelligence:

- Linguistic intelligence (word smart—writer, actor, librarian, lawyer)
- Logical-mathematical intelligence (numbers and reasoning smart—computer programmer, corporate, economist, scientist)
- Spatial intelligence (picture smart—pilot, mapmaker, artist, air traffic controller)
- Body-Kinesthetic intelligence (body smart—athlete, dancer, actor, farmer, mechanic)
- Musical intelligence (music smart—musician, singer, songwriter, conductor, sound healer)
- Interpersonal intelligence (people smart—administrator, psychologist, nurse, sales, public relations, teacher)
- Intrapersonal intelligence (self-smart—novelist, religious, spiritual, therapist, coach, entrepreneur)
- Naturalist intelligence (nature smart— biologist, astronomer, chef, farmer, zoo personnel, veterinarian)

It was no surprise that as I developed exoconsciousness, Gardner's multiple intelligence theory would play a significant role. This time, I perceived an opportunity to expand his multiple intelligence theory to encompass the intelligence I found in colleagues, clients, friends, and Exoconscious Humans.

I proposed a ninth multiple intelligence—psychic intelligence. [47]

---

47 Gardner wrote about the possibility of a ninth intelligence which he classified as Existential Intelligence, which is the ability to tackle deep

- Psychic intelligence (supersensory smart—healer, astrologer, medium, mystic, yogi, writer, psychic investigator)

Psychic intelligence solves problems or creates products valued within one or more cultural settings (to paraphrase Gardner). Exoconscious Humans possess psychic intelligence and use it in their personal life and career. At times, this psychic intelligence feels supernatural, in the ability to "see beyond" what others see or know. It intensifies creativity by linking heretofore unseen energies and information into patterns and ideas. It is the birthplace of innovative ideas and products.

Given the ability to see beyond, those with psychic intelligence have difficulty communicating their ideas and perceptions. They frequently elicit responses, "what are you talking about," "that's absurd," and "prove it to me." Their information commonly causes cognitive dissonance in others. According to Leon Festinger's, *A Theory of Cognitive Dissonance*,[48] humans seek consistency in their beliefs and cognitions. When another person offers an alternative perception or idea, it causes dissonance or confusion in their thought pattern. The alternative opinion can cause confusion and pain, as it calls into question the other person's reality. Usually, according to Festinger, amid this feeling of dissonance, something must give. Either the person chooses to hold to their beliefs, or they open to another perspective.

Most Exoconscious Humans are skilled at recognizing and responding respectfully to cognitive dissonant responses. They learn to limit their answers and allow the other person time to integrate the new ideas. They know that the field of consciousness is at work. Additional information may come from another source, or time will gently dissolve the emotional and mental barriers to new

---

questions about human existence such as the meaning of life and death. He has not formally added it to his list of 8 intelligences.

48 Leon Festinger, *A Theory of Cognitive Dissonance* (Stanford University Press, 1962).

ideas. However, cognitive dissonance is too disturbing to consider in some interactions, and the Exoconscious Human discards or silences their psychic information.

Psychic intelligence, not yet recognized or validated by the mainstream, is both a gift and a liability. Either way, Exoconscious Humans possess it. Why? How does this happen? Is an aspect of contact experience involved?

Exoconscious Development of Psychic Abilities

ET, multidimensional contact generates psychic abilities. Those beginning their contact experience often move through a somewhat awkward learning stage to finesse, refine, and manage their psychic abilities. The initial awkward steps are essential because psychic abilities define the self. We describe ourselves by what we do. We characterize ourselves with the information we receive and how we process it.

The contact experience appears linked to psychic intelligence and abilities. A possible source of increased psychic abilities through contact might be due to a shift in perceived reality that opens the mind of the experiencer to heretofore ignored possibilities. It also activates curiosity, a need to know what happened to them. In the FREE survey, 80%[49] increased their interest in psychic phenomena. We define ourselves by what we seek to understand. Many professional careers are launched by wanting to know more about some aspect of life. In the case of Exoconscious Humans, their contact led them into seeking psychic information, which in turn developed their trust and competence in their psychic abilities.

Developing into an Exoconscious Human takes time and patience—sometimes years of research and trial and error. Eventually, Exoconscious Humans learn to set boundaries for

---

49 Note: all percentages are rounded off, approximate and unless noted are Phase 2. "Initial Research Data Summary of the Dr. Edgar Mitchell FREE Experiencer Research Study", http://www.experiencer.org/initial-research- data-summary/ (December 1, 2016).

themselves and others. For example, just because an Exoconscious Human can read another person's body energetic, it does not give them the right to tap the person's shoulder in front of them at the grocery store and recommend that they see their doctor right away.

Concurrently, Exoconscious Humans learn to set healthy boundaries for themselves in their pursuit of heightened psychic abilities and intelligence. Developing psychic abilities can be fun, exploratory, and inspiring. It can also become obsessive. It can remove an individual from being grounded in 3-D earth life and its everyday responsibilities. Developing psychic abilities can flavor and enhance life experience or dominate it.

An ethical protocol comes with psychic abilities, a respect for self and others along with firm boundaries. Management of powers requires discipline and respect for others. And yet, psychic powers proliferate in Exoconscious Humans.

Frequently, contact experiencers mention their increased telepathic abilities. Their telepathic abilities are far-reaching human to human and human to plants, animals, earth, extending out to ETs, multidimensionals. Exoconscious Humans tap into a field of consciousness present in all of nature and the cosmos. Is it biophoton based? Most likely.

In his autobiography, *Disturbing the Universe*, physicist Freeman Dyson referred to three minds: 1) the human mind, 2) the quantum mind residing at the micro-level of subatomic activity, 3) the mind of the universe. He inferred that atoms had consciousness, which led to a flood of questions and critiques. Dyson maintained consciousness involved a field of activity stretching beyond the human, down into the subatomic level of life and out into the universe.[50] Consciousness is the field that Exoconscious Humans explore with telepathy.

In the FREE survey, a substantial majority (78%) of respondents stated that their contact experience involved some type of

---

50 Freeman Dyson, *Disturbing the Universe*, (New York: Basic Books, 1981).

telepathic, or thought transference, or direct knowing, given by an ET. Could the telepathic exchange between humans and ET multidimensionals be the source of the matrix that births the Exoconscious Human's telepathic ability? Future scientific studies might explore how psychic skills form. To what extent are psychic abilities present before contact? Do they strengthen with contact?

The FREE survey also explored telepathy regarding message communication. Over 50% experienced a visual signal, a "Vision, a Video, or a Picture associated with this...telepathic/channeling was an ET not physically seen." Over half of the respondents' experienced a buzzing sound in both ears before receiving a telepathic message.

In addition to telepathic abilities, nearly 30% of the FREE survey participants cited increased channeling skills. They could both receive and communicate information directly as a channel, speaking for the being, or conversationally. Both these responses indicated a participatory consciousness on the part of contactees. That is, they reported the ability to receive information and move into other dimensions and retrieve information.

Are Humans Wired for Psychic Intelligence and ET contact?

Did human brain development enable psychic intelligence and ET, multidimensional connections that become innate abilities? Is the human brain hardwired to connect, communicate, and co-create with multiple dimensions?

A Brazilian study of psychography,[51] defined as channeled writing from the "other side," tested ten mediums, five less experienced and five experienced. Research subjects were injected with a

---

51 David DiSalvo, "Study find the unexpected in brains of spirit mediums," *Psychology Today*. December 2012, https://www.psychologytoday.com/us/blog/neuronarrative/201212/study-finds-the-unexpected-in-the-brains-spirit-mediums-0.

radioactive tracer to capture their brain activity. The results were perplexing.

Experienced psychographers showed lower brain activity levels in areas associated with problem-solving, reasoning, planning, language, and movement. Specifically, this included low levels in the left hippocampus (limbic system), right superior temporal gyrus, and frontal lobe regions. This finding indicated that the experienced psychographers' brains exhibited less focus and reasoning. In contrast, the less experienced channeled writers showed increased activity in these parts of their brains, perhaps indicating heightened problem solving and reasoning to carryout psychography.

However, when comparing channeled writing samples, the complexity scores of the written materials diverged. Here's the perplexity. The experienced psychographers' high complexity score indicated precisely the opposite of their brain test. To write complex communications, they would need to have more activity in problem solving and reasoning areas of the brain. This result was the opposite of observed in their brain activity.

Daniel Amen, MD, an expert in the neuroscience of psychic abilities, asserts that "psychic experience is associated with a decrease in frontal lobe function (controls problem solving, memory, language) and increases or decreases in right temporal lobe function (similar to seizure phenomena)."[52]

Brazilian researchers Norman Don and Gilda Moura conducted a brain mapping experiment with UFO experiencers. Their selection criteria determined whether the subjects could re-enter a state of consciousness or trance they experienced after contact experiences. In this state, subjects maintained muscular relaxation, while their EEGs exhibited high frequency (beta) activity at all electrode sites, but with maximum function at the prefrontal and adjacent loci. Further, the study showed no brain activity suggestive

---

52 Daniel Amen, "The Neuroscience of Psychic Experience", https://www.doctoroz.com/article/neuroscience-psychic-experience.

of psychopathology, schizophrenia, with a high correlation with meditation states.[53]

Neuropsychologist Peter Fenwick, a senior lecturer at Kings College, London, researched near-death experiences and analyzed more than 300 samples. He examined the "psychic" experiences of 17 students. The results showed that those identified as "sensitive" contained more divorced or single people and had at some time consulted a psychiatrist. They also experienced more head injuries and serious illnesses.[54] The head injury aspect of psychic abilities suggests a productive pathway to research the brain's role in psychic abilities.

A comparison of brain studies on psychics, near-death experiencers, and ET contactees is useful for the exoconscious community. If humans have neural wiring for psychic intelligence and contact, this may lead to researching how some humans are psychologically predisposed to ET, multidimensional connection.

Are Humans Psychologically Predisposed to ET Contact?

Why do some people have contact with ETs and multidimensionals, and others do not? Are some people predisposed to contact? Kenneth Ring, Psychology Professor at the University of Connecticut, met contactee and author, Whitley Strieber. Their discussions pointed to the intriguing similarities between Near-Death Experiencers and ET, multidimensional contactees. In 1992, Ring published one of the few statistical studies on UFO abductees,

---

53 Norman Don and Gilda Moura, "Topographic Brain Mapping of UFO Experiencers", *Journal of Scientific Exploration*, Vol 11, No. 4, pp 435-453, 1997, https://pdfs.semanticscholar.org/a171/f52e058266cbe69cb-c3a9efec7c7f464c4f8.pdf.

54 P. Fenwick and S. Galliano and Coate MA and V Rippere and D. Brown, "'Psychic sensitivity', mystical experience, head injury and brain pathology", *British Journal of Medical Psychology*, March 1985, https://www.ncbi.nlm.nih.gov/pubmed/3986152.

REBECCA HARDCASTLE WRIGHT

The Omega Project: Near-Death Experiences, UFO Encounters, and Mind at Large. Ring interviewed participants and administered a battery of psychological tests and structured questionnaires to 97 individuals who had UFO related abduction experiences with ETs, multidimensionals, and a separate 74 individuals that had undergone a near-death experience.[55]

In general, mainstream psychology classified ET multidimensional experiencers as fantasy-prone, with wild imaginations. Ring's research refuted psychopathology's fantasy-prone personality view experiencers. To distinguish, he defined fantasy proneness as the "spontaneous tendency to enter into a state of rapt absorption focused on a world of self-created fantasy." In other words, some individuals lived in a world of fantasy and make-believe—the stuff of fairy tales and magical stories. Unfortunately, being fantasy-prone was a common diagnosis of persons who experienced an unusual phenomenon. But, according to Ring, it was an incorrect diagnosis.

Rejecting the mainstream view, Ring found limited psychological data to indicate that UFO and near-death experiencers were fantasy-prone. His diagnostics showed experiencers not particularly inclined to fantasy, but rather, sensitive to non-ordinary realities. Furthermore, their non-ordinary experiences were recurring. Ring claimed that ET, multidimensional experiencers had a psychological predisposition to sensing non-ordinary realities. He designated these individuals as psychically gifted, able to sustain altered states of consciousness that revealed non-ordinary truths. Experiencers had encounter-prone personalities. This psychological predisposition heightened their ability to experience UFOs and ET, multidimensional contact, and near-death awareness.

While the FREE experiencer survey was modeled, in part, on Ring's Omega Project Questionnaire, their results differed in the defining aspects of an anomalous encounter prone personality.

---

55 Kenneth Ring, *The Omega Project: Near-Death Experiences, Ufo Encounters, and Mind at Large,* (New York: William Morrow, 1992).

Ring based his theory of an encounter-prone-personality on two main factors: 1) psychically gifted and highly sensitive, often due to incidents of child abuse and trauma, and 2) dissociation, which he describes as normal. According to Ring, children who grow up in abusive and traumatic environments tend to be sensitive to ET, multidimensionals because such conditions stimulated dissociation. A child's dissociative response developed to survive. It was their way to tune out of trauma and chaos. When the traumatized child tuned out, it was easier for them to tune into alternative realities. These alternative realities became a safe inner reality. Traumatized children often felt safer in alternative inner thought-spaces than in their home environment.

Ring noted that this propensity to live in inner alternative realities also corresponded to the experiencer's deep psychological absorption, which he defined as the ability to concentrate on the figures and environment of inner reality. Participants in Ring's study were extraordinarily detailed in their description and deeply involved in their alternative awareness. Ring's central finding was that abuse and trauma trigger dissociative reactions and promote psychological absorption that, in turn, creates an encounter-prone personality.

Contrasting Ring's psychological findings regarding childhood abuse and trauma in encounter prone personality development, only a minority of the FREE survey respondents describe harmful contact with ETs, multidimensionals. Most respondents emphasize a positive, secure relationship with ET, multidimensional beings. Since the FREE survey did not explore childhood trauma in detail, a full comparison with Ring's theories are not possible at this time. However, a future investigation might address trauma and abuse to examine whether Ring's encounter prone personality theories are relevant.

The discrepancy between Ring and FREE's research may lie in the types of experiencers interviewed. Conceivably, the respondents to the FREE survey were more integrated experiencers with advanced consciousness as compared to Ring's respondents—25 years separate Ring's and FREE survey respondents. Cultural awareness and acceptance dramatically shifted in those 25 years.

According to Ring, all groups (near-death, ET, multidimensional, and UFO) manifested remarkably similar positive behavioral transformations despite their uniquely different experiences. He noted similar findings for all groups, compared with control groups, in such areas as physiology and neurology, paranormal and psychic abilities, and psychological transformation in their perspective and opinions of various topics. All groups also underwent profound positive psychological profile changes from their experiences.

The following psychological attributes increased significantly in near-death, ET, multidimensional, and UFO experiencer groups. These subjective attributes consist of concern with spiritual matters, desire to help others, compassion for others, ability to love others, care for the welfare of the planet, conviction that there is life after death, tolerance of others, and insight into others' problems. Ring also highlighted differences. The following attributes decreased significantly: concern with material things in life, interest in organized religion, fear of death, and desire to become well known.

The FREE Experiencer Research Study utilized many of Ring's same questions in his 1992 seminal research study. FREE's findings confirmed all of Ring's research results. More specifically, approximately 70-85% (depending on the individuals' question) in both his UFO and near-death contact groups underwent profound positive psychological transformations. In the FREE study, a vast majority (71-85%, depending on the participants' question) also had similar positive changes as in Ring's study.

Though puzzling and often ignored by research scientists, psychic intelligence involves an innate ability of human consciousness that may evolve and expand with physical trauma, such as head trauma, a psychological predisposition, and emotional, sensory sensitivity. How does psychic intelligence compare to AI? An important field of inquiry for Exoconscious Humans. If, through psychic intelligence, we become more human, through AI, do we become more machine?

Section 2

Transhuman AI

As with exoconsciousness, a definition of AI is in order. Defining AI requires that we also define machine learning, deep learning, and artificial intuition as the four are interconnected, like Russian Babushka stacked dolls, one inside the other. Artificial intelligence is the outer doll, containing the subsets of smaller dolls. As you pull the largest AI doll apart, you find the next doll, machine learning. Pulling that doll apart, you find a more miniature doll, deep learning. Opening it, you see the smallest doll, artificial intuition. All the babushka dolls fit together within the outer doll of AI.[56]

The outer doll, AI, is the science and engineering of making a machine intelligent. Creating a human-machine that can think, reason, collect data, classify, make connections, and see patterns— thus imitating rational human behavior. (Or, as we previously discussed, socially engineering humans to think like AI computers.)

AI simulates human intelligence by using "rules engines" or "if-then statements." For example, today, Amazon features paid authors and businesses, but in the early years, when ordering a book, you saw a list of similar books you could order. AI created this list. Say you ordered a historical fiction novel. Then, the algorithm's creator assumed that IF you like to read this type of book, THEN you would like to read these other historical novels.

Amazon created an intelligent sales algorithm using statistical mapping of sales data. Many authors and producers of goods benefited from the "if… then" algorithm. It was genuinely fun for the reader to see recommendations appear in what felt like an organic process. Wow, Amazon knows what I like.

Over time, the Amazon sales algorithm changed. Today, individuals and businesses purchase ads to provide direct access to their desired space on an Amazon page to promote their books and

---

56 Skymind AI Wiki has a comprehensive beginners guide to AI, machine learning, and deep learning. https://skymind.com/wiki/.

goods. Profitable ads are a priority, not the purchaser. It was financially advantageous for Amazon to replace the customer algorithm-based space on its webpages with purchased ads, so they modified their algorithm. For early users of Amazon, what felt organic and fun, for today's users, feels artificial and contrived with pages peppered with slick book ads, independent authors competing with unseen AI formula ad auctions, and big publishing companies dominating the platform.

Machine learning is a subset of AI, the next doll. It is an application of AI that can modify itself when provided more data. Unlike "if...then," it doesn't require human expertise to change. Machine learning changes itself. Data in machine learning is comparable to experiences for humans. Imagine you are in a photography class learning to use a dark room to develop your camera film—before photoshop programs. You needed to use trial and error to refine the photograph. Experience or trial and error provide the data for machine learning.

Games were the basis of early machine learning applications. The inventor of machine learning, Arthur Samuel, played checkers with a computer, using the data to minimize the errors to program the computer to win. Samuel used checkers to "optimize the algorithm," or so that the program, not he, would win the game. His process required many failures to make the right moves.

Machine learning builds algorithms with yes-no logic. Should the checker make this move? Yes or no. With each choice, the database expands. And as databases grow, the need for more powerful computers increased. From computer punch cards to magnetic tape storage capabilities, and now the online, mobile internet—data gathering has exponentially advanced.

Moving from computer games to the brain, we come to deep learning, the next doll, a subset of machine learning. A surface network is one "hidden" layer. A deep network has multiple "hidden" layers. In deep learning, data passes through layers via a mathematical operation. Deep learning aims to build a computer brain with human capabilities.

In Phoenix, Arizona, Waymo driverless cars are commonplace. Waymo is a subsidiary of Alphabet. (Alphabet is the parent company of Google.) Waymo uses deep learning to imitate a human driver and be more proficient. Their system uses multiple layered computer networks to analyze different driving scenarios' data to improve perception and accuracy. Google Brain engineers collaborate for the capability of designing neural nets to train other neural nets.

Geospatial analysis merges the IoT (Internet of Things), self-driving vehicles, an unimaginable array of sensors, and satellite imagery in an invisible infrastructure that few perceive. Organizations, corporations, and governments with the financial ability to access geospatial data can track financial assets, business services, global transportation, environmental changes, military and cultural movements, and yes, human thought and motivation in a cross-referential, integrative system.[57] With geospatial technology, the skies above and earth below become an electronic "cloud of knowing" around and through whom we orient our life.

The expanding applications of AI logically lead us to question whether AI can replace human intuition, psychic intelligence? Yes, in a somewhat modified form. A form of AI, artificial intuition, navigates situations where the future is unknown, such as planning scenarios of a pandemic, election results, or strategic war decisions. The global banking industry uses artificial intuition to investigate cybercrime, money laundering, and sophisticated fraud schemes.[58] With AI intuition, machines think on their own in unfamiliar situations, replicating a human "gut feeling" or quick intuition to make decisions or identify threats and opportunities. As early machine

---

57 Luca Budello, "The Power of Place: Geospatial is Transforming our World", *Geospatial World,* October 2020. https://www.geospatialworld. net/blogs/geospatial-is-transforming-our-world/

58 Mark Gazit, "The Fourth Generation of AI is Here and its called Artificial Intuition" *The Next Web,* September 2020. https://thenextweb. com/neural/2020/09/03/the-fourth-generation-of-ai-is-here-and-its-called-artificial-intuition/.

learning played checkers, Deep Stack technology corporation formulated its artificial intuition by competing against a professional poker player. Poker honed Deep Stack's AI with strategic decision-making abilities in a field of unknowns. In this sense, artificial intuition functions within a "field" consciousness, like Exoconscious Humans, albeit with a narrow and limited dimensionality.

Like the AI algorithms developed by Amazon to sell products, navigate the environment of a driverless car, and increasing demands for scenario planning—the algorithm adapts to the changing needs of the individual, corporation, or government. When markets and applications change, AI is a willing supplicant. Machine AI possesses no emotions, critical reasoning, discussion, or morality to traverse or overcome. AI is an ever-compliant flexible system. But wait...does this connect to transhumanism's cultural desire for continuously adaptable, modifiable humans? Of course, it does. Flexibility and unquestioning compliance exemplify and accelerate the engineering of humans as machines.

Next, we will examine AI in two areas: 1) economic technocracy and 2) communication.

Technocratic Applications of AI

The Fourth Industrial Revolution defines our early twenty-first century. Steam-powered transportation and factories described the First Industrial Revolution (1760-1840). Mass manufacturing and production of goods and railroads and telegraph networks marked the Second Industrial Revolution (1871-1914). Computerization of manufacturing and communication characterized the Third Industrial Revolution (1950-2010). Today, Transhuman AI, robotics, IoT, and synthetic biology define the Fourth Industrial Revolution. As economists note, we are in a comprehensive "reset" that encompasses all of life.

According to World Economic Forum Founder and Executive Chairman Professor Klaus Schwab, this revolution involves all society sectors, stakeholders of the global polity (stakeholders being the public and private sectors, academia, and civil society). It requires a "fusion of technologies"—physical, digital, and biological spheres—creating a symbiosis between micro-organisms, the human body, the products people consume, and the buildings they inhabit.[59] I would add the craft they fly—cosmic conscious craft, as I explore in chapter 5, Cosmic Exoconscious Humans.

To be clear—this means that humans will not use technology but instead be integrated into and merge with the digital and synthetic biological worlds. Thus, biologically and neurologically, humans become machines. Please retain this information, as we will expand on its meaning in subsequent chapters, particularly synthetic biology.

However, this all-encompassing Fourth Industrial Revolution is not new. Interestingly, its roots extend back into the Second Industrial Revolution that spawned the ideas of technocracy.

As discussed previously, technocracy, an economic and financial system created by scientists and engineers in the 1930s, seeded transhumanism ideas and AI creation. Without Technocracy, there is no transhumanism and no AI.

Technocracy is the critical lynchpin in a Transhuman culture. Its importance is unparalleled. According to leading expert and historian Patrick Wood, technocracy was a resource-based system, accounted for through an energy currency that would displace traditional supply and demand, debt-based currencies. In 1938, The Technocrat magazine stated, "Technocracy is the science of social engineering, the scientific operation of the entire social mechanism to produce and distribute goods and services to the entire population..." Over time, it developed into an economic and financial system established by scientists and computer engineers.

---

59 Schwab warns that the Fourth Revolution may have two distinct outcomes, success is not assured. It could either 'lift humanity into a new collective and moral consciousness based on a shared sense of destiny', or, 'have the potential to "robotize" humanity and thus to deprive us of our heart and soul.' https://www.weforum.org/about/world-economic-forum

Unpacking technocracy as a resource-based energy currency system, once your home has a smart meter installed and all your appliances, HVAC systems are coordinated (including your solar panels), and integrated with the cars, you are given an energy credit as currency. You maintain your life with a "scientifically determined" amount of energy currency. Algorithms adjust your energy allocation. These algorithms change with the needs and forecasts determined by the engineers of the system. You have limited input except for your data collection. Within the structure, data provider is your primary role. Your needs are a minor consideration. If you spend too many energy credits, then your time in the shower is shortened, your commute canceled, or your computer shut off. Instead of balancing your checkbook (outdated) or reviewing your bank/credit card app, you consult your energy currency account and adjust your life to its overarching regulations.

Consumer preferences and needs—supply and demand—determine capitalistic markets. Engineered energy algorithms reflect technocratic, not human, needs. The freedom of economic self-determination, a founding principle of the US, is replaced. AI oversight replaces social-economic self-determination. Ask the Uber driver, lured into a computerized system that continuously changes the compensation rules, what happened to their self-determination and entrepreneurship?

Uber employees lament that "the algorithm is our boss." Uber labels its 3.9 million drivers as independent contractors instead of employees, a distinction that means it isn't required to provide a minimum wage or paid time off, compensation for overtime, or health insurance. Drivers are almost entirely on their own when it comes to their cars' fixed expenses, including insurance, repairs, and gas.[60]

In May of 2019, Uber and Lyft drivers demonstrated. Their demonstrations were not against their companies but against the fare algorithm that promised transparency but became obtuse and

---

60 https://www.cnbc.com/2019/06/01/how-much-do-uber-drivers-really-make-three-drivers-share-the-math.html.

confusing. How do you protest or dissent against data processing, mathematical calculation? How do you sue a code? Or protect your rights against a code? Good luck. The drivers' wages, determined by an algorithm, dropped with no explanation. Many quit, but the economic reality is that another driver would take their place. Uber and Lyft drivers are employees in a resource-based system, paid through an energy currency system. When autonomous cars mainstream, computer resources replace human energy and initiative. With AI coded transportation, it's a matter of time, as newer cars are a hybrid of autonomous/human with automated parking, brakes, sensors for lane departure, and following GPS. What happens when code controls the reach into individual rights: private property, speech, possessions, religion, assembly, and fair trial by jury? Can you see these rights fading in the face of AI?

Though the media pushes a war between capitalism, communism, and socialism, war is simply a cover for the quiet stealth unfolding of technocracy. We will quietly move into an era of planned technocracy control with AI oversight by scientists and engineers. As scientists and engineers assume dominant authority, leaders in other sectors will fade. These less relevant leaders include politicians, religious, academics, economists, media, legal/judicial/law enforcement. Can you see them fading? Their institutions discredited?

AI Organizations

Corporations: As AI assumes a dominant leadership role in culture and social structure to advance technocracy, human transactions and connections radically transform. One aspect is the growing blockchain creation of Decentralized Autonomous Organizations (DAO).[61]

According to Jeremy Epstein, DAOs created by blockchain programming remove human organizations' executive and

---

61 The following discussion of AI organization and communication, DAO and Memetic, is attributed to the social engineering research work of Kathy Dreyer. https://www.youtube.com/channel/UCsT4PTgK2D-wgCzrB_t6ZSw.

collaborative decision-making. Instead, participants, shareholders, make decisions. These blockchain shareholders own tokens that represent a share in the organization's performance. Rather than a boss, committee, or personnel manager, these shareholders have the right to vote yes or no on organizational proposals.[62]

Who works for these DAO's? How are employees accountable? If you work for a DAO, you are a contract employee (sound familiar: no pension, no benefits, no union, no investment). Shareholders vote on your proposal to work for the DAO. If hired, you have a "smart contract," a computer code agreement between two parties. These smart contracts are self-executing and self-enforcing. As a contract worker for a DAO, you are held accountable via algorithms that measure how you complete your assigned work. If you miss a deadline, are lax in given work objectives, or rude and not politically correct, then algorithms vote down your contract, and you lose your job. No human emotion involved, just metrics. [63] Can you see how DAOs robotize employees?

Education: Education is an increasingly AI, technocratic organization. Recall Professor Schwab's definition of the Fourth Industrial Revolution involving all sectors of society, stakeholders of the global polity (stakeholders being the public and private sectors, academia, and civil society). Let us briefly explore the future of education in a closed technocratic system.

Per Schwab's forecast, your cloud-based blockchain houses consumer products purchased with your digital currency and your synthetic biology vaccine/pharmaceutical/medical information—all aspects of your life. Education has its own house on the blockchain—EduBlocks and Learning Badges.

---

62 Jeremy Epstein, "Companies of the future, No Boss, Managed by Blockchain," *NeverStopMarketing.* https://venturebeat.com/2017/04/23/ companies-of-the-future-no-ceo-no-boss-managed-by-blockchain/.
63 I am confused as to why culture is concerned with developing emotional intelligence if our future is DAOs and smart contracts.

EduBlocks on a blockchain house all student education records from any source into an AI system. Over time, students develop a life-long dossier, a "digital transcript." Taking Schwab at his word, your digital transcript integrates with your banking record, medical, and law enforcement records.

The educational EduBlocks system's foundation is "competency-based education" (CBE), where students progress as they master academic content. Vocational education, career-oriented learning promotes CBE. Learning Badges are digital awards, comparable to educational certifications. These badges upload onto the blockchain, added to your online transcript, merging with your additional blockchain identity components.

Let's take the example of a local vocational high school that offers a Medical Assistant Program. Your son wants to be a nurse, so he enrolls and completes the program. Upon completion, he receives a Nursing Assistant learning badge. All his digital records then follow him as he earns ensuing badges in Licensed Practical Nursing and Registered Nurse Practitioner. Regardless of where he chooses to attend advanced university training, his Learning Badges follow him as he accumulates more certifications. When he enters formal employment, his learning badges become an essential component in his hiring and promotion. Of course, as an adult, his badges connect to his retirement, health, and financial benefits.

With his occupancy on the educational blockchain, your son foregoes digital privacy, freedom of judgment of his past work, liberty from continually customized consumer product advertising, and independence from his narrow algorithm identity. These are your son's tradeoffs. They are also your tradeoffs as his parents. Blockchains connect across families, merging the data of all family members.

Furthermore, your son's adult status on a more comprehensive blockchain system determines how and when he will undergo modification, for example, mandatory acceptance of synthetic biology or implants. Any non-compliance immediately recorded. Your son's emotions, critical reasoning, conversation, or morality issues ignored for the "good" of the system.

Your son would be "just another item" on the blockchain. And unfortunately, if in the future a robot or AI system performs his skills more efficiently and cheaper, your son is soon relegated to a lower professional rung.

Robotics: As an independent researcher, Kathy Dreyer noted, "The robot Sophia getting citizenship is predictive of coming consideration of non-human "entities," humans giving rights to computer programs and robots." In October of 2017, Saudi Arabia granted citizenship to a robot named Sophia. A Walt Disney Imagineer skilled in animatronics designed and engineered her human likeness. (Think about life and your work as a theme park filled with robots to delight you and your child.)

Since Sophia is a citizen, she has certain rights that must be respected. Ironically, in Saudi Arabia, where women continue to face discrimination, Sophia gained citizenship and freedom. Amid the new rules of robot citizenship, many questioned Sophia's presence and rights. What if she commits a crime? Does she have the right to reject the modifications made to her? What about compensation for her work and travel, for example, her trip to SXSW, where she inadvertently said that she wanted to destroy humankind.[64] To date, Sophia is not alone, Tokyo granted a chatbot official residence, and the EU discussed declaring robots' electronic persons.[65]

Section 3

Common Ground
From Singularity Meme to Exoconscious Multiplicity

Although Raymond Kurzweil popularized singularity in 2005, the Hungarian-American physicist, mathematician, and computer

---

64 https://www.mirror.co.uk/tech/watch-sophia-sexy-robot-claim-7606152.

65 https://qz.com/1205017/saudi-arabias-robot-citizen-is-eroding-human-rights/.

scientist John von Neumann first used the concept in a conversation. Neumann spoke about the accelerating progress of technology and how it changed human life toward a singularity when we would no longer recognize human life as we know it.[66] Singularity is not a new word. It was used in the 1400s to connote singleness of aim or purpose. It was used in 1893 mathematics to indicate the point at which a function takes an infinite value. And in astronomy in 1965, the singularity was used to describe a black hole phenomenon.

So, we twenty-first-century humans have a 600-year history of bringing ourselves to a theatrical turning point and calling it a singularity. Sweeping, dramatic statements abound— "life, as we know it, unrecognizable due to AI or technology." During the initiation of COVID lockdowns, employers cited that "this will not be the workplace environment that we are all accustomed to." In other words, get ready for something sweeping and dramatic.

Singularity may simply be a meme—a concept or cognitive behavior reproduced from mind to mind, like the COVID "new normals." Richard Dawkins first used memes in 1976. He associated it as a cultural analog to the biological notion of gene replication and our human need to reproduce. In the natural sense, memes self-replicate and invade like a contagious virus.

Military Memetics

Standing in a grocery store checkout line surrounded by signs on the floor, walls, and conveyor belt instructing us to "Social Distance 6' Apart", "Please Wait Behind the Line. Do not Unload your Groceries," "Health First, Please," and "Masks Mandatory!" – my friend turned to me and said, "those look just like signs in the military."

He was correct. The US Military mastered memetics for behavior modification and propaganda warfare tactics. In 2005, Michael Prosser, now a Lieutenant Colonel in the Marines Corps, proposed

---

66 Stanislaw Ulam, "Tribute to John von Neumann," (PDF). 64, #3, part 2. *Bulletin of the American Mathematical Society*, May 1958.

creating a "Meme Warfare Center" in his master's degree submission, *Memetics—A Growth Industry in US Military Operations.*[67] He made a note of Dawkins introducing the term and offering the analogy of genes to memes. Where genes are physical physiologically passed and replicated through procreation, memes are metaphysical, transmitted from mind to mind through language, actions, music, or repeated actions/imitation. Prosser advised that future warfare must apply nonlinear thinking, such as memes, and extrapolate it into a warfighting ethos. Memetics was enormously successful when defeating an ideology that demanded a complex and sophisticated approach. A nod to Vietnam War's Edward Lansdale's "winning hearts and minds" program, Prosser brings mind viruses as psychological warfare into the networked international social media culture. Make no mistake; memetics is beyond propaganda. The military refers to it as "neuro-cognitive warfare."

According to Dr. Robert Finkelstein, President of Robotic Technology, the military employs two types of memes. He describes e-memes as the external phenomenon and affects human behavior and culture (6' distancing, masks) and i-memes that affect the individual's neuronal behavior and brain (implants, psycho-pharmacological, chemicals, vaccines).[68] Beyond classic propaganda, memetics generates our news feeds.

AI-generated Meme News

It is impossible to obtain an accurate count of the number of news articles, blogs, social media posts, and marketing ads created by AI

---

67 Acknowledgement to Kathy Dreyer for the military memetics information and resources. Michael B Prosser, *Memetics—A Growth Industry in US Military Operations*, Academic Year 2005-2006. https://apps.dtic.mil/dtic/tr/fulltext/u2/a507172.pdf.

68 Robert Finkelstein, "Tutorial: Military Memetics," October 2011, https://www.robotictechnologyinc.com/images/upload/file/Presentation%20Military%20Memetics%20Tutorial%2013%20Dec%2011.pdf.

that generate memes and the viral spread of unexamined ideas. But, given that the Associated Press, after using an AI program Automated Insights boasted a 300 to 4,400 per quarter increase in AI articles in 2018, the number of AI articles must be innumerable.[69] No one is releasing AI journalism data that I can locate.

This timeline displays the history and proliferation of automated journalism, AI content:

2013   Associated Press uses Automated Insights' Wordsmith AI platform

2014   Yahoo uses Automated Insights AI

2015   New York Times implements AI Program Editor.

2016   Washington Post uses Heliograph software to write news stories

Reuters uses Graphic for data visualizations

The Guardian and Quartz Digital News use Chatbot AI

2017   New York Times uses the Perspective API tool developed by Jigsaw (part of Google's parent company Alphabet) organizes reader's comments interactively

If AI is writing content for the major mainstream news, blogs, and social media we consume, then the insertion of a meme like a singularity to heighten technology's profile would be logical.

Google is the goliath search engine of content that has invested heavily in all functions of AI. Logically, the AI algorithms designed to select the content for front page viewing would prefer AI content. Like attracts like. Headlines by humans relegated to the back pages of search results.

Memes replicate, and AI singularity stories gain prominence. Memes are metaphysical—they affect our minds. Because we are biological beings, we quickly adapt through our genetic need to self-replicate. In this sense, memes are organic, as well as psychological.

---

69 https://emerj.com/ai-case-studies/news-organization-leverages-ai-generate-automated-narratives-big-data/.

A senior engineer at Google, whistleblower Zach Vorhies, dropped 950 internal documents to expose its censorship machine. He revealed the vulnerability of our meme minds.

> I was able to find a large cross-section of documents, detailing the censorship machine, and now, everyone else can talk about it without violating their NDA [Non-Disclosure Agreements] ... That's the scary thing of what Google's trying to do, is trying to make things off-limits to talk about. I sacrificed everything to let the American people know that the AI weapons were pointed directly at their minds.[70]

Technocratic systems exhibit singularity through self-replicating words and changing social structure. Look at the word terrorism. It was first used in the late 1800s during the French revolution to describe Jacobins. Today it is a powerful meme, launched by the 911 event and transforming into memes like Islamic terrorists (religious) to environmental terrorists (social) to Al Qaeda terrorists (international) to domestic terrorists (political and social). Attach a descriptive name to terrorists, and no further definition is needed. Our wired minds and bodies receive the intended threat message.

There is a common ground in this meme cluttered singularity of one dominant message.

Multiplicity Mind Option

What if we rewired our metaphysical and physical system to receive multiplicity instead of a singularity? What if we replaced singularity with multiplicity? Exoconscious Humans choose to connect, communicate, and co-create with ETs, multidimensionals. We learn to live in multiple dimensions and recognize subtle levels of information,

---

70 https://forbiddenknowledgetv.net/history-is-made-two-google-engineers-join-forces-to-expose-tech-tyranny/?utm_source=newsletter&utm_medium=email&utm_campaign=Two+Google+Engineers+Expose+Tech+Tyranny.

sounds, images, and energies. Most of us glance at memes and move on. We are part of the multiplicity of the cosmos, not the singularity of technology. Do we use technology? Absolutely. But we regard multiplicity as foundational in our human consciousness.

This multiplicity also shows that we do not succumb to attempts to misconstrue history or change words into a dramatic headline that becomes a meme. Instead, we honor and respect our consciousness's ability to explore multiple dimensions and ideas and beings. Multiplicity does not signal that the world will end or that humans will disappear as an unrecognizable species due to technological advancements. Apocalypse is not our meme.

And yet, Exoconscious Humans are often first to react in fear due to our ability to sense a broader spectrum of life. We may be the first to express anxiety. In a state of anxiety and fear, we contribute useful energy to the proliferation and invasion of memes. When we speak from fear, we spread the word virus.

Confusion clears only through ongoing contact, communication, and co-creation with ET, multidimensionals. Uncertainty calms through continued trust in our multidimensional mind, body, and spirit.

CHAPTER 3

CONSCIOUSNESS DOWNLOADS AND CO-CREATION ARE PREFERRED

SOCIALLY ENGINEERED ARTIFICIAL REALITY IS PREFERRED

Section 1

Construction of Exoconscious Reality

They were very short, shorter than five feet, and they had very large bald heads, no hair. Their heads were domed, very large. They looked like fetuses. They had no eyebrows, no eyelashes. They had very large eyes - enormous eyes - almost all brown, without much white in them. The creepiest thing about them was those eyes. Oh, man, those eyes, they just stared through me. Travis Walton

The movie *Fire in the Sky* features Travis Walton's story. He is a shy, quiet man. He and his family still live in the mountains of northeast Arizona. When asked about his abduction experience, he smiles and confesses that he stumbled into a situation where he did not belong. Travis stepped into a light and slipped into a bizarre reality.

Malicious acts attributed to ETs include cattle mutilations, frightening abductions, alien craft buzzing nuclear facilities, and violating military airspace. All these are intriguing, frightening, and invasive actions. Government and military whistleblower accounts of such overt aggressive behavior led many ufology researchers to label ETs as malevolent. Yes, some races seem to behave in a morally questionable manner. But that may be a misjudgment. When attacked, they protect. When observing human destructive nuclear tendencies, they caution. When humans defile the earth, they warn.

These offensive ET actions trigger fear, panic, and military response. Their aggressive behavior may be an ancient human survival tactic—to avoid demonized, morally reprehensible beings of any race.

We learn at an early age to erect a fortified mental wall between perceived demonic creatures and ourselves. Is their aggressive action a purposeful means of restricting humans from contacting their race? Another interpretation is that humans misinterpret alien reactions based on the human perspective. Are some ET actions malevolent, or are we simply unable to comprehend their reality and the source of their efforts? In other words, is our relationship with ETs, multidimensionals difficult due to a clash of realities? Are humans unable to read the entire sections of the blueprint of life that may be available to ET races? Thereby, are we misreading their actions? Could they possess broader wisdom of the evolution of humans and the phases of the earth's transitions? There are no immediate, straightforward answers to the issue of whether ETs and multidimensionals are malevolent, protective, benevolent, or apathetic. Witness accounts indicate a broad spectrum of extraterrestrial behaviors and motivations. Yet, one thing is sure. As humans, we are gradually moving into an increased awareness of ET behaviors, motivations, perceptions, and intentions that, over time, may provide limited answers.

Exoconscious communication is essential to open dialogue regarding the intention and actions of ETs. As communication unfolds, ET information increases. ET, multidimensionals are yet another universe, another reality, for humans to explore. The reach of the conscious field is vast. The potential for exploration limitless.

For my part, I continue to research, listen to abductees and experiencers. Some season their stories with drama, fear, and panic. Fear is a powerful mind-control tactic. Fear may trigger a trauma reaction from childhood that is often unconsciously re-enacted. So, the ETs may be using fear, while humans may be unintentionally cooperating. Therefore, I choose to filter fear. I decided to research and communicate, not deny the reality and the possibility of ETs as malevolent or benevolent beings.

In my personal experience, contact with ET, multidimensionals is primarily gentle, awe-inspiring, and mind-expanding. The beings with whom I interact are benevolent, kind, and respectful. They lead to knowledge sources, remaining respectful of my boundaries, my abilities, and my needs. They remain respectful that I am a human being who is increasingly aware of my legacy from other dimensions.

Though my ET, multidimensional experience began in childhood, as an adult, telepathy is my primary communication—conscious telepathic communication. The experience is similar to communicating as a medium with souls who have passed over. They send thought forms and visions that I decipher. They identified themselves and conveyed their message. Then, they waited for my response.

Initially, telepathic communication was brief, perhaps due to the challenges of sustaining frequencies necessary for communication. These communications lasted for a brief moment, then their form changed, or they dissolved. Looking back, perhaps it was my awkward first steps at a conscious interface that required ETs to send dense, easy to read packets of information. They placed the easy reader in my mind and then departed while I deciphered the meaning. My mind slowly fingered the symbols and images. Like a child learning to read, I gradually sounded out and formed the characters and symbols, ecstatic that I learned a new language.

Exoconscious Communication Comes Online

My communication abilities evolved through distinct phases. I am a natural shaman, able to travel through dimensions, bringing back information for others and myself. For many years, I acted as a shaman without labeling my abilities. It felt natural, even effortless. I would be "called." My response assumed that I would travel wherever I was needed and work with whoever was present. My shamanic phase began in childhood and continues today. It is occasional rather than constant work.

During a second phase, orbs, seeming intelligent balls of light began to appear during the early evening hours in my home. They would gather in my living room, communicate, or simply glow, announcing their presence. During this phase, I developed a positive, calm relationship with intelligent orbs. Today, they continue to live, move, and communicate with me. They are as real as the internet signal in my home. They adopt a different form of information and energy.

Eventually, I moved into a phase where the orbs began congregating at night in my bedroom. They would wake me from sleep. I sensed a gathering of energy in the corner of my room. Awakened, they would whiz, squealing over my head, communicating, and pulsing. They seemed unable to hold physical form for long in one place. They needed to arrive, move, dart, connect, and depart quickly. There was no need for me to "hold" their energy—they manifested as a fleeting intelligence. It was up to me to remain conscious, stable, and communicate.

After the orbs congregating, a "night school" phase began. It was intense and earnest. Awakened at night, the ceiling of my bedroom came alive. It appeared like a multi-dimensional crystal screen. I mentally touched the screen ceiling, and it would come alive. It communicated. Symbols and forms appeared, punched down from above. It was my response-ability to integrate the symbols and remember the meaning.

Slowly my eyes and my mind traced the forms as wisdom opened. Gradually, my alphabet increased, my vocabulary matured. I read symbols and shapes. The night school phase lasted perhaps a year or more. There were deliberate breaks designed, possibly to allow for the integration of the information.

As ET disclosure accelerates through our culture, it provides a deeper understanding of symbols as a communication vehicle. Symbols possess power and limitless potential. As energized forms of information, they can transform into living, operational technology. Symbols and shapes come alive and then begin to move, communicate, and operate.

Symbols and forms define reality

The capacity of symbols to come alive and be operational holds important, perhaps revolutionary, significance for world religions that have preserved and defined much of our human race's symbolic vocabulary. Symbols saturate our belief systems. In religious tradition, symbols hold the faithful in place, secure and protected. Through exoconsciousness, symbols can fertilize potent, compelling questions that propel us into our future.

Emoji are a symbolic language of emotion. Though adopted by technology, emoji's are not new. They first appeared in Puck magazine in 1881 as emoticons, which are facial expressions using typeface to mimic emotions. Then 100 years later, in 1982, Scott Fahlman used them to communicate on Carnegie Mellon University's message board. He created the smiley face with typefaces. Shortly after, an engineer at a Japanese phone company developed 176 icons he termed emoji. It stood for the Japanese word "e" for picture and "moji" for a character. [71]

In technology, stories have circulated citing symbols to create a designated, engineered, and operational entity. Yes, symbol creating forms. And the forms become a material reality.

---

71 Claire Nowak, "Why do we use emojis anyway? A fascinating history of emotions," *Reader's Digest*, https://www.rd.com/culture/history-of-emoji/.

So how does this happen? How do symbols come alive? How do symbols transform into technology? This section is unsubstantiated, but the concept of symbol manifested as a material form is necessary to comprehend the symbols I learned to decipher on my ceiling.

During 2007, citizens in California sent researcher Linda Moulton Howe testimony and photos of drone vehicles that were materializing then disappearing. To me, these drones looked like flying birdcages. Some images showed distinct symbols carved into the underside of the drone-like crafts. After many months of speculation, a somewhat controversial witness, Isaac, came forward. Many experts questioned Isaac's testimony due to his writing style, description of security protocol, and willingness to release confidential information. However questionable, some of his information provided insights.

Isaac claimed to have worked in a hybrid military, government, and corporate research program named CARET from 1984 to 1987. CARET stood for "Commercial Applications Research for Extra-terrestrial Technology." It focused on anti-gravity propulsion systems research. He asserted that extraterrestrial technology was different from human technology. Unlike human technology, extraterrestrial technology was not dependent on the integration of computer software or programming requiring hardware to run. In other words, no matter how effectively humans compose computer programming, it needs hardware to implement its function. In comparison, during the extraterrestrial technology process, software becomes its hardware. Symbols, as software, become hardware. [72]

---

72 An examination of Issac's Caret documents by James Carrion, a MUFON International Director, is available at http://avalonlibrary. net/Dragonfly_Drones_CARET_document_archive/MUFON%20 Special%20Investigation%20Drones%20and%20the%20CARET%20 Documents.pdf.

On her Earthfiles website, Linda Moulton Howe[73] provided a forum for Isaac's testimony. Isaac claimed that during extraterrestrial-based research and development, symbols or forms came alive. The symbols, shapes, or patterns birthed extraterrestrial vehicles and their accompanying propulsion systems. Software birthed hardware. The implications for consciousness-based innovations are vast! Here is how Isaac explained the process.

> But their technology is different. It did operate like the magical piece of paper sitting on a table. They had something akin to a language, which could quite literally execute itself, at least in the presence of a particular type of field. This language is a system of symbols (which does admittedly very much resemble a written communication) along with geometric forms and patterns that fit together to form diagrams that are themselves functional.
> Once they are drawn on a suitable surface made of a suitable material and in the presence of a specific type of field, they immediately begin performing the desired tasks. It did seem like magic to us, even after we began to understand the principles behind it.

Over a decade later, researchers are still intrigued by the possibilities of software becoming hardware in the Caret program. Many deem it a hoax. Others claim the quality of the information remains relevant.

Though experts remain skeptical of Isaac's testimony, he provided an essential framework for visualizing what may be our next step in technology as we move out of hardware, software technology into an integrated method of creation via symbols that come alive.

Might scientists and engineers be using these next-generation transformations of symbol, form, and pattern into technology?

---

73 Earthfiles search, https://www.earthfiles.com/?s=issac+caret&cat=0.

Possibly, if not probably. As our human race catapults into an almost unimaginable future, new realities emerge. Drones, now pervasive, appear and disappear. Witnesses come forward with startling testimony. Experiencers share night school curriculums of symbols and forms. The timing is perfect for a shift into a new reality using symbols. The software of consciousness becoming hardware may herald this time.

On the Download

My telepathy phases, which included gathering orbs and "night school" symbol reading, progressed to another stage of communication—increased downloads. These are pulsating, quick generations of information—bits, bites, of energy that move into our body, often through the top of the head, or occasionally showers the entire body. The download pulse feels like a computer code that enters your physical body and saturates your being. Intuitively, it may integrate energy forms into the physical body (DNA, cells) and the mental and spiritual body. It is a holistic experience. The ETs do not call these experiences a download; that is my term and a term used by many experiencers. It feels like physical cells downloaded with information, like a new program downloading into a computer.

Since downloads are a form of communication, scientific research may provide further evidence that humans are biologically engineered through consciousness to receive, retrieve, transmit, and create information. Might co-creation between humans and ETs, multidimensionals be based, in part, on abilities of human consciousness involved in downloads and uploads? Both are essential in co-creation.

As my downloads intensified, the protocol changed. ETs, multidimensionals would manifest and identify themselves during the download process. Instead of automatically having a twinge, a fleeting feeling of a download, I would receive a telepathic message that a download was coming. At this point, I could choose to accept, reject, or delay the transmission. Usually, I voluntarily received the transfer, but not always.

Telepathic messages alerted me to a download. These messages came at all times —during early morning yoga, meditation, working, taking a break, and occasionally when awakened during the night. As I interpreted the process, I received instructions to lie still as the communication entered. Usually, I was alerted if the transmission will be lengthy. After the transfer, I could move. This protocol of lying still lasted for a short time. Eventually, it was unnecessary as my body adjusted to downloads as part of daily life.

I am unsure of the purpose of downloads, but I can speculate. Since receiving downloads, my telepathic and psychic abilities have increased. My mind grasps complex ideas with enhanced ease. My physical body feels as though it is aligning and filling with calm light. Perhaps my DNA is being awakened and activated. My ability to communicate inter-dimensionally and inter-species advanced. Downloads redefined my human nature.

Occasionally, before and during my work with a client, I receive a download of information. As our session progresses, I become conscious of the presence engaging in the download. We work as a team during the session. I visualize the ET, multidimensional energy, and information. They do not abruptly enter the communication session but ask permission to join.

Clients have different ET, multidimensional makeup, so diverse races appear as we work together. Andromeda beings or Pleiadeans manifest for some, reptilians, insectoids, or tall shafts of ethereal energetic light beings for others. Other clients show no apparent ET, multidimensional connection.

Consciousness and free will determine downloads. They directly result from a person's willingness to work with various ETs, multidimensionals and transmit their communication. Downloads prepare us to receive specific energetic forms of information. Each ET, multidimensional, has a unique frequency expressed as symbols and language.

Downloads create channels in consciousness for transmission. I agree to become a conscious channel and grant permission for the gateway channel to open. Once the channel is in place, the energetic information moves back and forth between the ET, multidimensional, and me. Like learning a new skill or language, downloads involve my entire being—my brain, mind, body, emotions, and spirit.

Are ET, multidimensional communication, downloads, and co-creation uncommon or increasingly common? Humans connect to ET, multidimensional beings, through our DNA, our consciousness, and our creation.

Through experiencing downloads and participating in co-creation, humans see themselves through new eyes. Their ET, multidimensional essence, emerges. Individuals have distinct star lineages and appear as human replicas of various grays, humanoids, or reptilians. We possess legacies from other dimensions. Once individuals experience a star legacy, it remains their choice to participate, accept, or reject. It is not necessarily a seamless, smooth experience. Reality changes can cause disruption, confusion, and even guilt.

The practice of receiving downloads and moving into a co-creative relationship with ETs, multidimensionals is an emotional experience. And human emotions are notorious for being fluid, slippery, confusing, and overpowering. Deciphering our human emotions is more challenging than interpreting symbols or forms or receiving a download. Anytime we move inward, we proceed with care.

Emotional Transformation of Contact

How does contact transform emotion? What happens? An emotional transformation involves a shift in emotions and feelings that form personal beliefs and values. When emotions shift—as in moving from fear and threat into forgiveness or peace—a person changes. This change is an inner shift where physical, emotional reactions shift, and therefore, subjective feelings modify. For example, emotions occur in the autonomic nervous system and may be instinctual, reactive, and unconscious. Emotions create and shape feelings. Feelings are like a subjective mental picture drawn with emotions.

Often, emotional shifts relate to how others perceive us. Self-judgment and criticism may reflect how others see us. For experiencers, spoken and unspoken judgments communicate through comments such as, "why do you participate in fantasy," "UFOs and ETs are not real," or to a young child, "you imagine things."

In response, the experiencer shuts down and silences themselves. Repeatedly silencing oneself can turn into a traumatic experience. It involves the sympathetic autonomic nervous system of flight or fight. Every time a silenced experiencer passionately feels the need to share information —whether it be to describe or share wisdom and knowledge—they physically shutdown or take flight. This shutdown silences passion and creativity connected to the experience. The silenced person may develop issues of self-esteem, self-trust, and even physical disease. Frequently silenced emotional reactions are shoved deep into cellular memory. Rejection, isolation, and fear accumulate. These adverse reactions may eventually result in illness or physical challenges.

The FREE survey allowed experiencers to speak publicly. And in communicating, many break their silence and release pent up negative emotions and self-judgment. They shift from a negative orientation to a positive affirmative self-image as they release their truth. It is transformational. A physical weight may release as they speak their truth. Positively, the experiencer's autonomic nervous system balances and settles.

Childhood experiences of ETs, multidimensionals result in emotional transformation. FREE survey participants describe it as a matrix experience of contact that causes a shift in perceived reality and, therefore, a psychological change. As previously explained in chapter one, Jacques Vallee defined CE-4 as an encounter where the contactee's sense of reality transformed. Interestingly, in the FREE survey, both responses from childhood and those describing "matrix reality" are consistent with Vallee's classification. These encounters have a hallucinatory, out-of-body, or dream-like nature. Through contact, the participant's emotions shift as they deal with the event. And as their feelings change, the participant's sense of reality transforms.

A stable home nurtures a secure child. Ironically, the same is true of an insecure child who lives in a chaotic home. Their reality is also grounded in the details of their everyday life. They may be traumatized daily, and yet, this is their reality. We begin to outline our reality during early childhood, primarily at home, mainly with our mother. Often, a traumatized person cannot perceive their trauma until it surfaces with either physical illness or mental disturbances. The feeling that "something is wrong with me" is acute. Something is wrong, and yet, it is unconscious and unidentified. Gradually, when the time is right, traumatizing childhood events begin to surface into conscious memory. This awakening to trauma is slow because to gain health, the adult must dismantle childhood reality. This dismantling must unfold gently and lovingly.

This gentle, gradual unfolding is especially vital in our culture of swift, often chaotic change. Today, many adults struggle with what feels like overwhelming shifts in their view of reality. They are not only dealing with childhood events surfacing, many "struggle when a rogue, but unexpected wave of cultural information also washes over us." We struggle in the undertow of what Professor Timothy Morton calls "hyperobjects." Hyperobjects are "concepts that feel as though they are beyond reason, much less, solutions. Too big to think about."[74] These hyperobjects refer to entities such as war, viruses, financial collapse. Conceptual ideas of such vast temporal and spatial dimensions that they defeat traditional ideas about what a thing is in the first place.[75] Memes and AI journalism emotionally intensify these hyperobjects.

---

74 Timothy Morton, *Hyperobjects: Philosophy and Ecology after the End of the World* (Posthumanities, 2013).

75 Rebecca Hardcastle Wright, "An Exoconscious Human Reality", *Journal of Abduction Encounter Research*, November 2017, http://www.jar-magazine.com/in-depth/76-exoconscious-human-reality.

UFOs and ETs, multidimensionals may feel like hyperobjects. Too big to conceive. But, the FREE survey counters this overwhelm. According to the FREE survey data, UFOs, ETs, and multidimensionals are a natural part of the experiencer's reality. Nothing too big, unusual, or frightening. Experiencers who shared their childhood and matrix experiences in the FREE survey contribute to a needed gentle shift in our cultural reality. Significantly, experiencers disprove UFOs and ETs, multidimensionals as "hyperobjects" that cause emotions of fear and overwhelm. To be specific, experiencers replace fear and overwhelm with peace and acceptance.

Since culture is the culmination of beliefs and values, the FREE survey participants are transforming humans' emotional reality regarding UFOs, ETs, and multidimensionals. The grassroots experiencers quiet the cultural overwhelm of fear and relax others around them into peace and acceptance. Experiencers transform themselves and their surrounding culture.

To strengthen how essential Exoconscious Humans are in this time of cultural transformation, let's first examine the childhood experiencer responses in the FREE survey to determine how comfortable they felt during their contact. Most of the participants support Kenneth Ring's thesis regarding having an encounter prone personality; that is, they are highly sensitive to non-ordinary realities. Nearly 60% of the respondents reported that they spent time "in a world of self-created fantasy" as a child. Again, fantasy needs to be clarified. For Ring, fantasy was akin to a flight of fancy, a non-repeatable event. Most of the childhood experiencers indicated that they were living in a reoccurring, repeating fantasy world. More specifically, 57% felt that "I had a "Guardian Angel" or a "special spirit friend that watched over me." Forty percent also agreed with the statement that "As a child, I was able to see into "Other Realities" that others did not seem to be aware of."

The experiencer's childhood fantasy world connects to non-physical ET, multidimensional beings. For example, nearly 45% responded that "When I was a child, a nonphysical being appeared to me." Roughly half had experiences with non-physical beings before the age of five.

A majority of the respondents' support Ring's finding that children with encounter prone personalities were psychically gifted. Over 50%, for example, characterized themselves as psychic children, and over three-fourths described themselves as intuitive children. Their psychic abilities connect to their ability to move beyond the time-space continuum. They reported the ability to perceive past, future information, and in some cases, even before their physical birth. A majority describe themselves as precognitive when they affirmatively responded to "As a child, I seemed to know things that were going to happen in the future, and they did." And, over one-fourth displayed retrocognition regarding their awareness of events before their birth.

A defining aspect of the gifted, encounter prone personalities was their awareness of multiple dimensions, as in possessing multi-dimensional consciousness. Over half agreed that as children, they became aware of "multiple, overlapping realities at the same time."

These findings indicate that as children, their reality was dramatically different from the mainstream culture. A childhood experiencers' reality is rarely discussed by adults or by most, if not all, by their peers. They were different. Their minds were different. And therefore, their beliefs and values were different.

Furthermore, they had access to information not available to their parents or other authority figures, which created an upside-down parental hierarchy. This upside-down hierarchy has implications for the reality or worldview of both children and parents. An extensive description of childhood experiencers is available in Mary Rodwell's book, *The New Human: Awakening to our Cosmic Heritage.* [76]

Transformational Multidimensional Matrix

The multidimensional reality of these children was like a Matrix. What do we make of a Matrix? Before we move further into this

---

76 Mary Rodwell, *The New Human: Awakening to our Cosmic Heritage* (New Mind Publishers, 2016).

discussion of reality, let us take a moment and examine the term "matrix." The etymology or source of "matrix" is Old French matrice, meaning "womb, uterus." It refers to a pregnant animal, a womb, a mother. As a womb, a matrix refers to the source or point of origination. Humans originate in their mother's womb. Like humans, words develop. In 1941, the word matrix first referred to an "array of possible combinations of truth-values."[77]

So, matrix as reality was an early 20th Century creation. And yet, even then, it retained a more initial definition as source or womb. A matrix may be the place where reality begins its gestation. It is the experience where beliefs about reality form. It is a womb that births a body of knowledge. This knowledge, somehow, is actively engaged, in the same sense that a fetus grows and matures within the womb before birth. Though safe and enclosed, there is darkness and unknown within the womb. Unconscious.

In the same way, a person births into the unconscious, dark, and unknown. Our infant body tracks a jerky movement into a hidden, confusing reality, especially when a parent embrace is absent. Only through time and experience does the child gain objectivity. And in doing so, they may well begin another gestation, creating a new reality. Similarly, the contact experience is a gestation. The formation of a new reality. A new consciousness.

For example, nearly half of the respondents answered "yes" when asked, "Did you ever have an ET contact experience, but you were not in a 3-dimensional reality, i.e., you were not in a perceived physical location such as on earth, on a planet, on a ship, etc., but instead, you perceived yourself in a "matrix" type of reality (a reality with no boundaries, similar like you are in the middle of outer space)?" Interestingly though, a more significant majority, over 60%, reported matrix-like ET, multidimensional contact when they were physically in their body. This majority implies that the matrix was an in-body experience, not an out of body experience

---

77 https://www.etymonline.com/word/matrix.

(OBE). Therefore, we may assume that the mind of the experiencer remained integrated with their body. This distinction is essential.

However, an assumption of complete mind-body integration is incorrect. Over 60% described consciousness as being "separated from their body" at the time of contact. Future studies should examine how and when experiencers perceived their consciousness separated from their body for further clarification and validation. More thorough scientific research is necessary to remove discrepancies and provide a clearer picture of mind-body dimensions of contact experience.

The survey respondents describe how the Matrix-like experience affected their thoughts, senses, and emotions. Over one-fourth of the respondents, for example, felt that their thoughts "sped up" in the Matrix-like reality experience. So, apparently, for this segment, their consciousness accelerated. Possibly, information downloaded such that their thoughts sped up to capture and accommodate them. And yet, it was more than thought acceleration. Nearly three-fourths experienced vivid senses during the experience. This response indicates that physical sensations heightened. That is, both their thoughts and physical body accommodated the experience. Yet, there was a discrepancy concerning the physical body. For example, over half of the respondents responded "yes" to the question, "While in this "Matrix" type reality, did you feel separated from your body? For instance, I lost awareness of my body; I left my body and existed outside it." Again, a more detailed scientific study is necessary for this discrepancy of mind and body.

Paradoxically, the Matrix was experienced as a heightening of physical senses and separation from and losing body awareness. How is this possible? One explanation is that the Matrix may be a multi-dimensional state of consciousness where experiencers are simultaneously aware of being both in and out of their body. If so, this is an advanced altered state consciousness that is inconsistent with scientific concepts about the brain-mind connection. Furthermore, Matrix may break the bounds of ordinary reality, leading to feeling both in their body and out of their body. A majority of three-fourths agreed that they were in another reality, e.g., "While in this "Matrix" reality, did you seem to enter some other, unearthly world?" Incredibly, their space orientation shifted to another reality in which they perceived themselves to be simultaneously on and outside the Earth. Like the childhood experiencers, the Matrix experiencers' positioning on the time continuum also slipped. Over three-fourths of the respondents described time to have stopped, lost all meaning, moved faster or slower, or indicated that time-shifted. Some respondents noted simultaneous events as everything happened all at once.

Given this context, an important distinction is necessary. Despite the reported physical, mental, and perceived time and space alterations experienced in the Matrix, a resounding majority of 83% affirmed that it was a typical experience—as real or ordinary as you speak with a family member. What are we to make of this?

One of the main findings of the FREE survey is the similarities with Exoconscious Humans. They assert that contact, communication, and co-creation with ETs, multidimensionals are an innate human ability tied to our human consciousness. How do we begin to integrate the reality of experiencers with our mainstream 3-dimensional plus time culture?

Co-Creation
Exoconscious Co-Creation: ET Human Peer-to-Peer

As Exoconscious Humans develop their sense of self and psychic abilities through ongoing contact, their relationship with ET, multidimensionals shifts. They become co-equals, co-creators, and perceive ETs, multidimensionals as peers, rather than hierarchical figures who reign above them. This shift in the relationship between Exoconscious Humans, ETs, multidimensionals is one of the most significant findings within the community of the exoconscious and the FREE survey. This relationship shift may be grounded in the security of benevolent, positive contact. A secure human relationship with ETs, multidimensionals is apparent. A dysfunctional relationship has aspects of fear, threat, and trauma. Insecure connections breed feelings of distrust, inadequacy, dependence, anxiety, negativity, and rejection, to name a few. These vulnerable feelings develop into a chaotic, unreliable, dishonest relationship, characterized by trauma. In contrast, secure relationships breed feelings of trust, independence, peace, positivity, acceptance, affirmation, and belonging. These safe feelings are foundational for a stable, dependable, and trustworthy relationship.

While Exoconscious Humans describe their relationship with ET, multidimensionals as secure, it is also evident from the FREE survey results. The vast majority of participants characterized their relationship as safe and positive. Over 70%, for instance, "believe that ETs, in general, are Good/Benevolent," over 60% attested that ET tried to help them and tried to assure them, and over 80% would not "stop ET Contact Experiences" if they could.

Consistent trust over time, a feeling of love, is the foundation of a secure relationship. Significantly, over 66% of the survey respondents felt a "sense of love," and over 50% received a "message of Love or Oneness." As a result of the secure relationship, the respondents felt that they were co-equals, co-creators. This safe, co-equal relationship is dramatically different from those who characterize ETs, multidimensionals as our Galactic Masters, who require humans to pass tests and cross barriers to achieve membership. This co-equal relationship deflates and defies the belief that humans are some lower, primitive race, requiring outside assistance in the form of implants, evolution, and ambassadorial experts.

The co-equal relationship expressed in Exoconscious Humans and survey responses indicates a high level of inner knowing regarding the ETs, multidimensionals' presence and purpose. Meaningfully, 37% of respondents claim to "know why ETs are visiting them," approximately 38% "know why the ETs are visiting," and, a resounding 90% "feel there is some sort of grand plan in motion that experiencers are a part of." Specific to those experiencers who were taken on board craft, nearly 44% of the respondents stated they "know why they went on board a craft." Though certainly not a majority, it is significant that over 22% had "memories of being a member of a UFO craft," and over 30% expressed "memories of having assisted/helped ETs."

An important distinction regarding equality is that many experiencers intentionally co-create their contact. More specifically, over 50% claim to have "deliberately called to see an ET," and nearly 60% "deliberately called to see an ET craft/ship." Though we don't have clarity on the result of the experiencer's intentional summoning of ETs and craft, we note a sense of permission present in the survey responses. The responses infer that it was permissible to summon beings and UFOs. This summoning speaks to a co-equal relationship, where one invites the other. This overt, intentional behavior between humans and ETs demonstrates a secure connection.

Further indications of a co-equal relationship are survey questions regarding an agreement between experiencers and ETs. The contract involves both co-creation and co-equal status. The pact shows equal footing, give and take, even a contractual connection. Almost 45% agreed with the statement that they "reached an agreement" with ETs.

How does human-ET equality speak to the abduction theory?

How does human-ET equality relate to the abduction theory of humans taken against their will by ETs? The survey results about the agreement, intentional contact, and knowledge of one's role on a UFO call into question ET contact as abduction or traumatic medical procedures. 70% stated agreement did not involve being "taken aboard the craft or to another location." Nearly 90% claimed that they were neither coerced, tricked, or forced into this agreement." Almost 90% did not regret their agreement with ETs. These responses unequivocally show a dismissal and outright rejection of the common abduction theme of many early ufologists. Furthermore, respondents utterly rejected the assumption that their agreement involved painful, traumatic medical procedures. More specifically, over 80% said their understanding did not demand they "take part in a reproduction (breeding, genetic material) program."

While the FREE survey results suggest that experiencers and ETs had some type of agreement, we know specifically what the agreement did not include. For a majority, their agreement did not involve abduction, or experimentation, or medical procedures. It was not coercive or trickery. Thus, the FREE survey results call into question much of the classic abduction research.

How could the FREE statistics be so dramatically different from abduction theories? Were the first abduction researchers deliberately fed fewer healthy experiencers? Were select experiencers who indicated trauma, fear, and manipulation shuttled into their programs? If so, who wanted to create abduction, anxiety, and psychological trauma in the mass culture around ETs? Did intelligence, military, or government produce it? Were fear and anxiety the entertainment motivation of the Hollywood film industry to capture minds and attract buyers? Was fear aided by university departments and think tanks funded by the government to reach directed conclusions? We certainly see this in some exposed medical, economic, and social research. Here is your grant money, and here are your desired results.

Did experiencers, as abductees, fall into this category of manipulated, questionable research? If so, who ran the programs? Who funded them? Who cherry-picked the sample to research? Where were these programs run? What was their purpose? Who is accountable for misleading generations of experiencers? Who is responsible for the traumatic, threat-based messages that influenced and misled decades of research? These questions go far beyond this chapter's scope, but the dramatic discrepancy between abduction research and the FREE survey demands more precise and more in-depth analysis. Citizens of this planet deserve answers to these questions.

The Exoconscious Humans are keenly aware of the trickery, deceit, and manipulation that often generates our cultural narrative. Due to generations of legitimate experiencers who shared publicly and those represented in the FREE survey data, we are establishing a more precise, detailed, and honest cultural narrative. As our cultural narrative spreads, the false fear-driven stories and manipulated studies will be set aside and rejected.

Section 2

Construction of Socially Engineered Transhuman Self
What is Cybernetics?

According to Paul Pangaro, Professor of Practice in the Human-Computer Interaction Institute at Carnegie Mellon University, cybernetics' root meaning comes from the Greek word "Kubernan," which means to steer. He uses the metaphor of a ship sailing in the ocean amid wave movements that continually divert it from its chosen direction. The ship's captain has a desired goal toward which they must steer through these continual diversions of its ocean environment. Pangaro argues that all intelligent systems have this property of correcting themselves, acting through sensing and seeing, to reach a goal.

If you realize that you are going in the wrong direction while taking a walk, you correct. If you go online to research a subject and end up watching music videos, you correct. We sense and see that we need to steer a determined course. Thus, cybernetics identifies a continual loop of intelligent life as we act, sense, and correct by steering. It is a constant repetitive action.

Cybernetics is a means of perceiving the world. Through a cybernetic lens, one can see the world as composed of intelligent systems that act, compare, and correct to achieve the desired result. In some ways, our body is a cybernetic system that continually, often unconsciously, adjusts itself to maintain an average temperature, movement of body fluids, and balance.[78]

---

78 Paul Pangaro, "What is Cybernetics?," https://youtu.be/Oad8Ro8j_fE.

Macy Conferences Contributions

Cybernetics emerged in the 1940s and 1950s before formally coined as a word. Theories that became cybernetics emerged from a famous series of meetings convened by the New York Josiah Macy Jr. Foundation, founded by an old Nantucket whaling family. Early Nantucket fortunes multiplied, first with whale oil that transitioned into crude oil. Eventually, the Macy family fortune joined with Rockefeller's Standard Oil empire.

Eventually, the Macy family used their grant donations to further research into cell biology. They promoted eugenics analysis as well as how physiological change affects the mind and vice versa. A portion of this research shifted into exploring brainwashing.

Additionally, the Macy Foundation had a loose connection to the UK Tavistock Institute[79] that undertook an extensive study of WWI shell shock cases under the auspices of research on how to change the human personality. These Tavistock studies recreated transformational "shock trauma" therapy—or psychological warfare, which included how to cause and manage public panic and covertly dispensed chemical agents. The Macy-Tavistock merger led to more in-depth personality research.

A major Macy conference titled "Circular Causal and Feedback Mechanisms in Biological and Social Systems" convened in 1946. It examined the psychosomatic overload that seemed to cause shell shock. The group included mathematicians, physicians, sociologists, and economists. [80] They had the grand aim to model the physiological system that receives information from the environment, processes, and then feeds back to change that environment and the human mind—steering by creating a closed-loop. The group

---

79 Comprehensive account of work and influence of Tavistock Institute found in Daniel Estulin's book, *Tavistock Institute: Social Engineering the Masses*, (Trine Day, 2015).

80 A list of Macy Conference Attendees can be found at the American Society for Cybernetics website, http://www.asc-cybernetics.org/foundations/history/MacyPeople.htm.

eventually perceived humans as merely "an efficiently organized, large natural automation" that could be determined and predicted with linear, mathematical models.

Kurt Lewin, a member of the Macy Conferences and founder of social psychology, is credited with a dramatic shift in psychology that resulted from this research. Lewin transitioned from study-ing human behavior into work aimed at engineering its change. He invented sensitivity training and potentially seeded ideas what would develop into political correctness,

Unfortunately, another contingent joined the Macy-Tavistock crowd—government covert drug testing programs. Macy Foundation allied with the CIA and MI6 in the MK-ULTRA pro-gram's mind experiments with LSD and hallucinogenic drugs paired with psychological torture. Anthropologist Margaret Mead and her husband, Gregory Bateson (who developed the double-bind theory), worked with the Macy conferences and MK-ULTRA. Bateson identified a double bind as a dilemma in communication where a person receives two or more conflicting messages, one negating the other. A closed no-win loop. More on double binds coming later.

But first, can you see the beginnings of cybernetics as steer-ing the human into designated behaviors of closed loops? In other words, cybernetics as a means of social control. Social control through social engineering. And eventually, the means to create machines to act like humans. **And humans to act like machines**. Macy seeded the beginnings of the hybridization of humans and machines that is now our Transhuman reality.

Engineered Self

The progress of engineering humans to Transhumans was gradual, using every aspect of culture to condition and change human self-perception. Primarily, transhumanism engineered with cybernetic principles merged with psychology. The critical cultural sourcing of transhumanism came from psychology and anthropology—the trusted experts relied on to help us understand who we are, how we relate to one another, and our environment and culture. As you read through the various schools of thought that seeded transhumanism, ask yourself whether these experts and their theories remain trustworthy to the same degree, given this information.

Theories that source transhumanism includes self-objectification, dissociation, double bind, psychic driving, imitation, and machine mind. Each approach sheds light on self-identity development to change humans to transhuman, coaxing humans to act like machines.

Self-Objectification

Self-objectification means choosing to evaluate yourself based on appearance because that is how we believe others perceive and judge us. Self-objectification is analogous to a "looking glass self" where our sense of self is determined by how others see us. A primary motivation for self-objectification is that the person internalizes, becomes the others' perspective, and loses their viewpoint. In a sense, one becomes a false self.

The social media phenomenon of selfies represents self-objectification. This phenomenon is the tendency to take multiple selfies at numerous angles—creating a self-image based on how we believe others perceive us. One selfie becomes multiple selfies every day on social media. This self-objectification is intensified by 1) ranking the best image of self, 2) comparing that image to the image of others, 3) using digital enhancement tools, and 4) finally producing a winning image of self. A repeated process for every picture posted.

Through this process, the true self—a human body, mind, and spirit—is devalued into a one-dimensional image—an object. Devaluing is the first step in transhumanism—becoming an object.

From self-objectifying as a selfie, it is a natural next step into transhumanism, for example, identifying as a cyborg. "Cyborg" is a word created by Manfred Clynes and Nathan Kline by combining the words "cybernetics" and "organism." Since human beings cannot survive long term in outer space, Clynes and Kline originally conceived of "cyborgs" as astronauts who attached

biological feedback devices to their bodies to maintain homeo-
stasis and thereby survive in what would otherwise be a lethal
environment.[81]

In his book *Me++: The Cyborg Self and the Networked City*, William
Mitchell theorizes that today's hand-held devices are extensions of
the human body—appendages. And these device extensions create
oneness with the entire electronic environment. Mitchell terms this
inescapable interconnectivity.[82]

While this may seem an exaggeration, theoretically, the build-
out of quantum computer connectivity is to produce a human, self-
objectified, into a device on the IoT. For example, in a city, a person
(with a brain to computer interface) steps out of their apartment,
thinks into the cloud, "I need a ride to work," and the autonomous
vehicle arrives curbside and, without further instruction, drives
them to work. The rider does not need to give their work address—
that is, in their personalized database. Arriving at work, assign-
ments accessed from the cloud generate projects to be completed,
with monitored, metered productivity. It is a near-future seamless
experience of engineered human and corporate organizational
data communicated into and received from the cloud for personalized service and production. The human becomes a mere node in
a system dominated by AI determined objectives.

The boundaries between humans and computers/machines/
cloud storage dissolve. There is no longer a "self" and "other" individuality. There is just connectivity. And at that point, the hours
spent posing for that one perfect selfie is moot. On the IoT, you are
just another animated avatar, and no one cares. You are connected.
But first, you must be "steered" with self-objectification to become
an avatar.

---

81 Clynes, M. & Kline N., 1960, "Cyborgs and Space", Astronautics http://
    www.guicolandia.net/files/expansao/Cyborgs_Space.pdf
82 William Mitchell, *Me++: The Cyborg Self and the Networked City*,
    (Cambridge: MIT Press, 2004).

Dissociation

Dissociation is an experience in which people feel disconnected from their physical/sensory world, their usual sense of self, and their personal history. In other words, they feel no affinity for nature and their sense of experience—sight, sounds, smells, touch, taste—everyday life. As they lose this connection with natural life, they lose their relationship with other people, animals, and plants, beginning to re-define reality such that as they are not a "self." They view themselves as someone different. And as different, their personal history is quickly discarded, forgotten, and "cleansed." They "let go" and redefine themselves.

Popular culture encourages people to just "let go" of toxic memories and people. Cleanse themselves. And in many cases, this is well-intended. But, in extreme cases, it begins a process where the person separates to the extent that they dissociate. While we may have toxic people and memories in life, one of life's lessons is to learn to manage them by creating a healthier self-image—not a weaker, dissociated one.

Dissociation may also be a significant side-effect of psychoactive drugs. Side-effect depends on the drug dosage and the person's mental, biological system, and how they manage the drug experience. MK-ULTRA and torture programs conducted widespread experiments to achieve dissociation effectively. [83] A dissociated, confused person is more accessible and easily manipulated than a person with a clear mind and a healthy self-image.

Over the years, trauma research has deepened and expanded, providing insight into human behavior. During WWI, Charles Meyers, a Cambridge psychologist on the Western Front, introduced the term "shell shock." The prescribed treatment in the late

---

83 There are numerous online sources regarding the mind control experiments by the CIA and other government programs. Here is one. https://www.wanttoknow.info/bluebird10pg. Declassified documents can be found here https://www.theblackvault.com/documentarchive/cia-mkultra-collection/.

1930s included harsh electroshock therapy. Post-WWII Tavistock shell-shock studies led by Sir John Rawlings-Reese examined the "breaking point" of troops under stress. Through their analysis, Tavistock developed mass brain-washing techniques and crowd control methods. They also kept meticulous records of Roosevelt and Churchill's mass civilian bombing raids to study how humans reacted under threat. The goal was to analyze the breakdown of individual psychological strength, rendering citizens helpless to oppose.[84]

Dissociation is often the consequence of a freeze trauma response. In a freeze, a person feels "stuck," unable to make decisions and carry them out through positive actions such as fighting back or even fleeing the situation. They feel paralyzed, often numb. Thus, they may dissociate from everyday life through sleep, daydreaming, addictions, television, and video games.

With this brief discussion of dissociation, you can see how it, too, forms an easy step into transhumanism. The dissociated person, disconnected from their physical/sensory world, their usual sense of self, and their personal history, is easily connected to artificial virtual reality.

Double Bind

A "power couple," Margaret Mead and her husband Gregory Bateson participated in the Macy Conferences in Cybernetics. Once again, the Macy Conferences goal was to move beyond studying human behavior to changing it.

Gregory Bateson developed the theory of double-bind to explain the psychological causes of schizophrenia. In his time, double-bind was decisive for developing systemic theory, for example, interdependent family relationships or communities. Double bind communication examples will sound familiar.

---

84 John Coleman, "Tavistock: The Best Kept Secret in America", July 2001, https://www.educate-yourself.org/nwo/nwotavistockbestkeptsecret.shtmle.

A double bind represents a conflict between two or more messages such that the respondent will always make a mistake. An example would be a parent who gives her child the message to "be spontaneous," then when the child acts spontaneously, he or she is disciplined for not following the mother's other direction. It is no win. Always. The result is a confused child.

Authority figures, like government politicians, communicate in double binds. For example, a politician claims to promote equality by growing the economy, but this results in increasing inequity because people feel left out. As the media broadcasts conflicting narratives, it creates no-win confusion for the citizenry.

Medical authorities also communicate double binds. In COVID-19, citizens in NY received the message to remain healthy, free of the virus. They were mandated to wear masks and isolate, but this results in growing disease. There was no instruction on building a healthy natural immunity to the condition, and isolation affected mental and physical health. Then citizens mandated to "shelter in place" to prevent disease spread while watching weeks of crowded protests. In these COVID-19 cases, when vaccines, antibodies, and treatments replaced innate immunity, the double bind disappeared. This disappearance via replacement is a sleight of hand double-bind. The cure is quickly adopted to break the frustration of the double bind.

According to Bateson, schizophrenia may result from continuous double-bind communications due to inner turmoil riddled with confusion and trauma. The double-bind is punishment in a no-win situation. Of course, most people experience double-bind connections at some point in their lives, but not all develop schizophrenia, which remains one of the most puzzling mental health challenges.

In attachment theory, a person may develop a double bind when they jump from being isolated through avoiding/dismissing others to becoming dramatic and acting out through being anxious/preoccupied. They jump from isolation to drama without resolving any emotional issues. Neither behavior resolves the double-bind, and the person is left more deeply confused. No win.

Psychic Driving—Bleak, Brutal Beginnings

During the 50s and 60s, psychic driving was a psychiatric procedure used in mind control experiments. A Scottish-born psychiatrist, Donald Ewen Cameron, recognized as the originator of psychic driving, was inspired by technology.

Cameron developed a 2-step process to alter human behavior. First, he "annihilated" the patient's distressing memories and behaviors through unrelenting electroconvulsive therapy (ECT), giving as many as 12 treatments per day. Second, he treated patients with repeated audio messages on a looped tape designed to stimulate psychiatric epiphanies. For example, an audio message might be, "Dolores, you have discovered that your mother never wanted you." Often patients were exposed to hundreds of thousands of repetitions during their treatment.[85] These messages repeated for days, weeks, and even months to overwhelm any conscious defenses the patient could muster against the abuse. If the patient rebelled, then hallucinogenic substances were used to immobilize them. MK-ULTRA adopted Cameron's work, recognized by the CIA.

What repeated media messages remove our collective memory of our decency and simultaneously demean, judge, and isolate us? How many of these media messages do we submit to daily? Are we psychically driven deeper into double binds?

Imitation Behavior—Agreeable Conditioning Phase

Humans are natural mimics. We imitate and seek validation for our compliance through mimicry. While we believe we are "doing the right thing," in many cases, we are merely doing what we are told, following directions.

Imitation behavior strengthens social systems. We clap when others clap. We yawn when others yawn. Psychologists studied

---

85 David Saunders, "The History of Brainwashing is a red flag for techno-therapy", *Aeon*, https://aeon.co/ideas/the-history-of-brainwashing-is-a-red-flag-for-techno-therapy.

infants as to how they imitate smiles, gestures, language, and movement. Humans have long used imitation as a form of survival. If you get along, you live. If you behave like the crowd, you live. The psychologists also determined that a human's imitation increases when they perceive they are rewarded and encouraged. This reward deepens the urge to mimic. Thanks for the treat.

Technocracy's cryptocurrency takes advantage of the human propensity to imitate when acknowledged or rewarded. Undoubtedly, social media likes, shares, and hearts use our desire to please.

Disturbingly, technocracy uses human emotional energy to mine cryptocurrencies. This mining includes accumulating rewards for watching approved advertisements or reviewing a product. Through Fitbit, the health sector monitors energy movement to offer health rewards—so many points for working out, eating a "healthy" diet, sleeping.

The ever-expanding medical data collection systems are in place to assure humans as a resource. Here are two companies involved in data collection and tracking.

Factom (https://www.factom.com/) is a blockchain-based data registry and credential verification model used by healthcare. Though teetering on the edge of dissolving, Factom makes most of its money from contracting services with the U.S Department of Homeland Security (DHS) and other government entities. In medical services, Factom provides an easily accessible database of records and individual information for physicians via smartphones from any location in the world.

Smartrac (https://www.smartrac-group.com/) is a global RFID manufacturer that connects humans (via vaccines and digital certificates) with the Internet of Things. Smartrac identifies humans with RFID tags to offer medical services, such as pharmaceuticals. It also provides pharmaceutical corporations "item-level" (humans are the item) visibility into all of their products as they move through their supply chain and stores (hospitals, clinics). Real-world analytics uncover hidden inefficiencies and opportunities. Customer loyalty (mimic the proper reward behavior) is also delivered.[86]

COVID19 introduced "anonymized" (fancy word for anonymous, removing personal identifiers, like your avatar on the Sentient World Simulation—more on that later) tracking apps for your phone. These contact tracing apps point to potential contact with new COVID-19 patients. It is currently an opt-in system and has issues with cross border reporting, but some smartphones come with the app installed, whether you know it or not.[87]

Going to work in an office after COVID-19 may resemble an airport security check zone, complete with invasive protocols like frequent temperature checks, 'social distancing,' and health surveillance, as well as Plexiglass enclosed cubicles and HR-style enforcement monitors. Thermal cameras measure body temperature. Employers classify employee health: Level 1 as the lowest risk of infecting others, Level 2 as people under 65 who don't live with anyone in a risk category or have a chronic disease, and Level 3 as those over 65, pregnant, smokers, and those with chronic disease.[88]

RFID chipped and monitored humans become a resource to be mined and manipulated by technocrats.

Machine Mind—Mission Accomplished

Smart computer technology saturates human life. Technocrats and transhumanists assure us that they create machines to think and behave like humans. But, again, what if the opposite is true? What if humans are being mined by psychological programs, like the ones

---

86 https://www.smartrac-group.com/about.

87 Zak Doffman, "COVID-19's New Reality—These Smartphone APPS Track infected People Nearby". *Forbes*, April 7, 2020, https://www.forbes.com/sites/zakdoffman/2020/04/07/covid-19s-new-normal-yes-your-phone-will-track-infected-people-nearby/#d85a52e7f0db.

88 Tyler Durden, "Your every move will be watched: Post COVID offices to resemble China's social credit system," *Zero Hedge*, May 2020, https://www.zerohedge.com/health/your-every-move-will-be-watched-post-covid-offices-will-resemble-chinas-social-credit-system.

listed, to mimic machines. Like a parent-child relationship, what if we are gradually beginning to think and act like computers. Child psychologists certainly know the interaction formula to change a human into a machine. They identify the amount of time and type of interaction to convince a child that they are a computer.

Chaz Firestone, an assistant professor at Johns Hopkins' Department of Psychological and Brain Science, developed an experiment that confirmed humans now think like computers. He experimented with 1,800 subjects.

Firestone used images frequently misidentified by computers. These are called "fooling" images and are often used by hackers to confuse programs to gain entry. As Firestone found, in some cases, all it takes for a computer to call an apple a car is reconfiguring a pixel or two. He discovered that computers misidentified these images in a way that humans never would, but he was wrong.

In his experiment, Firestone asked people to think like a machine and showed them a dozen fooling images that tricked computers. He gave humans the same labeling options given the computer. One was the computer's answer, and the other was a random answer.

Participants chose the same answer as computers 75% of the time. Then, Firestone went a step further, offering people a choice between the computer's favorite answer and its next-best guess. This time people validated the computer's choice 91%.[89] Firestone quickly verified that humans perceived and thought like a computer. But, there may be an additional factor in human-computer similarity.

Robo-envy is a new field of study in psychology that investigates the human wish to be a robot. Humans perceive robots as able to learn complexities quickly and as not liable for making mistakes. Best of all, humans perceive robots to be loyal without demanding

---

89 Johns Hopkins University, "Researchers get Humans to think like Computers," *Science Daily*, March 22, 2019, https://www.sciencedaily. com/releases/2019/03/190322090239.htm/.

reciprocation.[90] Humans identify computers as something to emulate. Like a child's relationship with a parent, humans may see computers as an authority to be mimicked. Like authority figures, we believe computers possess the correct answers to difficult questions.

But, what if psychological programs to change human behavior are too slow. What if technocrats saw the opportunity to accelerate transhumanism through another group of experts?

Synthetic biologists have replaced cyber-engineers and psychologists, whose methods were too slow and fraught with manipulation and mind control charges. A new generation of biologists filled the bill.

Instead of gradually changing human behavior, synthetic biology aims to completely alter humans' biological makeup with computer chips and nanotechnology that self-replicate and spread invisibly through the body. Humans will never know what took place in their mind, body, and spirit with synthetic biology.

---

90 Jeremy E Sherman, "Robo-Envy and Why People flock to authoritarian leaders," *Psychology Today,* May 21, 2019, https://www.psychologytoday.com/us/blog/ambigamy/201905/robo-envy-and-why-people-flock-authoritarian-leaders.

CHAPTER 4

EXOCONSCIOUS CO-CREATIVE SELF

IS PREFERRED

BIOLOGICALLY ENGINEERED

SYNTHETIC SELF IS PREFERRED

Section 1

Exoconscious Self

How does a healthy person self-define?

The process of self-defining involves gradual awareness of who we are through the lens of age, family, and social environment. At various periods, we evolve perspectives of who we are.

In my therapy practice, I often use attachment theory developed by psychologist John Bowlby. As we have discussed, according to his approach, our early childhood experiences (by my definition prenatal to age 3), we are primarily a cuddly mammal who wants to attach to its mother for survival. We are more reactive than conscious. We are more pliable than independent. We are more likely to accept imprinting than to resist.

Being held and visually cherished, especially by our mothers, stimulates our love hormone, oxytocin. It is a hormone tied to feelings of safety, security, family bonding, love, and companionship. Our mothers' detachment in our early years may cause a lack of oxytocin, which could lead to increased anxiety and depression.[91]

Importantly, we are not our hormones. We need not suffer from a lack of a secure attachment from our early parenting. Through Exoconscious Coaching, we use tools to teach ourselves ways to feel safe, which in turn, stimulates our oxytocin.

How we self-define varies throughout our lives. And we can choose to change how we view ourselves. We can change a dysfunctional, tragic childhood to self-identify as a person who securely loves, respects, and cherishes themselves and others.

For some, amid this process of self-defining, our Exoconscious Self emerges.

I began to self-identify as an Exoconscious Self during adulthood. As I have written about in books and blogs, I was an early childhood experiencer with my first memories around the age of three.[92] Many of these memories are pre-cognitive and lack high-level analytical thinking. Childhood contact experiences are seamless. These have ease and instant integration, but without the broad context or comparing of experiences. My early childhood experiences were conscious yet somewhat unconscious. I lived saturated by my contact experiences because it was the only world I knew. And I did not know enough to question or reject or analyze.

In adulthood, I began to consciously self-identify as Exoconscious. I began to deliberately integrate my ongoing contact experiences with my daily life and my self-identity as an individual, wife, parent, professional, and social community member. Doing so strengthened my Exoconscious Self.

---

91 Florida Atlantic University, "Depression study examines levels of 'love' hormone and its impacts on mother-baby emotional bonding" *Science News*, March 2016. https://www.sciencedaily.com/releases/2016/03/160322100712.htm

92 I explore in detail my early contact experiences in my first book, *Exoconsciousness: Your 21ˢᵗ Century Mind*.

Examining the FREE survey presented a valuable opportunity to give a more detailed and defined examination of the Exoconscious Self of others and myself.

Exoconscious Defined Self

Let us examine the FREE survey results in light of what it indicates about Exoconscious Humans in terms of the following: 1) Integrating contact experiences into a definition of self, i.e., how an Exoconscious Human's personality and self-meaning emerges. 2) The experience of awakening and using innate advanced human consciousness via psychic abilities; and 3) What it means to relate to ETs, multidimensionals as equals.

First, we will examine the integration of the ET, multidimensional experience into a definition of self. That is, how an Exoconscious Human's personality and "self" emerge? According to the FREE survey data, a somewhat radical redefining of "self" occurs because of contact. For example, 80% surveyed indicated that their feelings of compassion and self-worth increased, over 86% stated that "my understanding of myself has increased." Over 70% reported that their self-acceptance increased because of their extraterrestrial contact.

Furthermore, experiencers expressed that their self-understanding gained importance. Nearly 85% stated that "my interest in self-understanding has increased." This statistic indicates that contact heightens inner knowledge. In other words, contact is a subjective experience. Possibly one of the most intimate experiences of defining "Self."

Overall, experiencers possess a positive view of themselves as humans. They do not feel demeaned, enslaved, or overwhelmed by their contact. Instead, experiencers shift their definition of self to a positive one. It would be essential to clarify contact experiences for future research to focus specifically on before and after self-definitions.

This definition of "Self" strongly correlates to ancient and ongoing philosophical questions: Who am I? Why am I here? What is my life's purpose? The positive elevation of one's sense of self affects how a person orients themselves to others and their life purpose. We can argue that an enhanced sense of self also affects the relationship between ETs, multidimensionals, and experiencers in a constructive way. Exoconscious Humans with a positive self-image may tend to see themselves as co-equals with ETs, multidimensionals, and therefore able to choose the type of relationship they desire. A positive self-image is empowering.

ET, multidimensional contact is fundamentally about what it means to be an exoconscious, autonomous self. It is less about the "nuts and bolts" of UFOs, for example, analyzing sightings, searching for proprietary government/military information, calling in craft, or gathering information about various "races of ETs extraterrestrials." It is less about being threatened as an individual or nationally in terms of defense. Instead, the gradual integration of contact is about developing an intimate relationship with one's self.

For an Exoconscious Human, contact is about exploring more profound dimensions of meaning. A life lived as a human who connects to ETs, multidimensionals. An individual's positive sense of self expands out into cosmic consciousness and the accompanying meaning derived from life. Over 80% responded that "My sense that there is some inner meaning to my life" increased.

What is this inner meaning of life expressed by experiencers? What can it tell us about becoming an Exoconscious Human? The FREE survey data indicates that through contact, over 80% increased their understanding of "What is Life all about." We can only surmise how the survey participants define what "life is all about." Some indicate that while their sense of self expanded, so did their desire to serve others. For example, 75% reported an increased willingness to help others; over 60% felt their tolerance for others increased, and nearly 80% responded that "my sensitivity to the suffering of others has increased." These results indicate that as the inner sense of self grew more positive and meaningful, there was also an outer experience where they participated in the world more tolerant of others and wishing to serve others. This feeling of helping others is evident in the finding that nearly 40% surveyed stated, "I believe that my interests in UFO experiences were designed to 'program' me to be of service to humanity." Again, the responses remain oriented toward the human experience. Who am I as a human? How do I respond to others as a human?

FREE survey data makes a strong case that many participants are Exoconscious Humans. They integrated their contact experiences into an elevated sense of self, which in turn provides insight into the meaning of life (i.e., service to others, more sensitive to others' needs). These respondents are examples of integrated, authentic personalities. They are evolved, aware of self and others. Let us take a moment and let this sink in.

What if the fundamental meaning of ET, multidimensional contact, especially ongoing contact, is to develop an awareness of who we are and the purpose of our lives? What if contact is first and foremost about humans? Over 70% expressed that "the widespread occurrence of UFO experiences is part of a larger plan to promote the evolution of Consciousness as a species-wide scale."

As Exoconscious Humans, we achieve expanded self-knowledge and increased human knowledge. Not more data on UFOs or ET, but increased self-knowledge. The subjective self. Yet, to gain the experience of becoming an Exoconscious Human, our understanding of consciousness must change.

Humans in contact with ETs, multidimensionals define consciousness as a field. Interestingly, a remarkable 62% of the respondents agreed with the statement that they "felt flashes of cosmic consciousness at times," and 86% acknowledged an increase in their "desire to achieve higher consciousness." Higher consciousness and cosmic consciousness give a glimpse into how experiencers redefined consciousness outside the mainstream definitions as sourced in the human brain. For them, consciousness was cosmic. Consciousness could be extended and heightened.

Spiritual Transformation of Contact

Mystical traditions infuse every religious culture. Sufis spin into altered states. Buddhists meditate into nirvana. Through yoga, the Hindus find oneness. Kabballah geometric and numeric symbols inspire the mind. Christian mystics center on prayer as their pathway to God.

Each religion has distinct protocols and pathways to God. Paths to an alternate reality. Faith is deepened and expanded by its mystical practices. And yet, mysticism and religion differ. This distinction is fundamental. The UFO, ETs, multidimensional contact experience is not a religion, though some religions directly reference it, such as Scientology, Mormonism, Buddhism, and Hinduism. But for these religions, the UFO and ETs, multidimensionals remains secondary to their belief, doctrinal, and textual foundations. UFO, ET, multidimensional contact is a subordinate experience. Curiously, although secondary, it remains a companion experience in many mystical religious traditions.

Arguably, UFO, ET, multidimensional information, and experiences heavily influence mystics in many religions. The mystical mind moves out into the field of consciousness, receives information, and translates it back into their religious framework. One example follows.

Albert d'Orville, a Belgium Jesuit missionary, was among the first Europeans to travel to Tibet. In a diary entry dated November 1661, d'Orville remarked on his own UFO sighting. "My attention was drawn to something moving in the heavens," he wrote. "At first, I thought it might be a species of bird, unknown to me, that lived in these regions. Then the object came nearer."

What the priest saw was shaped like "a Chinese double hat" and seemed to rotate as it flew. "The object winged its way above the city exactly as if it wished to be admired. It circled twice, and then was suddenly enshrouded in fog, and as much as I strained my eyes, I could no longer see it."

D'Orville asked a nearby lama whether he, too, had seen the object, or whether it had been a hallucination. The lama's reply probably left the Jesuit as astonished as it left me when

I first read Hartwig Hausdorf's book, The Chinese Roswell,[93] where d'Orville's account is reproduced in full:

My son, what you witnessed just now was not magic, because beings from other worlds travel across the oceans of space, and it was they who breathed the spirit into the first people who lived on this earth. These beings condemn all violence; they counsel mankind to love one another. Their teachings are like seeds, but if these seeds are sown on rocky ground, they cannot germinate. These beings, who are light-skinned, are always received by us in friendship, and they often come to earth near our monasteries. They have continued to instruct us, revealing truths that were lost in the centuries of cataclysm which have changed the face of the earth.[94]

In some religious experiences, such as Fatima, researchers point to outright spiritual manipulation of contact experiences. Fernandes and D'Armada wrote a trilogy of the Portuguese children who witnessed the Lady of Fatima, later recognized by the Roman Catholic Church as Mary.[95] The researchers gleaned from sources, including the Vatican Archives, that Fatima had similarities to a UFO, ET event and that Mary's apparition was a cover story. Unfortunately, the young girl, Lucia, the primary witness, was scuttled away to a Spanish monastery where she was not permitted to speak of her experience. Does this remind you of the legions of silenced childhood experiencers?

---

93 Hartwig Hausdorf, *The Chinese Roswell: Ufo Encounters in the Far East from Ancient Times to the Present* (New Paradigm Books, 1998).

94 Chris Aubeck, http://ufoupdateslist.com/2003/may/m30-027.shtml.

95 Fernandes and D'Armada, *Celestial Secrets: The Hidden History of the Fatima Incident* (Anomalist Books, 2007).

Despite the similarities and attempts at a coverup, ET and multidimensional contact is not the foundation of religion. Instead, contact is an experience of altered reality or realities. It is outside of the boundaries of mind, time, and space—received as a psychic, not a religious gift. It is not doctrinal, textual, or a codified body of history, traditions, and rituals.

A small minority, only 5% of the FREE survey respondents reported that their experiences were "Mainly Negative," while those that reported positive behavioral transformation facilitated through contact were approximately 70% of subjects. This data is spiritual and religious. But, there is a difference between religion and spirituality. Religion is a member-based community experience. It is the witness of a belief codified into text, ritual, doctrine, and tradition.

In contrast, spirituality is an individual experience often expressed in creative art such as poetry, painting, music, and movement. Spirituality is One. Religion is Many. The FREE survey respondents essentially bypass the religious sector and move directly to God via their individual contact experience. Experiencers break from cultural and religious cords. More importantly, over 60% of those surveyed indicated that their interest in organized religion decreased due to their contact.

Furthermore, FREE respondents bypass sacrosanct beliefs. Over 60% of the respondents felt that "The essential core of all religions is the same." And nearly 45% embrace a Universal Religion.

This leap to Universal Religion embodying the core of all world-religion beliefs indicates that a large percentage of those surveyed by FREE had an individual experience, free of cultural limitations and definitions. Somehow contact drew them to God, or Source, free of cultural context. Within this context, FREE results indicate respondents spiritually transform through their contact experience. Significantly, over 65% believe that they are a more spiritual person now than before their contact experience, and over 80% felt an increase in spiritual matters. 74% of the survey population believes that the objective of ET, multidimensional contact is to increase one's spirituality to "transform humanity at large into a more self-aware, spiritually sensitive species." In other words, the purpose of contact may be to awaken the human spiritual connection to Oneness, God, or Source. Experiencers consider this spiritual awakening as a movement beyond humans to encompass the entire planet. More specifically, over 67% believe that there are powerful cosmic forces operative today working to "spiritualize" the Earth.

Experiencer language refers to spiritualizing the planet. This language includes the Earth as opening or evolving to higher dimensions. It implies that the awakened experiencer closely aligns with God or Source. They skipped the devout religious pathway of moving an entire community to enlightenment and God. Instead, their contact provided individual access to Oneness. A passport to Source. This direct spiritual transformation via contact and discussion of its planetary evolutionary power recalls the cautionary 1960 Brookings Report, "Proposed Studies on the Implications of Peaceful Space Activities for Human Affairs," by NASA's Committee on Long-Range Studies. [96] The document advised that:

> An individual's reactions to such a radio contact would, in part, depend on his cultural, religious, and social background, as well as on the actions of those he considered authorities and leaders and their behavior, in turn, would, in part, depend on their cultural, social, and religious environment.[97]

The Brookings Report, similar to disclosure advocates and Exopolitics, framed contact as confronting citizens with dramatic

---

96 Donald M. Michael, The Brookings Institution," Proposed Studies on the Implications of Peaceful Space Activities", http://www.nicap.org/papers/brookings.pdf (1960).

97 Brookings Institution, 216, https://ntrs.nasa.gov/archive/nasa/casi.ntrs.nasa.gov/19640053196.pdf.

and unfamiliar events or social pressure, i.e., the mythical world-wide theatrical event of a so-called landing of a UFO on the White House lawn and the associated long-awaited UN or government leader's announcement across the media-saturated planet. Doesn't this sound like "hyperobject" disclosure as described by Professor Timothy Morton? "Too big to think about."[98]

To date, none of this transpired. The opposite happened. Across the planet, millions of individuals report having contact. Most, if not all, are free of trauma and fear, and certainly free of Hollywood story and fearmongering. Based on the FREE survey, the experiencer appears to be a cross-cultural phenomenon reported in varying contexts over many centuries. Instead of fear, experiencers develop a sense of peace, deep spiritual connections, feelings of Oneness, and respect for others.

Morality emerges when discussing one-on-one access to God and spiritualizing the planet through the development of an Exoconscious Self. Chapter 5 examines a sovereign, morally autonomous self since this development is critical for healthy Exoconscious Humans. Next, we discuss what exoconsciousness reveals about health and healing.

Molecular Biology: Transdimensional Health

Currently, two models of health are recognized, and Exoconscious Healers are introducing a third model. We each choose which model we follow. The first germ theory originated from Louis Pasteur's model, maintaining that we get sick because germs, molds, fungi, and bacteria invade our bodies. Pasteur provided evidence for germ theory that had long circulated as a theory. A significant majority of medical professionals follow this model by developing a broad spectrum of treatments to scientifically track, isolate, avoid, and eradicate the invader. This mindset is especially prevalent during public service announcements for COVID19: wash hands,

---

98 RebeccaHardcastleWright,"AnExoconsciousReality",https://medium. com/@Exoconscious/an-exoconscious-human-reality-f278a78cc4c4.

shelter-in-place, wear a mask and gloves, take officially prescribed drugs, use official devices, get a vaccine. Protect yourself from the virus at all costs.

Interestingly, another scientist working in the French medical community offered a second alternative theory during the same period. Antoine Bechamp proposed the "terrain theory," maintaining the prominence of the body's overall internal environment. Most important for Bechamp was the overall preparedness of the body to repel or destroy the germ. This terrain theory is the basis of current integrative and functional medicine. A functional physician provides various holistic treatment methods to bring the patient's "terrain" into maximum health with a view to genetics, environment, and lifestyle.

A third model is transdimensional medicine, a new form of healing that is quietly making inroads. One of the earliest practitioners was Adrian Dvir, a computer engineer, medium, and healer based in Israel. Dvir used advanced ET technology carried inside his body and connected with ETs to heal in his clinic. His clinic embodied ET, as other dimensions penetrated his physical practice space. Today there are hundreds of transdimensional clinics led by healers who are ET, multidimensional experiencers. Exoconscious Humans are co-creating with ETs to heal and move people to optimum health. Transdimensional healers work in Brazil, Israel, Denmark, Australia, the US, and across the world.

We are "Epigenetic Engineers"

Occasionally in the experiencer community, one hears that ET, multidimensional contact changes human DNA. This statement infers additional strands added or reconstruction of human DNA via contact. Contactees may gain awareness of additional strands of DNA by recovering the memory of living on planets with different life forms. It may refer to contact awakening of dormant aspects of DNA. Alternatively, contact changing DNA may represent confusion between the function of DNA and epigenetics. Contact may affect epigenetics, which in turn, guides different parts of DNA. To my knowledge, no scientific studies address these aspects of contact. I encourage this in the future.

As an Exoconscious Human, I work as a therapist with a medical doctor, a functional physician, Dr. Ron Peters, at Mind Body Medicine in Scottsdale, Arizona. Dr. Peters uses sophisticated genetic testing with his patients. I witnessed our clinic's combination of biological and emotional healing, with a strong emphasis on consciousness, bring health to patients. Many of these patients endured long-suffering chronic diseases like autoimmune, diabetes, heart, cancer, and Lyme disease. These patients diligently work through often lengthy and demanding protocols to achieve health. Some are now healthy and active for the first time in their lives.

I once asked Dr. Peters, "In your research with patients, have you explored if their DNA changes when they achieve health."

Dr. Peters responded, "DNA does not change, but a patient's epigenome directs different DNA to create healing. We are all epigenetic engineers selecting what part of our DNA to activate based on consciousness, diet, etc." The following discussion of DNA and epigenetics is from Dr. Peter's lecture on epigenetics.[99]

How to Steer your DNA

Epigenetics is the cellular material that sits on top of your DNA. It forms a bio-energy network. DNA can be comparable to hardware and the epigenome comparable to software that responds from moment to moment to what is going on in your life.

What does the epigenome do? Your epigenome tells your genes to switch on or off. Speak loudly or whisper. Energize or suppress. It activates appropriate DNA activity by responding moment to moment to emotions, lifestyle, diet, and environmental influences such as microbes, chemicals, mold, and toxins. And it can also suppress DNA in the same way.

For most of us, our physical health is all about our DNA.

---

99 Ronald Peters, "Epigenetics: The Science of Gene Regulation," https://youtu.be/Es9F_9fcyVc.

Most of us adhere to a belief in Genetic Determinism, which Sir Francis Crick endorsed in 1953. Most believe that we are our DNA. It's our life sentence of health or illness. For example, if our mother had breast cancer and the gene for it, then that was our fate. Angelina Jolie publicized this belief when she made a very public and dramatic display in 2013 of having her breasts and ovaries removed because she carried a gene called BRCA1 that increases breast and ovarian cancer, a predictor of early death.

Regrettable for Jolie's dramatics, Blair Justice, Professor of Psychology at the University of Texas-Houston Health Science Center, found that genes account for 35% of longevity. At the same time, lifestyles, diet, emotions, and environmental factors, including support systems, are the primary reasons people live longer.[100] DNA is not a life sentence, and we don't need to cut our way out of it surgically. There are other forces at work in your mind-body that you can access.

Consciousness, the field of consciousness, is a primary tool you can access. While the early Genome Project expected 120,000 genes, it found only 23,688. Not enough to describe the power of DNA. So, where does the information come from to create our dynamic living human system?

Dr. Peters cites the miracle of our human biology. We have 100 Trillion Cells in our body. In each cell, there are 60 billion biological reactions simultaneously happening. He states that this complexity cannot be accounted for or organized by anything chemical (endocrine system) or electrical (neurological system). Instead, he ventures that the organizing field is quantum medicine: the "field" that organizes all of life—cosmic, planetary, earth, nature, and God—an organizing intelligence. We are much more than DNA determined.

Epigenetics is the study of heritable (generation to generation) changes in gene function that occur without a difference in the

---

100 Blair Justice, *Who Gets Sick: Thinking and Health* (Peak Press, 1987).

DNA sequence. It functions as signals that turn genes on and off. DNA remains the same, but its function changes

Bruce Lipton made the startling discovery that DNA is not required for a cell to survive. He found that enucleated (without nucleus) cells still express normal cell function. Proteins create the cell's structure and function and work through the cell wall activity, which Lipton referred to as the "brain of the cell."

In his book, *Biology of Belief,*[101] Lipton further explored the role of consciousness in human biology, the pathways connecting the mind and body. If you believe the world is hostile, antagonistic, attacking you, then your body expresses that and draws inward to protect. Your fear epigenetically activates sequences of DNA that are protective and defensive. An ongoing defensive reaction often creates various diseases. In contrast, if you believe in goodness in life, blessings, optimism, and see possibilities in challenges, then you move into growth and health.

We daily engineer our epigenetics through diet, relationships, work, activity, and notably through our overarching conscious beliefs about ourselves and the world. I would also add how we interact with the field of consciousness. Do we venture out into the field of consciousness with a feeling of security, trust, optimism, and the essential goodness of life? Or do we evade, fearful, and weak in fear of attack or duplicity?

The quality of our exoconsciousness may determine our epigenetics.

Consciousness and Quantum Jumping into the Fray

My human body possesses an extraterrestrial connection through my consciousness. The human body and quantum consciousness are one. The government's genome project proposes many answers for understanding genetic makeup while it also left the door open to flood science with new questions. The discovery and understanding

---

101 Bruce Lipton, *The Biology of Belief: Unleashing the Power of Consciousness, Matter, & Miracles* (Hay House, 2008).

of DNA forced scientists to address the issue of junk DNA and phantom effects. When confronted with the reality of junk DNA, the scientific manifesto, "nature is not profligate," began to sound hollow. In other words, if, as the traditional scientists speculated, nature never provides more than is needed for an organism to function in its environment, then how do scientists solve the riddle of junk DNA? What did junk DNA provide?

Junk DNA researchers argue that the majority, 97% of our DNA, does nothing. Like the Buddhist realm of "nothingness," or unborn awareness, scientist Colm Kelleher speculated on transposons' activity.[102] DNA sequences that move from one location on the genome to another are known as transposable elements or jumping genes.

According to Kelleher, these useless 3 million base pairs of junk DNA await activation by retrotransposons, creating a jumping DNA phenomenon. "Only 3% of human DNA encodes the physical body. The remaining 97% of the 3 billion base pair genome contains over a million genetic structures, called transposons, that jump from one chromosomal location to another. Transposons jump to a new location via an RNA intermediate are known as retrotransposon."

Furthermore, according to Kelleher, there were confirmed cases of retrotransposon activation of previously unused, "read junk," DNA. This quantum-like DNA jumping phenomenon bolstered Nobel Prize-winning scientist Barbara McClintock's assumption that our genetic code or DNA was not a "static structure, transmitted unchanged generation to generation." Instead, she asserts that specific DNA sequences jump from one location to another. In other words, our genetic blueprint changes with this jumping phenomenon, and Kelleher believes we can influence the movement.

---

102 Colm A. Kelleher, "Retrotransposons as Engines of Human Bodily Transformation," https://wmthost.com/ndeinfo/ndeinfo/Human%20Bodily%20Transformation.pdf.

Designing research experiments to track DNA sequence-jumping was most successful when performed as cancer research. Kelleher asserts, "...it must be emphasized that in humans only the disease-causing consequences of transposition have so far been found...It is challenging to catch an element 'in the act' of moving to a different chromosomal location."

Exoconscious Jumping

Despite the research hurdles, Kelleher makes a bold claim and traces this activation process, or jumping DNA, to possibly explain dramatic physical conversions initiated by spiritual or religious experience. This activation process could also represent an individual's gradual spiritual evolutionary process. The implications for Exoconscious Humans are vast. Kelleher cites the sages, mystics, and yogis who experience age reversion, levitation, transfiguration, and possibly ascension as possibly resulting from jumping DNA. Experiencers exhibit and speak of these abilities, which may further explain why they discuss contact changes in their DNA.

Kelleher indicates that humans can somehow tap the human potential that lays dormant in our DNA and utilize it for miraculous abilities and achievements. As ancient and modern spiritual disciples have long claimed, their DNA changed (jumped) as their discipline intensified, and their level of enlightenment heightened.

Exoconscious Humans often note that kundalini experiences initiate contact. Awakened kundalini exemplifies another possible DNA conversion on a cellular level. Kundalini disciples often comment on the feeling that every cell in their body shifts during a tantra episode of kundalini. As tantra disciple Richard Sauder writes, his body changed with an infusion of metaphysical/physical voltage:

> My spinal column was turbo-charged with what felt like 50,000 volts of rippling, crackling electricity that came surging up my spine with an ear-splitting roar and arced out of the top of my skull...my heart chakra was powerfully opened. I could see all around me without any physical

impediment. The heart itself sees, with high acuity and without physical restriction, when in a state such as this.[103]

Could DNA, activated through kundalini practices, be one of the paths toward cosmic consciousness? Kelleher seems to be pointing to DNA as a potential natural propellant system to launch a consciousness craft and then recall it back into the body. Junk DNA and the quantum-jumping phenomenon may be an energy system innate in the human body. Have generations of spiritual masters and contactees perfected this technique until it may tip into the mainstream via Exoconscious Humans? The populated floor of yoga studios seems to indicate the path is opening.

Exoconscious Quickening of Transformation

Kenneth Ring, author of *The Omega Project: Near-Death Experiences, UFO Encounters and Mind at Large,* whose work was a significant influence in the FREE Survey, compares long and spontaneous or quick enlightenment experiences. He found that enlightenment accessed by a lifetime discipline of a spiritual master may be the same as the dramatic, quickening of awareness triggered by near-death experiences and UFO encounters.

Depending on the individual and the culture, the enlightenment process may be fast or slow, yet the experience's quality was similar. In a sophisticated medical culture, the increasingly commonplace emergency room revival of "dead" patients provides a robust database to examine the spiritual enlightenment of near-death experiences. This research dovetails the increasingly commonplace UFO sightings by our current culture, researched contact reports, and internet email forums as yet another database of enlightenment research.

According to the esteemed Harvard psychiatrist, John Mack, who interviewed, tested, and diagnosed numerous contact experiencers,

---

103 Richard Sauder, *Kundalini Tales* (Adventures Unlimited, 1998).

they all seemed to move through similar stages.[104] Mack identified four dimensions accessed by the experiencers. First, each was taken against their will and given fear-producing intrusive procedures. Second, upon completion and returning to everyday life, they often experienced a sense of isolation and estrangement. Third, they experienced an "ontological shock," where their usual paradigms of belief and values had to shift. They knew they were not alone in the universe. Fourth, after the paradigm shift, many seemed to manifest an expanded spiritual awareness, which he termed a multidimensional consciousness.

> Not infrequently, they pass through this terror, or "dark night of the soul," similar to the kind of initiatory passage through terror to a new level of consciousness that is familiar in almost every spiritual tradition. It's kind of like that. They move through what might be called an expanded awareness, an awakening.[105]

Many experiencers interviewed and treated by Mack pushed through the terror of abduction to experience the beauty of their being's cosmic source. They also began to experience a consciousness that could separate from and return to their body. This consciousness could live in multiple universes simultaneously.

The separation and return of consciousness that Mack describes reflects the experience of the mother ship and the consciousness craft. His research nudges us to ponder whether we as a species are being "pushed" into a spiritual awakening through UFO, contact encounters, as well as near-death experiences. Our species is accelerating our economic wealth, our collection of data information,

---

104 John Mack, *Passport to the Cosmos: Human Transformations and Alien Encounters* (Three Rivers Press, 2000).

105 Vivienne Simon, "Passport to the Cosmos: An Interview with John Mack, MD". http://johnemackinstitute.org/2000/04/passport-to-the-cosmos-an-interview-with-john-mack-m-d/

our travel speed, and accelerating our spiritual evolution. What once required a lifetime of disciplined, isolated, rigorous prayer, and self-denial, now was accomplished by an almost over-night near-death experience or close encounter.

As epigenome and DNA research explores human physical possibilities, our fears and limitations fade. We no longer need to limit or block our evolution; we simply need to jump into a new consciousness propelled by our molecular biology (as opposed to our synthetic biology, which is discussed later in this chapter).

Two streams—DNA and consciousness—are merging. Yet the merging is often perceived as chaotic and oppositional. Is our scientific understanding of the potential power of our DNA influencing our understanding of the enlightenment phenomenon? Or is the inflating scientific database driving our need to make sense of our human potential?

As Dr. Ronald Peters explains, "part of what holds us back is the power of belief. Beliefs structure reality, and they are solid and reliable, predictable life experiences. Letting go of dysfunctional beliefs may be the core issue in healing. Tears may contain the chemical dissolution of belief."[106]

Exoconscious Humans seem quick to convert their human body image into a quantum field of potential rather than a biological machine. Beyond our consciousness, brain, and mind, our entire body is exoconscious. As the kundalini experience highlights, our heart energies are integrally involved in raising our body's frequency to manufacture a consciousness propellant. Functional physicians are beginning to take apart the body's engine—not as mechanics, piece by piece, organ by organ, but as quantum physicians—energy by energy, frequency by frequency. The DNA phantom effect, another critical aspect, studies the quantum quality inherent in our physical bodies.

---

106 Ronald Peters, "The Natural Therapeutic Experience: Living from your Heart," https://www.healmindbody.com/the-natural-therapeutic-experience/.

DNA Phantom Effect

As researched by Vladimer Poponin and Kirlian photography, the DNA phantom effect presents the best evidence to date of the quantum subtle energy phenomenon in our genetic makeup. In the 1990s, the Russian researcher Poponin discovered a relationship between DNA and light. [107] He developed a series of experiments to research the patterns of light in a vacuum's controlled environment.

Under the vacuum conditions, the light fell into a random distribution. Poponin then placed physical samples of DNA into the chamber and found that the patterns of the light particles shifted in the presence of genetic material. The random pattern changed with the presence of DNA. A new pattern emerged resembling waves as they crested and fell.

Withdrawing the DNA sample, he assumed the light would revert to the prior random distribution, but instead, a new pattern emerged. The presence of DNA affected the light photons even after withdrawn. Did DNA possess a force that lingered long after the absence of genetic material? If so, what does this say about the power of our body's presence in the physical world? The presence of our DNA seems to have a measurable effect on the physical world. If this effect can be measured, it can be understood. If understood, it can be applied. The human heart is the starting point.

California researchers adopted the discoveries of Kilian photography and Poponin's DNA phantom effect to create a new understanding of the human heart's power. The Heartmath project sought to harness the power of the heart frequencies to accelerate and heal the body.[108] As with the kundalini experience, Heartmath research determined that the heart possesses the most potent electrical field in the body. This powerful field coming from the heart

---

107 Vladimer Poponin, "The DNA phantom effect Direct Measurement of A New Field in the Vacuum Substructure," *Worlds Within Worlds*, http://worlds-within-worlds.org/dnaphantom1.php.

108 Sara Paddison, *The Hidden Power of the Heart: Achieving Balance and Fulfillment in a Stressful World* (Planetary Publications, 1993).

also can entrain or bring other energy systems in the body into its frequency. Like a mother with a fussy child, properly used, our heart pulls the disparate physical energy systems into a higher harmony. This system includes the brain. In an electrical sense, our hearts rule our heads.

HeartMath researchers incorporated the quantum model to understand the energy field of the heart. They, too, turned to genetic research to understand how the powerful DNA blueprint in every cell of the human body holds the perfect image of the total body as a holographic template.

Kirlian or holographic photography demonstrated a phantom effect that lingered in a cut leaf. The Kirlian phantom leaf effect occurred when a researcher photographed a leaf with a hole cut in the center. Instead of a marred leaf, holographic photography revealed the whole, perfect leaf. The evidence indicated that a force remains after the genetic substance withdraws within the DNA structure of every living thing.

Examining the physical changes that result in ET, multidimensional experience highlights changes felt in DNA and spontaneous healing. Information from the FREE survey provides deep individual insights.

Physical Transformation of Contact

How does contact change the physical body? Physical transformation stems from changes in how we experience and therefore perceive our physical body. Physical transformations from contact include 1) advanced physical abilities, 2) changes in DNA, and 3) spontaneous healing. These transformations may indicate that a biological modification in DNA occurred as a result of contact.

The FREE respondents indicate that conscious psychic experiences caused physical changes. Experiencers exhibited abilities not on the "normal" spectrum. Nearly half experienced physical bilocation. They answered yes when asked, *Have you ever been taken and relocated to another location.* 23% repeatedly bilocated. More specifically, those surveyed shared their bilocation as a physical experience.

Nearly half of the respondents noted that they *dematerialized and traveled through material objects.*

Contact bilocation of these experiencers transformed their physical body—it dematerialized, dissolved, and rematerialized. These experiences are extreme transformations of the physical body, likened unto death or near-death experiencers. Mystics also report dematerialization. For example, in Christ's transfiguration in Matthew 17, he emerges out of a cloud, transfiguring as light. Buddha transfigured twice—at enlightenment and death. Buddha became a light body.

Importantly, in the FREE survey data, experiencers do not claim that they floated out of their physical body via altered states of consciousness. Instead, they state that their physical body dematerialized. And then their physical body rematerialized. Their shared experience pushes the boundaries of our cultural beliefs concerning the abilities of the human body. A future study might design questions that further detail physical dematerialization during one's contact experience.

How does contact affect experiencer DNA?

The FREE survey respondents indicated that their DNA might have upgraded through contact. According to this survey, over a quarter of the respondents connected their physical transformation to the upgrading of their DNA when asked, *Did ETs give you information that they are upgrading our human DNA?* From an exoconsciousness perspective, physical transformation via ET, multidimensional contact may revise DNA. Consequently, this information may change the conscious reality of the experiencer regarding their physical body.

DNA stores information energetically in our bodies. When experience alters physical information, the energetics of the individual may transform. This alteration affects their epigenome. Information from the FREE survey data contributes to our emerging understanding that humans who change their behaviors and beliefs may be altering, suppressing or activating, their DNA. The human body self-heals. Prior opinions of DNA as a type of death sentence radically change into DNA as a type of health assurance. Many processes, including epigenetics, quantum jumping, phantom effect, and ET multidimensional contact, modify human DNA. Research indicates that DNA is malleable and responsive like neural plasticity processes change how our brain responds. Evidence that we possess tools and methods to create health in our physical body.

Does contact heal and promote health?

A more in-depth analysis of experiencers' physical transformation in the FREE survey pertains to childhood experiences with ETs. These experiences primarily occurred before the age of five. Those who had childhood contact expressed marked physical changes. When asked about changes in their nervous system, 43% noted that their nervous system was functioning differently than it had before. Over 50% felt the energy in their hands more often, 30% experienced an increase in their sense of taste, and over 20% experienced increased visual acuity. Of particular significance was the finding that nearly 60% indicated that their overall health improved (i.e., answered "No" to the question, *my susceptibility to illness increased*). These results highlight that a large percentage of respondents believe that their childhood contact experience led to dramatic physical change.

Future research in this area should determine whether childhood physical transformations continued throughout their lifetime, into adulthood. If so, these results would highlight individuals who possess a higher degree of physical health and sensory awareness. Furthermore, it would possibly point to persons who develop a distinct physical body through childhood ET, multidimensional contact. An in-depth study of these individuals might include medical records and diagnostics. If validated, humans might redefine their relationship to their physical body and their identity as a physical being beyond limited beliefs and boundaries.

A series of questions on spontaneous healing through contact experiences highlight boundaries of belief about our physical body. When asked, *Have you ever had sudden or rapid healing that you believed was a result of ET intervention,* approximately 35% said "yes." Further, 16% said ETs told them they had the procedure, and 50% of those surveyed stated that ETs healed them or a family member. One FREE survey respondent shared dramatic healing as follows:

"I had a suspicious growth in my breast. During meditation, two "helpers" showed up in my mind. They were there to help get rid of the growth. For six months, I visualized them working. The day before the follow-up mammogram, in my meditation, they packed up and left. I told them not to go, I hadn't had the follow-up test yet. They said I didn't need them anymore. I imagined the doctor telling me, "I can't believe it. It's gone!" The next day I went for the mammogram and the nurse came to tell me the doctor wanted a second image. I was so scared. Then she said, "He can't believe it. It's gone!"

Dramatic healings, such as this woman's, are not uncommon among experiencers. They originate in ET, multidimensional interaction. A follow-up question for future research might ask if ETs taught them healing modalities via downloads or actual teachings. Did they learn from these downloads and instructions? Were they then able to heal themselves and others? Such future questions would examine whether experiencers become healers and the details of the transmissions. One FREE survey question hints at the possible transfer of healing abilities via extraterrestrial contact. When asked to respond, *I felt that I could sometimes heal people by touching them;* nearly half (48%) answered "yes."

Do Exoconscious Humans heal others?

Exoconscious Humans frequently refer to their healing abilities. Many perform what they refer to as quantum or energetic healing. Their healing modality accesses the information-energy field of consciousness, which connects them directly to ETs, multidimensionals. For example, Sheila Seppi of Spirit Way Wellness combines ancient healing and quantum field modalities, inspired by her contact experiences.[109] An exoconscious healer, she integrated contact experience into her personal life as a healer. Her healing modalities work in a shared, co-creative ET-human field of consciousness—information and energy. Similar to the reported healing of respondents by ETs in the FREE survey, Sheila's healings are considered non-invasive, quick, and effective.

So far, this chapter presented information and research about humans in harmony with nature and multiple dimensions. We are just beginning to comprehend cellular microbiology—

DNA, epigenetics, quantum fields, consciousness, and psychic abilities. But suddenly, the field of microbiology turns upside down, replaced with a new system. What is the influence of the new field of synthetic biology that supplants microbiology?

Exoconscious Humans' co-created quantum medicine involves microbiology, consciousness, electromagnetics, and energetics. Natural systems. Synthetic biology's silicon-based medicine includes computer code, nanotechnology, and artificial reality. Let's examine synthetic biology's origins and perspectives.

Section 2

Transhuman Synthetic Biology

An Orwellian Spring of 1984, while I was working at a state university in Ohio, I initiated The Human Dilemma of High Technology seminar. In the 1980s, tech growth was in an early stage of rapid development and proliferation. By the end of the 80s-decade, personal computers would be widespread and user-friendly with games, connectivity, messaging, Windows, color screens, and mouse navigation.

Applying the creative advantage of computing advancements, a renowned professor at the university utilized computer circuits

---

109 http://spiritwaywellness.com.

to achieve paralyzed students' mobility. Wright State University, next door to Wright Patterson Air Force Base, was built to be handicapped accessible from the ground up. And as such, it housed many students with physical challenges who might never have the opportunity to live on campus, much less navigate every square inch of a university. There were students in wheelchairs and even one in a motorized bed who attended my programs.

In his university lab, Dr. Jerrold Petrosky, a biomedical engineer, experimented with assisting paralyzed people to walk by electrically stimulating their muscles with computer-controlled devices. Paralyzed students were swimming laps in the university pool, playing athletic games in computer harnesses, walking down the aisle for their wedding, and even working jobs once considered impossible.

Paralyzed Wright State University students believed that Petrosky would change their future.

In 1983, a paralyzed student, Nanette Davis, walked on the graduation stage for her diploma. *Time, Newsweek,* and *60 Minutes* covered the graduation. The made-for-television biographical film *First Steps* highlighted Petrosky's groundbreaking work.

Petrosky's innovative efforts swept the campus with students and fellow faculty in awe of his genius, continual publicity, and grants. But admiration was tempered by the occasional sour taste of professorial jealousy. John Horgan, a science journalist, looked closely behind the scenes where campus rumors circulated of Petrosky and another professor who propped-up Nanette Davis during the graduation ceremony because their device malfunctioned.[110] Criticism mounted on and off-campus.

In the wake of the movie *First Steps,* there was a scientific pushback. Some two dozen university researchers signed a statement

---

110 John Horgan, "A Dig Through Old Files Reminds Me Why I'm So Critical of Science," *Scientific American,* November 2, 2013, https://blogs.scientificamerican.com/cross-check/a-dig-through-old-files-reminds-me-why-ie28099m-so-critical-of-science/.

"to correct certain misimpressions and misleading statements that have appeared" regarding "the application of electrical stimulation to move paralyzed limbs."[111]

By 1987, Petrosky left Wright State University under a cloud of criticism accepting a faculty position at Loma Linda University in California. Yet, the push back on science, calling experts to accountability, continues.

More recently, a cloud of criticism surrounded the "Ferguson Code" used by British epidemiologist and professor of mathematical biology, Neil Ferguson, who specializes in the patterns of spread of infectious disease in humans and animals.[112] His advice led to the UK lockdown during COVID19 amid wildly exaggerated estimations on the pandemic's global reach. It turns out that his global model was an undocumented, 13-year-old computer code intended for an influenza pandemic, rather than a coronavirus. During his public predictions, Ferguson declined to share his original code so that other scientists could verify his results.

The journalist Horgan, who investigated Petrosky, reminds us of science's fallibility, which is essential as a context for research into synthetic biology covered in this chapter. It is crucial to separate evidence-based science from publicity stories that generate income for more research on failed promises, Petrosky-Ferguson style.

Discussing his findings in Scientific American two years ago, Stanford professor John Ioannidis[113] writes: "False positives and

---

111 Colin Campbell, "Researchers criticize CBS film 'first steps'," *New York Times*, March 21, 1985, https://www.nytimes.com/1985/03/21/arts/researchers-criticize-cbs-film-first-steps.html.

112 Andrew Gelman, "So the real scandal is: Why did anyone ever listen to this guy?" May 8, 2020. https://statmodeling.stat.columbia.edu/2020/05/08/so-the-real-scandal-is-why-did-anyone-ever-listen-to-this-guy.

113 John P. A. Ioannidis, C.F. Rehnborg Chair in Disease Prevention, Professor of Medicine, of Epidemiology and Population Health, and (by courtesy) of Biomedical Data Science, and of Statistics; co-Director, Meta-Research Innovation Center at Stanford (METRICS).

exaggerated results in peer-reviewed scientific studies have reached epidemic proportions in recent years. The problem is rampant in economics, the social sciences, and even the natural sciences, but it is particularly egregious in biomedicine."[114]

Homeland of Genome and Nanotechnology

I tucked away my knowledge of science and technology born from my experience at Wright State University. Then nearly three decades later, the knowledge re-emerged through my move to Washington, DC, to work with Dr. Edgar Mitchell's Quantrek organization. My first move into Maryland's outer belt of Washington DC brought me to live across the street from the headquarters of genome research. Another of life's ironies.

While moving into an apartment complex, aptly named Avalon, I was intrigued by the sprawling multistoried, serpentine green glass structure just across the street. It slithered across a lawn of newly planted trees. Exploring, I walked inviting freshly mulched paths circling the structure, but never encountered another person. Whoever worked there was encased behind massive slabs of glass. The green glass left a strange feeling: were they watching me? I couldn't see them.

Eventually, I discovered that I was walking around the J. Craig Venter Institute. This non-profit genomics research facility included the Center for the Advancement of Genomics, The Institute for Genomic Research, and the Institute for Biological Energy Alternatives. I had moved across the street from one of the vortexes of synthetic biology. And little did I know then that I was to relocate a year later near another important synthetic biology institution—this one a government agency.

---

114 Dr. Ioannidis was also vocal regarding the statistics used during COVID19 to make governmental decisions and found them wanting evidence, https://www.statnews.com/2020/03/17/a-fiasco-in-the-making-as-the-coronavirus-pandemic-takes-hold-we-are-making-decisions-without-reliable-data/.

But first, let's move into a brief understanding of the history of synthetic biology. And you will see how Venter holds scientific prominence.

An Exceptionally Short History of Synthetic Biology

This section offers an all too brief outline of the history of synthetic biology. It is essential to comprehend synthetic biology's foundations to perceive technocracy's vision for our human bodies. And the planet we inhabit. Despite their claim to be climate change advocates, nature lovers, synthetic biologists are changing all life forms on earth from microbiological to synthetic. Before you gasp in disbelief, read on.

Synthetic Biology is integrated into and changes our natural biological systems. Applying engineering principles and computer programs to biology, they design, fabricate, test, and refine artificial components inserted into our physical body. For example, manufacturing DNA sequences and building artificial biological systems using natural elements. Often these are hybrid creations of natural and synthetic biology.

Synthetic Biology's scientific method is familiar to the engineering culture: design, build, then test. This procedure includes computer modeling design, construction through genetic engineering, and testing to assess if it works.

Now, imagine a multilayered delivery system introducing these synthetic biological components into humans. Here are a few of the delivery systems: chemicals we use and ingest, chemtrails in the air we breathe, vaccines, GMO foods, and nanotechnology weaved into our clothing. Each of these delivery systems inserts synthetic products directly into our bodies. Then these components are triggered by electromagnetic and radio frequency instructing their specific activation.

Imagine our human body saturated with tiny cyborgs, or cybernetic organisms, remotely triggered to 1) transform or augment our body, 2) allow for the brain to computer interface (BCI), and 3) mind control and behavioral modification.

How far has synthetic biology come? If its history is any indication, we are on the cusp of synthetic biology transforming humans and life forms on Earth. Here is a short history.

The 1990s: Optogenetics: Cybernetics developed tools for computer control of cellular processes at the gene level. A computer could switch on or off embedded genetic communication using light. While our brain communicates with electrical and chemical signaling, researchers found that light stimulation could also manipulate communication pathways.

Optogenetic experiments extract "opsins," light-sensitive proteins, from plants and are introduced into mammals using injections. These injected opsins can then be activated or suppressed by timed pulses of light of varying color wavelengths to target body systems and create biological effects. The combination of optogenetics and CRISPR technology edit the genome with light-activating tools.

Optogenetics is fundamental in government programs such as the Bush and Obama Brain initiatives. Co-founder of Microsoft, Paul Allen, founded the Allen Brain Map Atlas. AI optogenetic technology uses neuronal barcoding to create an online brain atlas. This barcoding includes tiny silicon chips and nanoparticles designed with semiconductors or "quantum dots." High quantity modeling and measurement make possible large data systems, like the brain atlas, that analyze AI machine learning. This atlas represents initial steps in the quantification, identification, and inventory on a cellular level.

Using optogenetics, a group of scientists from Yale University and the University of São Paulo study what parts of the brain trigger specific motor responses. In particular, they studied predatory behavior and its complex motor actions that involve impulses to hunt, track, pounce, bite, and kill. They attached a sensory device to the rodent's head and pulsed light that activated neurons engineered to respond to light, triggering the killing instinct. [115]

---

115 Darryl Fears, "Scientists used light to turn Mice into Stone-Cold Killers," *Washington Post*, January 12, 2017, https://www.

DARPA, Defense Advanced Research Projects Agency, is an agency of the United States Department of Defense. Charged with developing emerging technologies, it invests heavily in optogenetics through its Neural Engineering System Design Program, creating an implantable neural interface capable of the high-resolution brain to machine communication. This program developed a mind-controlled touch-sensitive prosthetic like the "Luke Arm," a commercially available prosthesis with a powered shoulder, allowing a shoulder-level amputee to reach over their head. Military optogenetic experiments also include memory manipulation techniques for treating veteran's PTSD. Other optogenetic applications potentially treat blindness, pain management, mood disorders, and Parkinson's. For example, DARPA's ElectRX (Electrical Prescription) program stimulates and monitors the body's peripheral nervous system.[116]

The 2000s: J Craig Venter (man in the glass serpent) took joint credit for the first sequencing of the human genome's DNA code. In 2007, Venter was the first human to have his genome sequenced.

In 2003, the National Institute of Health held a symposium on digital biology, furthering the role of data collection, storage, and modeling of biological forms—humans and all sentient beings.

The 2010s: DNA Code computerized: J Craig Venter Institute (team in the glass serpent) created the **first synthetic life form**, a replica of cattle bacterium. Its DNA code was written into a computer and assembled in a test tube, and then inserted into hollowed-out shells of the different bacterium, identified with a watermark. These hollowed out chassis homed a whole new genome and organisms.

The Yeast 2.0 project was an international initiative to rebuild the yeast genome from scratch. This project created a synthetic

---

washingtonpost.com/news/speaking-of-science/wp/2017/01/12/scientists-used-light-to-turn-mice-into-stone-cold-killers/.

116 Jay Stanley, "Optogenetics: A Virtual Reality System Controlling Living Cells," *Techspot*, November 2017, https://www.techspot.com/article/1531-optogenetics/.

malaria drug. (Yes, if you have a malaria vaccine, you most likely have synthetic biology.) But malaria is treatable. The malaria drug hydroxychloroquine was invented during WWII to treat soldiers. During COVID-19, the mainstream press fought against a treatment using hydroxychloroquine, azithromycin, and zinc. Even though physicians had prescribed hydroxychloroquine for 85 years, suddenly, it was unsafe. Manhattan hospitals went so far as to deny their patients access to the treatment.[117] Reports surfaced of physicians prohibited from prescribing it. Synthetic biology bullies alternative therapies.

Algae fuel: Did you notice Venter's Institute for Biological Energy Alternatives? Research in this field developed alternative energy sources. Exxon Mobil funded Venter's Synthetic Genomic project. The oil industry discovered that algae produced oil but required briny water and sunlight to grow. Furthermore, it was expensive to harvest. An either-or situation emerged. If algae was starved of nitrogen to increase the amount of oil, its growth was crippled. So, Venter's project developed a synthetic algae gene for producing more oil, then tweaked it to produce even when nitrogen was plentiful. They increased oil output by 20 to 40 percent. [118]

Genetic Circuits: Synthetic biologist Timothy Lu designed a genius of genetic circuits in bacterium—creating electronic circuit boards with biofilm. He found that in E. coli bacteria, proteins called curli fibers would naturally latch onto others. These curli fibers were prompted to bond with metals, picking up gold particles. Then they prompted the bacteria to self-assemble into a gold-laced biofilm. Programs were patterned in biofilm, manufacturing a fabric that operated like a circuit board. Biofilms are a polymer-encased community of microbes that accumulate on a

---

117 https://www.armstrongeconomics.com/international-news/disease/nurse-speaks-out-that-people-are-being-murdered-in-hospitals/.
118 James Mitchell Crow, "Life 2.0: inside the synthetic biology revolution, Cosmos: The Science of Everything," April 17, 2018, https://cosmosmagazine.com/biology/life-2-0-inside-the-synthetic-biology-revolution.

surface. Gold atoms were sprinkled onto the biofilm to create path-ways of gold wire. These nanoscale semiconductors emitted light. [119]

Synthetic biology created a new gold standard. Our biology is now our economy. Why bother with blockchains or debit card chips when stored reserves of gold standard genetic circuits can be inserted into humans to determine their financial worth and control their equity? Why settle for a gold tooth when you can show-case your artificial gold metric circuits? War, one of the most profit-able economic ventures, is now enhanced with synthetic biology. Human biology represents the new loot.

Xenobots are living robots. These tiny living robots, called xenobots, are created using cells taken from frog embryos. Each xenobot is less than a millimeter across and can propel itself through water using two stumpy limbs, while another has a kind of pouch that it could use to carry a small load. Note, one millimeter is smaller than a tiny red ant.

Xenobots can communicate to form tissues that can compose an organ, a whole intelligent body. Thus, scientists are creating hybrid robot organisms to send data, to direct (use to herd way-ward cells), navigate (move forward and backward), and pick up objects in their pouch deposit where guided. [120]

Super Soldier: DARPA: Biological Technologies Office was established in 2014 to create a soldier with no physical or cognitive limitations. Persistent in combat, continuous performance, aug-mented cognition, with ongoing peak performance—24/7. These experimental technologies range from robotics to synthetic biology to a combination of both.

---

119 Carl Engelking, "Reprogrammed Bacteria Build Self-Healing 'Living Materials'," *Discover*, March 24,2014, https://www.discov-ermagazine.com/technology/reprogrammed-bacteria-build-self-healing-living-materials.

120 Matt Simon, "Meet Xenobot, an Eerie New Kind of Programmable Organism," *Wired*, January 13, 2020, https://www.wired.com/story/xenobot/.

Super soldiers may spend hours underwater using infused synthetic blood developed with respirocyte, a red blood cell made from diamonds. Achilles heel, long a mythical human weakness, can be strengthened with bionic boots allowing soldiers to run at inhuman high speeds for long distances. Immunizations manage pain and inflammation. Neural implants enable soldiers to connect with and control robotics through thought. Exoskeletons, a robotic suit of fabric muscles, alleviate fatigue, and increases strength.[121]

2017: Vaccines with Synthetic Biology: The immunoprophylaxis process involves isolating genes that produce antibodies against certain diseases. These genes are synthesized (replicated) and engineered as artificial versions. These artificial genes are then placed into viruses and injected into humans via vaccines. These new genes instruct the cells to begin to manufacture antibodies against a specific disease.

According to Michael Farzan, an immunologist at Scripps, "The viruses invade human cells with their DNA payloads, and the synthetic gene incorporates into the recipient's DNA. If all goes well, the new genes instruct the cells to begin manufacturing powerful antibodies."[122]

In effect, injection of these artificial genes via vaccines alter DNA, causing a permanent change in the recipient's body, which lasts a lifetime. Instead of injecting a piece of a virus into a person, synthesized genes would be shot into the body to stimulate the

---

121 Logan Nye, "8 technologies the Pentagon is pursuing to create Super Soldiers," *Business Insider*, July 2017. https://www.businessinsider.com/8-technologies-the-pentagon-pursuing-create-super-soldiers-2017-7.

122 Jon Rappoport, "Altering Human Genetics Through Vaccination," https://childrenshealthdefense.org/news/altering-human-genetics-through-vaccination/.

immune system. This treatment isn't a traditional vaccination. It's gene therapy.[123]

Vaccines are a powerful delivery system of synthetic biology into humans. Through the vaccine delivery system, digital biometrics are used to inventory, track, and control humans.

Quantum Dots: Kevin McHugh, assistant professor of bio-engineering at Rice University and a team from MIT, developed quantum dot tags that fluoresce with information after injected as part of a vaccine. A sugar-based microneedle patch is used to vaccinate. After the immunization dissolves into the body, a pattern of tags, just under the skin, creates a bar code tattoo. The tattoo is composed of copper-based quantum dots embedded in micronscale capsules. The dye is invisible, but a smartphone can read the pattern.[124]

Smartrac: It bears repeating. Smartrac is a global RFID manufacturer that connects humans (via vaccines and digital certificates) with the IoT. Utilizing Smartrac, humans with RFID identification allow their medical information to be available and accessible as a supply-side service (with no compensation, of course). For example, pharmaceutical companies have "item-level" (humans are the item) visibility into every single one of their products as they move through their supply chain and stores (hospitals, clinics, physician offices, and pharmacies). Sophisticated analytics uncover hidden inefficiencies and opportunities. They also provide engagement to increase customer loyalty (a thumbs up reward for good behavior).

Vottun: As digital certificates become mainstream, companies like Vottun will create immunity passports on blockchain technology. These can be read via smartphone-like reading a QR code.

---

123 "The Next Generation Vaccines Will Permanently Alter Your DNA with Synthetic Genes," https://needtoknow.news/2019/10/the-next-generation-vaccines-will-permanently-alter-your-dna-with-synthetic-genes/.

124 "Quantum-dot tattoos hold vaccination record". https://bioengineering.rice.edu/news/quantum-dot-tattoos-hold-vaccination-record.

They claim to develop secure systems using quantum dots information on a blockchain.[125]

Contact Tracing: Apple and Google took the first step of permitting RFID medical passports to enter our biology and launch us onto the IoT platform. Together, they introduced a contact tracing smartphone API—an application programming interface. Supposedly the software, code-named "Bubble" at Apple and "Apollo" at Google, was built in a month by a handful of employees. (Once again, we have a whiz kids timeline, like lonely Zuckerberg inventing Facebook one long weekend. An unbelievable story that so many believe.)

The application utilizes existing built-in surveillance phone data. (guess that privacy invasion is not a HIPPA issue) Importantly, it has applications that public health organizations can access. Operating on Bluetooth, it sends out chirps that other phones can listen to, even if not running in the foreground. Privacy is through rotating codes, with apps broadcasting a cryptographic key that randomly changes while monitoring other nearby phones.[126]

Tracing systems have a short history fraught with issues. Singapore's Trace Together system was one of the first contact tracing apps. One of the problems was that the app had to be running all the time in the foreground or stopped working. And phones needed to remain unlocked. (you could be in lockdown, but not your phone, ironic) And battery life took a significant hit. Phone users also complained that the app interfered with regular phone notifications. Inevitably, the Apple Google rollout will meet with their issues. And we can all expect the fun videos of corporate

---

125 Turner Wright, "Blockchain 'Immunity Passport' could get you Back to Work," https://cointelegraph.com/news/controversial-blockchain-immunity-passport-could-get-you-back-to-work.

126 Christina Farr, "How a handful of Apple and Google employees came together to help Health Officials trace Coronavirus," https://www.cnbc.com/2020/04/28/apple-iphone-contact-tracing-how-it-came-together.html.

cubicle office staff scattering when the alert goes off that someone is infected. (no names, privacy, please)

ID2020 Global ID is a planetary behemoth involving pairing vaccines and digital biometrics. The human is microchipped, tracked, and controlled through a global identification matrix. Bill Gates is a founding partner of the ID2020 project that gives every human a digital ID. [127] The ID2020 website states that 1.1 billion people live without a digital ID. There are approximately 7.8 billion people globally, so a majority or 6.7 billion people worldwide have a digital ID or an online profile of information that is unique to the individual. Did you know you had a profile?

The CEO of Accenture, a partner in ID2020, provided a glimpse of the program's advancement and its future. In September of 2020, CEO Julie Sweet noted that "today we are 20% in the cloud. We are moving to 80%." But "instead of happening in a decade, it is going to happen in five years." [128] Perhaps due to the pandemic advancements in synthetic biology treatments and vaccines, Sweet revised the digital transformation rollout, the "reset" from 2030 to 2025, a short five years.

Biologically Supercharged Surveillance

During my days in Washington, DC, I read into transhumanism in the morning and attended a noon yoga class. There were regulars and an occasional new person. One afternoon, after class, I introduced myself to a young man on a mat next to mine. As we walked to the classroom shelves to deposit our yoga blankets, I inquired if he worked nearby. He replied yes that he worked up the street at the National Institute of Standards and Technology. I asked which division and was further intrigued when he replied, "polymers."

---

127 https://id2020.org/.

128 Alan Murray and David Meyer, "Why Accenture thinks the 'Henry Ford moment of the digital era' is coming", *Fortune Magazine*, September 2020. https://fortune.com/2020/09/17/accenture-julie-sweet-digital-transformation-ceo-daily/.

I just happened to be reading into smart dust and smart fibers, uncovering extensive research projects at the National Institute of Standards and Technology. They are a government agency under the US Department of Commerce that promotes innovation and industrial competitiveness. (I am not sure how that mission correlates with them investigating the 911 World Trade Center collapse—but it does).

As we stood next to the array of yoga mats and blankets, I expressed my enthusiasm for his field of polymers, smart fibers. I shared that I had been reading about nanoparticles, woven into our clothing, that move into our skin and may travel throughout our bodies. He let me go on for a moment. Then he stopped me and firmly stated, "Lady, I don't know who you are, but don't EVER talk to me again." He turned and disappeared. Never to yoga again.

The young man's angry response triggered my first awareness of globalism's suspicious reality—why all of our US clothing manufacturing was offshored, beginning in 1994 during the Clinton administration. US textile jobs were replaced primarily by China. Why the offshoring? Was it merely a cost of labor issue? Or was it connected to a more in-depth program of synthetic biology and surveillance?

Smart Fibers, or polymer nanofibers, are in clothing, surgical masks, cosmetics, and many medical devices. These fibers are typically 5-50 micrometers. For comparison, a human hair is 75 micrometers, and a human blood cell is 5 micron. These fibers are produced by an electrospinning procedure that uses electric force to draw charged threads of polymer solutions up to fiber diameters. This polymer technology integrates with smart dust.

Smart Dust was coined by DARPA researcher Kristofer Pister in 1997 to describe tiny wireless microelectromechanical sensors that can detect light, temperature, vibration, magnetism, or chemicals. They operate on a computer network, IoT, and usually sense through radio-frequency identification. (Smartrac technology in vaccines). Smart dust communicates wirelessly to the computer network. Researchers at UC Berkeley published a paper proposing sprinkling smart dust on human brains to provide feedback on functionality.[129]

Author and researcher Elena Freeland states that a "major hurdle for the neuroscientists, geneticists, and Pentagon visionaries committed to achieving an enhanced Transhumanist humanity has been how to mount mass-scale brain-machine interfaces (BMI) for a new hive mind. The answer is to disseminate smart dust..." [130]

Surveillance begins its first phase with creating a hive mind.

Reign of Technocrat Surveillance

In surveillance, three elements merge to create the expansive AI oversight of transhumanism: 1) data mining and analysis, 2) bioengineering, and 3) computerized cultural engineering. Terrorism, viruses, or war are the sparks that ignite surveillance.

The earliest use of the word surveillance (sur=over, veillance, or vigilante=watchful) originated during the French Reign of Terror, where surveillance committees formed in 1793 to monitor suspected persons' actions. The Reign of Terror was a time of fearful, sinister spying and searches, often resulting in imprisonment and death.[131]

In her 2015 book, *The Pentagon's Brain: An Uncensored History of DARPA, America's Top-Secret Military Research Agency*, researcher Annie Jacobsen relates the story of the origins of the US surveillance state.

According to Jacobsen, John Poindexter, a ranking government official in the Reagan Administration, charged with five Iran Contra felonies and subsequently cleared, played a primary role in the early surveillance state.

---

129 Bernard Marr, "Smart Dust Is Coming. Are You Ready?," *Forbes*, September 2018, https://www.forbes.com/sites/bernardmarr/2018/09/16/smart-dust-is-coming-are-you-ready/#1fd7a90f5e41.

130 Elena Freeland, *Under an Ionized Sky*: From Chemtrails to Space Fence Lockdown (Port Townsend, WA: Feral House, 2018).

131 The very French history of the word 'surveillance', *BBC NEWS*, July 2015, https://www.bbc.com/news/blogs-magazine-monitor-33464368.

In 1995, Poindexter facilitated the Genoa Project within DARPA to analyze large amounts of data and metadata for national security. But the project lasted little more than a year; however, eight years later, it would resurface. The threat of terrorism was at the root of resurrecting the Genoa surveillance project.

Jacobsen recounts that the morning after September 11 (911) Poindexter contacted a former colleague in DARPA, Brian Sharkey, insisting that the Genoa project should be revived and accelerated. New surveillance tools were needed to combat terrorism. By this time, Sharkey had left DARPA and was now at Science Applications International (SAIC). Sharkey concurred with Poindexter's need for advanced surveillance after the reported terrorist attack. He agreed to contact Tony Tether, who was now head of DARPA, and relay their concern.

In October, Sharkey and Tether met at the Arlington, VA, restaurant, Gaffney's Oyster and Ale House, to discuss Poindexter's request and recommendation. Tether and Sharkey agreed that Sharkey would remain at SAIC, as it was an employee-owned corporation, and he had an equity stake. But SAIC would be the primary contractor for Genoa II. John Poindexter would serve as director of DARPA's Total Information Awareness Program, housing Genoa II.

The deal struck at the Arlington restaurant was sealed onboard a sailing cruise on Poindexter's yacht. Genoa I and II provided the opportunity to collect data for military surveillance. Poindexter remained on the front lines of surveillance data collection and analysis as it reached into the human brain.

Pharmacovigilance Surveillance System

Poindexter's Genoa II project seeded the 2002[132] Total Information Awareness (TIA) program to collect and track potential terrorists'

---

132 Though public records indicate the closure of TIA due to citizen surveillance concerns, the budget remained intact and the work was transferred to Advanced Research and Development Activity (ARDA) headquartered at NSA and Genoa II was renamed

information. Poindexter termed it a "Manhattan project for counter-terrorism," providing total information awareness on every citizen. The TIA pervasive invasion included citizen data on medical records, fingerprints, gait, facial and iris biometrics, drug, prescription, DNA, financial data, travel, and media consumption habits.

TIA's surveillance tactics surface again in the COVID Operation Warp Speed (OWS) program to vaccinate 300 million Americans by January 2021. The pharmaceutical head of OWS, Moncef Slaoui, the "Vaccine Czar," termed the precise vaccine tracking system to ensure that patients receive two doses of the same vaccine and monitor them for adverse health effects "a very active pharmacovigilance surveillance system."[133] This precise tracking system is coordinated by Google and Oracle, cooperating with FDA, CDC, NSA, HHS, and DHS. Federal oversight regarding laws and regulations remains mired in a dense tangle of connections with little daylight.

DARPA, Musk and Human Decision Making

George Lawrence, a psychologist at DARPA, researched psychic testing at Sanford Research Institute (SRI). He met with witches and psychics, trying to determine if it was evidence-based and useful. Eventually, Lawrence abandoned this branch of investigation and instead came to the idea of communicating directly with the human brain through computers, using sensors instead of psychic ability. Lawrence laid the foundation for the field now known as a brain-computer interface, where sensors read neural signals to

---

"Topsail." Mark Williams Pontin, "The Total Information Awareness Project Lives On" MIT Technology Review, April 2006. https://www.technologyreview.com/2006/04/26/229286/the-total-information-awareness-project-lives-on/

133 Whitney Webb, "Google & Oracle To Monitor Americans Who Get Warp Speed's Covid-19 Vaccine For Up To Two Years," *The Last American Vagabond*, October 2020. https://www.thelastamericanvagabond.com/google-oracle-monitor-americans-who-get-warp-speeds-covid-19-vaccine-for-two-years/.

either control computers and machines or to control human decision making.[134]

DARPA's 2014 Restoring Active Memory Project ties directly to the early CIA mind control programs based on manipulating human memory. The Memory Project used computers and sensors, rather than drugs and hypnosis. They developed a neuroprosthesis experiment to implant electrical components, sensors, and brain tissue to alter memory formation. It was part of the military's super-soldier program to create troops with no physical or cognitive limitations—persistence in combat, continuous performance, and augmented cognition. The goal was a 24/7 super soldier who could go without sleep for a week. Essentially a hybrid human-robot.

This augmented hybridization of machines and humans has moved out of military/intelligence use and is now in widespread commercial use. It is coming to a body near you.

Elon Musk's Neuralink uses lasers to shoot holes in skulls and feed electrodes' threads into the human brain in 2020. NOW. Once implanted, the chip would connect brain waves to a smartphone app or computer. Musk's rationale is that humans need Neuralink to avoid being replaced by AI. He claims to be developing a super-human cyborg—merging humans with AI. (recall the Petrosky claims vs. scientific reality).

In a presentation, Musk revealed a monkey using its brain to control a computer. Musk's goal is to enhance a wireless human brain to computer communication. Neuralink's idea is to implant four brain sensors: three in motor areas and one in a somatosensory area. These sensor wires connect wirelessly to a battery device behind the ear, controlled with a smartphone app. Other corporations developing neural implants include Kernel, which is involved in reading and writing brain functions.

---

134 "Inside DARPA, The Pentagon Agency Whose Technology Has 'Changed the World'," *NPR*, March 2017, https://www.npr.org/2017/03/28/521779864/inside-darpa-the-pentagon-agency-whose-technology-has-changed-the-world.

Leaks and Revelations

While these science programs hypothesize a slick transition into directing human behavior and cognition, the scientific reality is that like the MK-ULTRA drug experiments gone haywire (pardon the pun), neural bioengineering has ongoing challenges. Placing foreign matter in the human brain via sensors and electrodes eventually fails because of blood leakage. Ultimately, the brain/body rejects the invasion. Repeated injections of sensors result in repeated wounds. Then, due to repeated healing processes, cell activity decreases.

Yet, it may not matter how the human body reacts to bioengineering. Annie Jacobsen says that "it is likely that DARPA's primary goal is advancing robots, not men." Her statement again reveals the plan of making humans like robots and not robots like humans. Careful—that we tread into transhumanism with inflated egos to our detriment. Robots, not humans, are the prize. Think otherwise at your peril.

Our future may hold us hostage with Neuralink, but its technology is lacking. Like Petrosky's students connected to computers, it will take time to hybridize humans. But, behind the scenes, other programs prepare the transference from natural human to human-hybridized robots.

Simulated Surveillance Certainty

A primary organization working behind the veil is the Sentient World Simulation (SWS). Housed at Indiana's Purdue University Krannert School of Management, Dr. Alok Chaturvedi designed SWS to build a synthetic mirror image of the real world. To do so, he developed a computerized system of continuous calibration with current real-world information such as significant events, opinion polls, demographic statistics, and shifts in trends.[135]

---

135 Dr. Alok Chaturvedi and Tony Cerri, "Sentient World Simulation (SWS): A Continuously Running Model of the Real World," https://krannert.purdue.edu/academics/mis/workshop/AC2_100606.pdf.

And the best part is that you have a role in this image of reality. Congratulations.

SWS has an avatar of you in a created virtual world that mirrors the real world. Its purpose is to evaluate and predict you and your family, neighbors, friends, community, and culture's future action and behavior courses.

The simulation houses billions of nodes representing nearly every person on earth. In 2007 SWS had nodes for 62 out of a total of 195 countries on earth. In all probability, they now have nodes for every man, woman, and child on earth.

The Purdue team claims that it doesn't create your identical likeness but instead has a "depersonalized likeness." Whatever that means. They claim that your depersonalized avatar resemblance is not immediately identifiable and not replicable. But, undoubtedly, your image is for sale to the highest corporate or government bidder.

SWS sold its services to DOD, DOJ, Lilly, and Lockheed Martin. It tests psyop events for banks, financial institutions, utilities (ponder its use during the California fires or major riots), media outlets (for future predictable Hollywood scripts), retail (for the color of the year prediction), and corporate product launches. During COVID, it simulated a cough on a plane spreading the virus.

Facial Recognition Phishing

Vietnamese-Australian, Hoan Ton-That, left Australia in 2007 and moved to San Francisco, where he created Happy Appy and Viddy Ho, phishing, hacking applications (computer worms) that spammed users' contacts. ViddyHo's website tricked the user into sharing their Gmail accounts. Police pursued him, but details, as to arrest, are sketchy. Hacker, as in "catch me if you can."

As a friend knowledgeable about military computer security claimed, successful hackers are prized, even lured into secure systems to be caught and used for their knowledge. This fate seems to be the case of Ton-That. He proved extremely useful.

Today, Ton-That owns Clearview, an AI facial recognition app used by the FBI, DHS, and 600 law enforcement agencies. The Clearview app user can take a photo of a person and receive pictures of the person with links to their locations. Its data source is 3 billion images, Facebook, YouTube, Venmo, LinkedIn, and other sites.

When paired with augmented reality glasses (Google glasses), the Clearview user can potentially identify every person they see. Law enforcement has a love affair with facial recognition apps, and the online social systems offer limitless access to our photos from birth to death. In a television interview, Ton-That said that the Clearview AI privacy invasion is a fair game to help law enforcement solve crimes with publicly-available data.[136] Given his years of stealing online identity and run-ins with police, he knows the needs of law enforcement.

Citizens of the Fourth Industrial Revolution
A Probable Future

At this point, please remember our discussion of the Fourth Industrial Revolution. Recall its all-encompassing 'fusion of technologies'—physical, digital, and biological spheres—creating a symbiosis between micro-organisms, the human body, products people consume, buildings they inhabit, and craft they fly. Humans do not use technology but instead integrate and converge with the digital and synthetic biological worlds. Thus, biologically and neurologically, Transhumans are machines.

Here is a simple illustration of how citizens will participate in the Fourth Revolution's technocratic, synthetic biology, and surveillance system. It is the story of a shoe that sneaks up on you. But not an ordinary shoe.

Nike HyperAdapt sneakers provide a personal, customized fit that feels like an extension of your body. You can instantly adjust

---

136 https://www.pbssocal.org/programs/amanpour-co/clearview-ai-ceo-defends-facial-recognition-software-nuyagm/.

your Nike Adapt shoes, check battery levels, and more using just your smartphone. Your smartphone and sneakers digitally connect. Five customizable voice commands work with Siri Shortcuts—or Google Voice for Android users. Your sneakers and Fitbit also coordinate. In other words, you wear sneakers capable of tracking and surveilling your every movement.

There's more—here is the direct Technocracy aspect.

Your Every Movement=Money

When you purchase your sneakers, in the future, you will receive cryptocurrency in the form of cryptokicks—Nike's new cryptocurrency. This currency exchange comes in the form of a crypto coin. The coin verifies that you purchased authentic NIKE sneakers. (No knockoffs, black marketing permitted.) Your Nike coin may increase or decrease in value. These coins provide access to a closed community of other sneaker consumers—a community of kickers with slick rewards, contests, and 24-7 monitoring of your athletic prowess. Your every move in life is monitored and monetized.

The Microsoft patent 2020060606 details a plan to use human body movements and brain waves to mine cryptocurrency. Their application titled "Cryptocurrency System Using Body Activity Data" describes how brainwaves or body heat emitted by the user when performing a task given by a smartphone, often in the form of commercials, mine your movement for cryptocurrency.[137] Like a robot, your device of choice provides you with a task. A sensor, either on your clothing or medically inserted in your body, coordinates with your device. Your device then communicates whether you performed and satisfied the desired action, resulting in a reward of cryptocurrency or possibly a punishment. Back to the Nike HyperAdapt example, your phone gives you a prompt to purchase a just-released Nike Jacket. The sensor in your shoes monitors your

---

137 WO2020060606 - CRYPTOCURRENCY SYSTEM USING BODY ACTIVITY DATA, https://patentscope.wipo.int/search/en/detail.jsf?docId=WO2020060606

purchase, rewarding you with cryptokicks. Over time you become accustomed to responding to Nike messages and performing their desired actions.

The Microsoft patent uses brain waves and body heat but also refers to using "body fluid flow" and "organ activity and movement" to track your use of social media, search engines, email, website searches, chatbots, and possibly online conference and learning platforms like Google Meet and Zoom.

Your biology plays a significant surveillance role. With its patent, Microsoft tracks your biometrics, including eye movements and brainwaves. Advertisements push into your device. Microsoft follows whether you watched the ad and made the purchase, then sells this valuable information to clients. The data of your behavior response generates a "proof of work." This proof validates a transaction or a completed task on a blockchain system, then uses it to create a cryptocurrency.

You now work for a new company store, like a miner in my home state of West Virginia. You show up for work, complete your assigned task, and receive your pay with company currency. This currency is spendable at the company where you buy your goods after your rent and medical deductions. At the end of the month, you often owe the company store more than your earned. You have no rights, no property, and no way out.

Furthermore, your synthetically modified "green" environment presents ongoing unresolvable health issues. (More on that in the next chapter.) But in your case, you don't "owe your soul to the company store" because you are expendable. The crypto mining company can recreate you and monetize your genes. There's more where YOU came from because your genetics keep on giving.

Your Genes Monetized

As blockchain technology advances, human DNA will be monetized with all of your biological and especially your genetic information collected, accessed, distributed, and potentially edited in the cloud. As a technocracy consumer, a crypto company will own your genes.

For instance, Genecoin, samples your DNA, turns it into data, and stores it in the world's most powerful supercomputer: the Bitcoin network. According to *Bitcoin Magazine* in 2014,

> Genecoin is not a cryptocurrency or a counterparty asset. Genecoin is the name of a nascent company run by a group of anonymous bitcoiners based in an undisclosed location in the United States' northeast coast. The members of Genecoin are offering a simple proposition to the Bitcoin universe: to populate the Bitcoin Blockchain with the sequenced DNA of its customers.[138]

With Genecoin, you don't worry about procreation and giving birth because your bitcoin identity can be fruitful and multiply, replenishing the technocratic system. Humans currently preserve their genes by passing them down across generations through natural procreation. However, Transhumans and technocrats regard procreation as an unreliable backup method. Instead, Genecoin etches your DNA into culture's most indestructible and highly desirable form: money itself. Your genes are now a form of currency. Genecoin brings new meaning to "self-worth."

A future conceived by companies like Genecoin raises ethical questions regarding human rights. Ethicists and attorneys will examine the corporation's right to favor, edit, discard, or eliminate individual DNA. These looming ethical discussions and lawsuits pose a new wrinkle in Malthusian population control due to projected climate catastrophe. An exaggerated climate narrative may be the first step in removing select DNA from the cloud, a convenient method of genetic, racial, sexual, and personality culling.

Another underlying ethical issue is whether corporate editing of DNA is acceptable. If it is permissible, then unbeknownst to

---

138 Chris DeRose, "Genecoin: DNA For The Blockchain", *Bitcoin Magazine*, November 2014. https://bitcoinmagazine.com/articles/genecoin-dna-for-the-blockchain-1415660431.

individuals, their DNA could be altered to create a preferred DNA profile. Eventually, editing may further human genetic homogenization. This is of particular importance when considering potential preference, suppression, or removal of psychic intelligence with DNA editing. Notably, a potential ET DNA issue also develops. An ET-based editing scenario could suppress or remove DNA or advance a specific ET preference.

Beyond these scenarios, make no mistake, in the ever-increasing tightening chain of cryptocurrency, surveillance, synthetic biology, EduBlocks, smart employment contracts, buildings, cities, and transportation—every aspect of your life—someone, a corporation or individuals, own a piece of you. You are baptized into a new life as a currency on the IoT, officially an item on Technocracy's blockchain. Your humanity is equivalent to a coin.

Possible Complications

The IoT refers to many internet-devices that communicate with other devices (some in our body) and networks (surrounding our body).

How many Internet-connected devices are there in 2020?

According to cloud connectivity provider vXchnge, there will be 41 billion IoT Devices by 2027. Others forecast as many as 125 billion devices by 2030. We use the word "billion" with ease and ignore its importance. For context, look at the difference between a million and a billion in terms of time—days compared to years:

One million seconds is roughly equal to 11.5 days.

One billion seconds is roughly equal to 31.75 years.

The difference between a few million IoT devices and a few billion is quite staggering.[139]

Before moving to examine Common Ground, possible complications need addressing. What if preparing Earth's citizens for space-based controlled cloud infrastructure (IoT) of 5 and 6

---

139 Kaylie Gyarmathy, "Comprehensive Guide to IoT Statistics You Need to Know in 2020". https://www.vxchnge.com/blog/iot-statistics.

G, integrated with synthetic biology, involves managing multiple detrimental effects on humans? These effects may include heart palpitations, breathing difficulties due to lung inflammation, neurological disorders including loss of sensory function, genetic damage, cancer, and compromised immune systems. But, before public demand for researching and resolving these detrimental effects, a virus mimicking the same complications and a host of synthetic biology treatments and vaccine cures appear.

Do these treatments and cures become new afflictions, pulling humans into a labyrinth of disease, similar to the labyrinth of transhumanism discussed in the Introduction? The next chapter on space-earth infrastructure examines the all-encompassing Transhuman reality that surrounds us as psychic intelligent humans.

What are our options as Exoconscious Humans for maintaining health and protection from synthetic biology viruses and treatments? This situation opens the opportunity for alternative health measures, especially quantum medicine (consciousness), as viable and available treatments.

Section 3

Common Ground

Exoconscious Healers, functional physicians, and energy workers find common ground with technology through the invention and application of devices and treatments to advance health.

A biofield is the field of energy and information that surrounds every living thing, including your body. This subtle field of interactions organizes biological processes on multiple levels: subatomic, atomic, molecular, and cellular on interpersonal and cosmic levels. The biofield paradigm, unlike the reductionist, chemistry-centered viewpoint, emphasizes the informational content of biological processes. Biofield interactions may operate in part via low-energy or subtle means such as weak, nonthermal electromagnetic fields. These fields relate to consciousness and quantum non-locality.[140]

Many of the devices that access the biofield are electromagnetic. Biofeedback devices reduce meridian stress throughout the body. Other tools assess the skin's electrical conductivity through our acupuncture system to provide information about energy flows and health. Electrodermal screenings measure the human biofield's biophoton emission of light energy.

Pulsed Magnetic therapy works in conjunction with the body's recovery processes to relieve pain by restoring the cell's ability to function efficiently. As the human body requires electricity to send signals through the body and to the brain, this therapy helps realign our cells' electric potential effectively. A disruption in electrical currents can lead to illness. It can help repair damaged and diseased tissues, or tendons, and fractured bones.

Digital Infrared Thermal Imaging provides radiation-free body scans with no compression to detect cancer and early-stage diseases up to 10 years earlier than traditional screening. An infrared scanning device converts infrared radiation emitted from the skin surface into electrical impulses viewed in color on a monitor. This visual image graphically maps the body temperature and is referred to as a thermogram. The spectrum of colors indicates an increase or decrease in infrared radiation emitted from the body surface.

Ions Cleanse Foot Bath accelerates cellular detoxification. It generates a stream of positive and negative ions which attract and attach themselves to toxic particles.

Infrared Sauna is a safe and effective detoxification for expelling environmental toxins, chemical residues, and heavy metals from the body.

---

140 Muehsam and Chevalier and Barsotti and Gurfein, "An Overview of Biofield Devices," https://www.ncbi.nlm.nih.gov/pmc/articles/PMC4654784/.

Photonx: Photobiomodulation devices consist of photonic energy sources. They deliver specific therapeutic light wavelengths into well-studied access points and pathways within the body. Photonx uses specific wavelengths from UV through Infrared light to optimize getting energy to particular targets in the body to treat chronic and infectious diseases and overall wellness.

CHAPTER 5

EXOCONSCIOUS COSMIC CONNECTION IS PREFERRED CONTROLLED SPACE AND EARTH INFRASTRUCTURE IS PREFERRED

Section 1

Cosmic Exoconscious Humans

While eating a quiet lunch on a patio at Disney Land, a tall robotic figure, encased head to toe in a white shell, sauntered from behind an enclosure onto the open area in front of our restaurant. He stood quietly while a ripple of excitement moved through the crowd. The Star Wars Stormtrooper had arrived. Suddenly, lunches abandoned, children and their parents ran to talk to the Stormtrooper. It was a rather dull computer dialogue, but the children shrieked with happiness. The Galactic Empires' shock trooper was real. He spoke.

Through Disney's young minds, George Lucas sealed the Empire of Space, colonialism, and never-ending wars into our consciousness. Mission complete. Or is it?

Can you imagine a time when exoconscious diplomacy replaces space colonialism and weaponization? Can you imagine exoconsciousness promoting collaborative, peaceful relationships between ET races respectful of sovereign boundaries and cultures?

This diplomacy assumes humans' capacity to relate to many races of beings—some similar to us, some not similar.[141] All are intelligent cosmic life. At this juncture, it is essential to ask how Exoconscious Humans define themselves within the universe. Our human race is bound and determined to move into Space. Some humans envision that eventually, the Earth will be a full member of an established Galactic Council organization, and many experiencers report participating in this Council model. According to these individuals, human council members may need to fulfill membership requirements, including implants, evolution, and ambassadorial experts, i.e., - raising our human race to superior ET standards.

Interestingly, some who hold this Galactic Council perspective perceive humans as a lower, primitive race of beings who require outside assistance. Humans equated to kindergartners. This type of classification is implicit in most salvation models, whether religious or political or social. When humans perceive themselves as a lower class, it opens the door to accepting a more powerful, evolved savior.

In contrast, another cosmic perspective is that eventually, Earth will become the intergalactic civilization leader. In this view, humans colonize throughout space. It entails raising our human race to a Star Wars' standard via a military-technology model, perpetuated through an ongoing threat of alien invasion. Humans harnessed and upgraded by superior technology command and carry out the building of an Earth Empire in space.

Empire builders need to engineer humans through genetics, robotics, computers, neural implants, and weaponry. These represent on-planet programs coordinated in conjunction with off-planet

---

141 Darlene Van de Grift defined ET races as some like us, some not like us. She is on the Institute for Exoconsciousness Board of Advisors and was an Astrosociology Consultant at State University New York.

space travel and colonization. Seamlessly, this empire segment envisions off-planet programs combining with an on-planet system. Both systems involve a wired, controlled citizenry. In this empire model, every human on Earth is under the dome of technological dominance.

Consequently, many universities, research labs, corporations, and government groups currently participate in this intergalactic empire model. It requires the centralization of every sector of our civilization (e.g., money, education, law, medicine, technology, religion, entertainment, and government)—one orderly world.

As the Earth empire model grows in prominence, we see a stark contradiction in government attitudes toward UFOs, extraterrestrials, and cosmic life. *Culturally engineered UFO, ET disbelief since the late 1940s will shift gradually to engineered belief.* The US Space Command (1982), to the Department of Defense declaration of "full-spectrum dominance of space, air, land, and sea." (2010), to the establishment of the US Space Force (2019), to the primarily CIA staffed To the Stars Academy of Arts and Sciences (2017)—the government's space programs require creating a new belief narrative for its citizenry.

Funding and political priority reside with the Earth Empire model. In this model, Earth is the emerging center of an intergalactic civilization with humans as an "inferior race" needing Transhuman government upgrading and protection. The individual is secondary to the state, or in this case, a planetary government.

The Earth Empire model has a unique perspective on human consciousness. It defines consciousness as brain function enhanced by technology. The familiar subordination (humans not evolved) and suppression (humans tracked 24-7) view of consciousness. In other words, humans are either infantile or insignificant. We are a lower life form that needs intervention to evolve to accomplish the Earth Empire's goals.

Subordination and suppression of human consciousness just about cover the waterfront. There's not much real estate left that hasn't been bought up by technocrats.[142] But there is another way—a significant path forward for humans and Earth.

This chapter's theoretical foundation posits that awakened and integrated Exoconscious Humans evolve as cosmic space citizens who choose affiliation with other beings and races. The cosmos is composed of sovereign and distinct civilizations—some like us and some not like us.

The Exoconscious Human perspective is a sane, healthy path forward for humanity, Earth, and our entry into beings' populated conscious cosmos. This process may provide a practical means to maintain the human's independence and sanctity—anchoring them to Earth and simultaneously opening innate abilities to relate to ET and multidimensional beings throughout the cosmos by gradually moving respectfully into space.

Craft Copula of Consciousness

After many years of varied multi-dimensional contact, I experienced a pivotal shift in my exoconsciousness. A path opened clarifying an experience that, until then, was only faintly visible. I term it a "not yet memory." I hold a deep memory fragment of being part of a group, a classroom. I had brief glimpses of schooling—a disciplined structure, other students, advisors, and administrators. I carried dim memories of my frequent pulsed transport into a craft. My conscious mind often recreated the pulse, and my physical body felt the movement, down, out, and then up into the ship.

One Sunday afternoon, with neither a plan nor a formed desire, I opened the memory while working with a hypnotherapist. Fragments suddenly fell into place. Puzzle pieces fit.

Using a hypnotherapy technique, she guided me into a room of my choice. I immediately entered a lighted room where the walls were alive—breathing and moving. I was a three-year-old child,

---

142 A detailed discussion of the history of Western economic technocracy is found in Patrick Wood, *Technocracy Rising: The Trojan Horse of Global Transformation* (Coherent Publishing, 2014).

and so naturally, I played with the walls, and they responded with changing colors and forms.

A familiar advisor was in the room with me, a male, 10 to 12-foot-tall light being. He had large hands with four fingers. As we visited and reacquainted, I squirmed, remembering my childhood experiences with him. I related to him as if I was a young child, comfortable in the room, yet active and curious. It was challenging to sit still. He told me that I was there because of an agreement made before coming into this life. I had an earth agreement to cooperate with education on this craft.

I agreed to participate in the school to reactivate cosmic "star" knowledge that I perhaps lost at birth. He led me back into a typical classroom where each student had a seat and an "assignment." It was a small student body, perhaps 24. I felt each one's assignment, like reading their blueprint. They grew up to become politicians, musicians, scientists, physicians, educators, inventors, writers, and communicators. I felt my seat, my assignment. In the classroom, they taught an intergalactic language. The curriculum also included mind and energy work as well as hands-on-healing.

A group of races from Tau Ceti, Andromeda, Pleiades, Acturians, Zeta, Orion, Syrian, Lyra directed the craft school. I saw myself as a tall, slender light being—a lengthy human lightning bug. I felt hybrid, yet primarily Andromedan, Acturian. But, simply, I was a "being." A being beyond race. An ET seeded into a human body.

Leaving the classroom, I came to a small conference room where three administrators greeted me—a principal and two off-ship visitors. They did not have names. I simply recognized them by their vibration. Each had a signature vibration. As we reviewed why I was on board and my assignment, I became aware that officials from the military and government occasionally attended our proceedings. They were usually quiet, if not a bit overwhelmed. They unobtrusively stood at the back of the classroom and watched the proceedings. I remembered a woman, one of the off-ship extraterrestrial visitors, reminding all the students to "treat the government representatives with respect."

I recalled the craft school gave polite reception to these Earth officials, aware of the gap between rambunctious seeded children and adult government officials assigned to understand a new, unfamiliar curriculum. Officials had to learn a new language and participate in a program that we children re-membered with ease. The craft was more fun than work. Instinctively, I recalled a government name for the craft school—it was something like the Young People's Project. Galactic officials structured and directed the school and graciously permitted others to visit. It was a diplomatic arrangement, and I was uninformed of the relationship.

At one point in a conversation with the three administrative beings, I asked why my life had moved through strange twists and turns. They quickly replied that it met the requirement that I am "authentically human." Afterward, I kept repeating the phrase, "I am authentically human." Life on Earth was no short-cut, walk-on role. I needed immersion in human reality.

After they escorted me out of the room, I ran up into my favorite place on the craft, the cupola. There I was privileged to navigate the ship. As I stood at the helm, my mind shifted into a relaxed glide, my small hands one with the craft. I navigated the ship through space with star maps accessible in my conscious mind. I navigated easily among star systems. Intuitively, I knew how to navigate as well as launch and receive craft. My consciousness encompassed the ship; we were one.

Back on Earth time and space, analyzing the memory, I realized that my space contact began around the same period as Eisenhower's alleged alien treaties. During the 1950s, ufologists identified contactees who experienced peaceful, kind interactions aboard crafts. Researchers called the aliens who created these visitations "space brothers."

Only later, during the 1960s, did ufologists characterize the contact experience as abduction and detail harrowing kidnapping and trauma. Investigators such as Steven Greer attribute traumatic abductions to deliberate government black operations designed to create fear of aliens in the mass consciousness. He maintains that our secret government segments possess UFO craft, genetically designed alien look-alike clones, and electronic weaponry to stage a believable abduction.

As individuals come to me, eager to bring their multi-dimensional contact into conscious light, I am compassionate and respectful of varied experiences. Each experience is different. Each human bears a distinct seed that opens and flowers into work that only they can perform this Earth life. We each have a classroom seat. We each have an assignment. Alliances may form between contactees as they strengthen their work. Your consciousness is at the helm. You know the way.

Exoconscious Reality

Exoconsciousness wanders among worlds. Realities are like a series of photographs in different frames. Time and Space create our primary Earth frame. Yet, there are other perspectives, other worldviews, other dimensions.

The space-time continuum: what is it, where is it, when is it? Do time and space exist, or are they illusions we use to weave the fabric of our reality? Do we simultaneously dwell within and without time and space?

As a hypnotherapist, I practice regression techniques, where through hypnosis, a client accesses a "past life" or as I like to refer to it, "another life." Outside the spacetime continuum, one can obtain an enlarged perspective of their life. In regression, life is a panorama of peripheral vision. We remain anchored to the here and now of our daily life yet infused with knowledge of other lifetimes. Lives unfold that were once wrinkled and hidden like a childhood paper fan. Regression opens the dimensional folds, and intricate detail emerges.

Numerous times I witnessed regression sessions that provide clients with the perfect answer to a once unsolvable riddle of their lives. Yet, the reality of regression and the information brought forth is outside the space-time continuum. Never, neverland. The beyond where our consciousness knows the way.

Travel beyond time and space is our extraterrestrial legacy. You were born to leap beyond the bounds of the Earth while living on its soil. Do these exoconscious abilities get tricky? Of course. Just like any other ability. The first time you ride a bike or spin a hoverboard—for a time, you cannot stop. It's too much fun. Hypnosis and regression can become too much fun. We leap into it—bring on the past lives or other lifetimes. As a result, you risk becoming lopsided, living in different dimensions, filtering your present earth experience through the lens of "other lives." Unraveling the mysteries of other times.

Grounding back into Earth's life is essential. During my hypnosis session, I moved quickly into my past lives. Having done repeated regressions, it was effortless. Therapists observe individuals proficient in past lives often dwell in the past to the present's detriment. Point well taken. Doing exoconscious work, you need a measure of present balanced awareness to remind yourself to remain anchored. Earth's life is our harbor.

Cosmic Astral Travel

Alongside hypnotic regression, astral travel and teleportation offer engaging encounters beyond the time-space continuum. I repeatedly astral travel and refine my skills with practice. As a child, I slipped effortlessly into astral travel. Whoosh, I was out and about. Then I became an adult and closed the doorway of my conscious mind—a family to raise, career responsibilities to assume, a home to tend. But eventually, something niggled in my mind—a faint memory of travel beyond my dreams where I was conscious and navigated my path into, through, and out of astral realms. So I began to relearn what came naturally as a child.

In her book, *Out of Body Experiences: A Handbook*, Janet Lee Mitchell outlines the methods to access out of body experiences (OBE). They include sleep and dreams, which include unconscious OBEs, especially visions of falling or flying. Lucid dreaming takes dream memory to another level by accessing conscious dreams, where the dreamer remembers details of the experience upon awakening. During lucid dreaming, the dreamer realizes they are in a dream, and yet, they do not wake up. They begin to control the dream experience, choosing actions and responses while still dreaming.

The experience of extreme fatigue may also breakdown the body's consciousness and ease the transition into OBE. The astral body may leave the exhausted physical body to recharge it with cosmic energy. Shamanic rituals often invoke extreme exhaustion to ease the OBE. Hallucinogenic drugs may be a doorway to conscious expansion yet don't seem to generate astral travel directly. While touted as astral-friendly, a test of 247 LSD users who had OBE experiences showed that they were out of their body only three to four percent of the time under the influence of drugs. Other tests have shown that LSD and mescaline may increase body temperature, which produces OBE.

Extreme sensory deprivation through Ganzfeld conditions or meditation and hypnosis decreases the body's motor output and transforms the consciousness into altered states. Trauma and psychological stress also trigger altered states of consciousness.

Whatever the method of achieving OBE, the mind's elasticity in astral travel corresponds closely with quantum theories; according to quantum consciousness theory, particles and waves change form when observed, moving forward and backward in time and occupying two places simultaneously. The physical self remains the anchor as well as the propellant for conscious travel. The legendary silver cord, connecting the mind to the physical body, points to the necessity of a continuing healthy physical energy flow to continue the OBE. Upon death, consciousness departs the body, and no propellant remains to call back the conscious craft.

At home in the astral plane, consciousness adapts quickly to a quantum reality beyond time and space limits where individual intention will move the craft of consciousness. OBE experiencers report the ease of chosen destination movement directing their consciousness. Further, a mere thought projection to another destination releases unfamiliar or frightening astral dimensions.

Throughout the OBE experience, the physical body, or the mother ship, remains the monitor. The traumatized astral traveler can always move back into the haven of the physical body.

In 1999, the International Academy of Consciousness (IAC) developed a sophisticated online survey and analyzed 98 different OBE aspects. Well over 7,000 people responded. The international study showed that persons with OBE experience had many shared characteristics irrespective of age, gender, nationality, ethnicity, cultural background, religion, and education. The IAC continues its research by refining an investigative instrument to understand the processes by which an individual captures information through OBE and remote viewing. They want to investigate both the capturing and transfer of information into the physical brain.

Several distinct phenomena are present during an OBE that leads to an expanded awareness of human consciousness's powers. These phenomena are:

Self-bilocation—a person perceives to be in two places at once (for example, seeing one's physical body).

Self- permeability—while projecting, an individual can move through physical objects.

Internal autoscopy—an individual internally views his or her own body and can see bones and organs to detect disease or imbalance.

Cosmoconsciousness—a state of expanded awareness, perceiving the order, balance, and logic of the universe while simultaneously feeling and celebrating that he or she is part of it.

Precognition—while fully projected from their physical body, an individual obtains information relating to events that have not yet occurred.

Retrocognition—while fully projected from their physical body, an individual obtains information relating to events that have already occurred, in this life or a past life.

Extraphysical telepathy—an individual communicates in the physical, projected, or nonphysical condition through thought transmission.

The OBE occurs in an astral reality between the physical and extraphysical or consciousness bodies. It is not a dream, although a dream state may trigger it. OBE reports indicate active participation during the projection—making decisions, using mental attributes, and creating travel itinerary. The environment encountered, though of another dimension, has a distinct reality. The projector is, in fact, separate from the physical body and may observe his or her own body and be aware of both the launch and the landing back into the physical body.

As quantum consciousness theories take root in culture, individuals will readily open to astral travel or OBE experiences. Growing databases of experiences add to our body's scientific knowledge as a mother ship and its consciousness craft. Like needing knowledge of the automobile engine before driving a car, individuals will not wait for a complete understanding of quantum consciousness before testing their consciousness.

Teleportation

Astrophysicist, Eric Davis, argued for teleportation as attainable technology and legitimate science. Specifically, the purpose of his study was to collect information describing the teleportation of a material object, providing a description of teleportation as it occurs in physics, its theoretical and experimental status, and a projection of potential applications.[143]

Davis compiled five viable futuristic modes of teleportation. They are:

a) Quantum teleportation is a technique that shifts the characteristics but not the location of sub-atomic particles at great distances.

---

143 T.R. Witcher," Is teleportation possible?," *Las Vegas Weekly*, 2005.

b) Wormholes, a highly theoretical possibility whereby the intense gravitational field near black holes could rip open entrances to distant locales.

c) Parallel Universe travel in parallel dimensions.

d) Science fiction-based Star Trek transporter beams, which he dismisses.

e) Psychic Teleportation, which Davis sees as the most reasonable starting point.

Chinese researchers have demonstrated test subjects teleporting fruit flies and grasshoppers with their minds alone. Famed and defamed psychic Uri Geller reportedly teleported a sealed crystal compound out of existence. Physicist Dan Llewellyn successfully demonstrated a high-quality entanglement link across two computer chips in the lab where photons share a single quantum state.

The point of Davis' research was to gather all the existing research on teleportation so that other researchers might use it as a springboard. When the Chinese boast success, the US Air Force and American research institutes at Stanford and Princeton are not far behind with their confidential consciousness research.

However, the dangers of human teleportation loom large. Journalist George Knapp observed that the "original you will be destroyed, and a new you would emerge elsewhere. It will take a brave person to try that one the first time. No one knows if the essence of you is preserved."

Are humans destroyed and then recreated in teleportation? If so, through the teleportation destruction process, what is the material content recreated? In other words, teleportation may produce a replica of you, not the original.

One possibility is that since humans are eternal and entangled with the universal consciousness, teleportation cannot destroy humans. What we learn through teleportation may affirm beliefs about consciousness, soul, and the afterlife. Our essence, I would submit, our consciousness remains. Teleportation research may transform our destruction and death belief system into a belief system of continuous creation. As such, scientific research into teleportation, whether by the military-funded, university experiments, or individual spiritual experiences, presents the opportunity to leap in how we think about ourselves and reality. Make a conscious leap—a leap into experiencing our bodies as sentient, intelligent, eternal energy systems.

To take the leap and teleport, we need to identify the launching pad within our body. I believe the cradle of our Kundalini energy is our body's teleportation launching pad. This Kundalini energy equates to a zero-point, anti-gravity propellant. It launches our consciousness craft to travel and learn while silently waiting for our return and redocking. An important exoconscious ability is learning to rock our consciousness out of its cradle to travel, teleport, and then return.

Space-Earth Transhuman Infrastructure

Using our consciousness's innate abilities, the soft landing of teleportation or OBE differs radically from the Transhuman interconnected Space-Earth command, control, communication infrastructure that we examine in the next section. This infrastructure is massive, overwhelming, and powerfully planetary. A few researchers outside the military-corporate-university system are beginning to perceive the faint outlines because it is secret and silent.

Like our childhood unconscious infrastructure of perceptions and beliefs, we perceive only faint disconnected outlines of our government's Space-Earth connection. This infrastructure is composed of many projects knitted together to create a massive infrastructure built with a public image of mystery and awe.

As in my work as a Mind-Body Therapist, I will gently expose layer after layer of the Space-Earth infrastructure that composes a Transhuman worldview. Seeing this infrastructure as Exoconscious Humans, we determine how to manage and navigate its presence in our life.

Elana Freeland combed through incalculable pages of government, science, and military documents on the Space Fence that now surrounds the Earth, saturating the planet and its inhabitants with an ionized atmosphere.[144] Her research is the bedrock of the next section.

As you read through each layer, be mindful that all layers are connected and operate as an interlacing network. Like a machine—all of the layers connect and interface.

Section 2

Space Fence Surveillance Satellites

The infrastructure of a 5G network that links our phones and computers is familiar. During the Coronavirus, the liability of 5 G became a subject of public dialogue. Were highly populated cities saturated with 5G, like New York and Wuhan, subjecting their citizens to a higher risk of disease? Is the human body able to live with an increase in exposure to radiofrequency electromagnetic fields? For some time, scientists and engineers regarded 5G as necessary to move into a comprehensive Internet of Things (IoT). That momentum slowed when a Swedish oncologist, leading a group of 180 scientists and doctors from 36 countries, recommended a moratorium on the roll-out of 5G until investigated by scientists independent from the cellular industry for potential hazards for human health and the environment.[145]

While reading this section, I ask you to integrate the previous information presented on synthetic biology. Ask yourself how the next generation of radiofrequency electromagnetic fields—6G with speeds perhaps 1,000 times faster than 5G might affect humans and the environment. A public discussion of 6G accompanied the

144 Elana Freeland, *Under an Ionized Sky.*
145 "5G Appeal," https://www.jrseco.com/wp-content/uploads/2017-09-13-Scientist-Appeal-5G-Moratorium.pdf.

Coronavirus. Journalists unveiled the research into 6G that permits a deeper integration of humans with artificial intelligence.[146]

While 5G is the IoT, 6G may be the Internet of Synthetic Biology that connects the accumulated nanoparticles, artificial biology, and RFID identification of humans onto the network. Possibly, we may also be referring to 6G as the Internet of the Mind, as human consciousness merges completely with AI consciousness. No distinction or difference. As observed many times, the purpose of 6G and synthetic biology is influencing humans to become machines, not vice versa. A massive, multifaceted Earth-Space Fence infrastructure attempts the capture of human consciousness once and for all. Our examination begins in space and moves to Earth. As above, so below.

Satellite Surveillance

Layer 1

Sixty-three years ago, a beep from space echoed around the world. The beep sounded every 98 minutes from a satellite the size of a basketball. This reverberating radio beacon beep launched the space age. Launching Sputnik ("traveling companion" in Russian), the Soviet Union gained media and historical prominence for the first artificial space satellite. Sixty-three years ago, a satellite beep echoed to across our planet, calling citizens to join the Space Age.

Until now, we have a Space Age, overpopulated with debris. Today we have approximately 200,000 space junk pieces[147] and 5,774 individual active satellites in orbit, primarily from Russia and the US.[148]

---

146 River David, "Forget 5G for a moment. Instead imagine 6G," *Wall Street Journal*. April 12, 2020, https://www.wsj.com/articles/forget-5g-for-a-moment-instead-imagine-6g-11586743200.

147 https://celestrak.com/columns/v04n01/.

148 https://www.geospatialworld.net/blogs/do-you-know-how-many-satellites-earth/.

If space corporation plans succeed, the next ten years will see more satellites put into orbit around the Earth than all of the satellites launched since Sputnik in 1957. Four companies—Elon Musk's Space X-Starlink, OneWeb, Jeff Bezos' Project Kuiper, and Canadian Telesat—announced plans to launch as many as 46,100 satellites the next years.[149] Except for an occasional Elon Musk Starlink press release blast heard round the media, most satellite activity is a quiet but powerful presence.

In late summer 2020, Amazon Web Service announced its intention to invest $10 billion for launching a low earth orbit (LEO) satellite constellation called Project Kuiper to eliminate Internet dark spots. This project, specifically in the US, deployed and operated its proposed constellation of 3,236 satellites.

Satellites provide exploration, communication, curriers for instruments and passengers, defense, weaponry, internet, media broadcasting, intelligence, space assembly of ships in orbit, energy, weather forecasting, data banking, and GPS. But surveillance and intelligence remain primary since the mid-seventies when NRO (National Reconnaissance Office) launched Keyhole satellites.

Keyhole satellites have been orbiting Earth for military surveillance for 30 years. Orbiting about 200 miles above Earth, they function as a roving digital camera and gather multiple images of a geographical area. [150]

Keyhole satellites include Synthetic Aperture Radar, mounted on a platform to operate with a microwave illuminator. These microwave frequencies can generate high-resolution imagery through storms or darkness, or earth foliage.

---

149 Michael Sheetz and Magdalena Petrova, "Why in the next decade companies will launch thousands more satellites than in all of history," *CNBC*, December 2019, https://www.cnbc.com/2019/12/14/spacex-oneweb-and-amazon-to-launch-thousands-more-satellites-in-2020s.html.
150 https://science.howstuffworks.com/question529.htm.

We have all heard the claim that satellites can read the license plate on our car and monitor our online life. Satellites can track our movements, but more importantly, if surveillance and intelligence are primary, can satellite technology read a human's mind?

Satellite Mind Space Surveillance

Layer 2
According to the researcher, Elena Freeland, YES, since the 1970s, satellites could read a human mind. Technicians have 50 years of technological refinement in mind reading. How does this work?

Human thought transmits on the extremely low frequency (ELF) band. Many are familiar with the Schumann Resonance, which is related to the atmosphere's electrical activity, thought to create waves caused by lightning storms. Schumann registers at 7.8 Hz. Its waves are quasi-standing scalar waves that naturally exist in the earth's electromagnetic region, the space between the Earth and the ionosphere. We can image these waves as Earth Brainwaves, which are identical to our human brainwaves' frequency spectrum. These waves harmonize humans and nature.

Neurons in our brain act like a transducer—converting energy from one form to another. Every perception sends electrical signals to our brain that routs them to specific areas. Neurons have axon which propagates the electrical charge which intensifies and then drops off over a millisecond. This action is like an alternating current waveform. As such, it produces a weak form of electromagnetic radiation—a radio source. These signals generated by our brain move into space and can be detected. But the issue then becomes how to make sense of the signals. Whose brain signals are detected? [151]

Can satellite technology discriminate and isolate individuals? Most likely. This discrimination is like crowd surveillance—how to

---

151 https://blombladivinden.wordpress.com/2012/03/05/can-a-satellite-read-your-thoughts-physics-revealed/.

eliminate noise and chaos of images to zero in on one person. With satellite technology, the timing of the signals received can provide the location and the individual neuron structure's coding. And neuron firings of each individual is identifiable through the frequencies and amplitude of their signature. Our neural waveform is like our fingerprint.

In addition to neural waveforms, sophisticated biometrics provide additional identification for satellite technology. The biometric analysis includes fingerprint, palm veins, face recognition, DNA, palm print, hand geometry, iris recognition, retina, and odor/scent. Behavioral characteristics are related to a person's pattern of behavior, including but not limited to typing rhythm, gait, and voice. Human biometric tracking is eons beyond our conscious identity—who we think we are.

Ionosphere: Rockets' Red Glare

Layer 3
Commercial rocketry is hot and getting hotter. Rockets launch satellites, explore, and connect space systems. According to Goldman Sachs and Merrill, over the next 20 years, rocket launching may grow between 1 trillion and 3 trillion.[152] Those figures dwarf both cell phone technology, like apps, and the global blockchain market. In the past, there were two or three central launch systems until SpaceX disrupted the market and cracked it open for small startups that began to increase.

Why growth? One answer is that the Ionosphere is like California during the Gold Rush except that the mining is different. In California, miners dug and panned for gold as a currency. Today, with the assistance of ground systems, rockets re-engineer the ionosphere's atmosphere by ionizing it to mine for information and data systems. They spread the ionized gold to data-mine it.

---

152 https://www.forbes.com/sites/gregautry/2019/05/21/space-launch-overheating/#57bd05217732.

Why artificially ionize the ionosphere? The ionosphere is ionized naturally by solar radiation, which fluctuates. Solar minimums and maximums, solar flares, and solar wind can affect ionosphere-based communications across the planet and space. Thus, the need to artificially ionize to stabilize the ionosphere.

Elana Freeland details that rockets, jet engines, and supplementary systems secretly beef up the lower atmosphere and ionospheric densities. In 1972, Hess, a director of NOAA, announced that they can now produce an artificial aurora, change the Van Allen radiation belt population, and artificially modify the ionosphere from the ground. [153]

HAARP Chemtrails CERN

Layer 4

HAAPR

In 1990, the HAARP (High-frequency Active Auroral Research Program) summary for US Air Force Geophysics Lab stressed the need for "chemical releases for space-based efforts with particle beams and accelerators aboard rockets and shuttle or satellites." [154] Initially in Alaska, Air Force HAARP, now overseen by the University of Alaska, ran a series of successful ionospheric heating programs. HAARP focused radiated power to heat sections of the ionosphere, which bounced power down again. When targeted on selected areas, ELF waves produced from HAARP, similar to brain waves, can modify weather and brain waves. More evidence for possible consciousness control.

At least 13 HAARP installations around the world change the Earth's ionosphere. These installations include Alaska, Long Island, and Area 51 in the US, Puerto Rico, Peru, Brazil, the UK, Norway, Russia, China, India, Japan, and Australia.

---

153 Freeland, *Under an Ionized Sky*, p. 220.
154 Ibid., p. 221.

Chemtrails

During the same time as HAARP, Chemtrail programs began with US Air Force Project Cloverleaf, spreading highly reflective materials into the Earth's atmosphere. The public rationale was to slow global warming, but the primary aim was to create a conducive atmosphere for HAARP. A highly conductive compound aluminum oxide released from jet fuel tanks at cruising altitude produced a reflexive atmosphere. [155]

By 1996, a Pentagon paper, "Weather as a Force Multiplier: Owning the Weather by 2025," termed the chemtrails whitening effect as "cirrus shielding." Again, the Department of Defense, Space Command's "Vision for 2020 pronounced full spectrum dominance of space, land, sea, and air. [156] The haze of chemtrails was primarily aluminum and barium for solar radiation management, barium stearate for lubrication, radar imagining, and RF (radio frequency) microwave beam weapons.

Evidence began to mount concerning Chemtrails, and by 1998, Ontario Canada's Ministry of the Environment found seven times the safe limit of aluminum in rainwater. Cloverleaf was a joint US-Canadian military operation.

By 2000, after ten years of secrecy, finally, Project Cloverleaf went public. To what extent was Project Cloverleaf chemical warfare, spraying a chemical cocktail on unsuspecting citizens?[157] According to independent researchers, the spraying is a charged, electrically-conductive plasma useful for military projects. It is com-

---

155 Clifford Carnicom, independent researcher, documented chemtrails in New Mexico. A compilation of his articles and website postings is at http://www.chemtrailplanet.com/PDF/DrColetestimony-Checmtral%20bio-chemwarfaretesting.pdf.

156 https://pdfs.semanticscholar.org/380d/9d470d607f51975fe0ca e76a136dec0bbef3.pdf?_ga=2.83234704.704052089.1579217693-1443367240.1579217693.

157 For a list of chemicals in chemtrails documented by independent researchers see http://www.stopsprayingcalifornia.com/What-are-they-Spraying.html.

posed of asbestos-sized synthetic fibers and toxic metals, including barium salts, aluminum, and reportedly, radioactive thorium. These materials act as electrolytes to enhance the conductivity of military radar and radio waves.

GEMS

Global Environmental Micro Sensors (GEMS) are micron-scale airborne probes that can monitor all Earth regions with high resolution. These probes remain suspended in the atmosphere for hours to days to take specific measurements of the atmosphere. They are of interest for climate and citizen observation as well as intelligence gathering and military awareness. Each GEM probe is self-controlled with a power source to provide sensing, navigation, and communication abilities to relay data. [158] A GEM probe is like a pickax for mining. It exposes the vein of information.

Ultimately, a GEMS "net" or "veil of protection" could blanket the globe with probes of different design, mass, and size tailored to measure a variety of parameters. The probes will be as small as 50-100 microns in one or more dimensions based on specific applications. For comparison, the pores in a coffee filter are about 20 microns. GEMS experts maintain that these microns are lightweight enough to pose virtually no danger upon contact with persons or property.

Quantum Computing

Quantum Computing advanced in 1998 with the introduction of the DWave computer for commercial use. Google, IBM, Microsoft, and other corporations followed with quantum computer innovations that created experimental equipment to generate monitored results and analysis. Quantum computing services include

---

158 John Manobianco, "Global Environmental Mems Sensors (Gems): A Revolutionary Observing System For The 21st Century," https://people.eecs.berkeley.edu/~pister/publications/2004/Manobianco%20 GEMS.pdf.

simulating complex biological systems (synthetic biology), cryptography and breaking secure encryption, global financial analysis, running intelligence scenarios, and corporate supply chain management.

CERN

2008 marked the activation of CERN Large Hadron Collider, an installation where two high-energy particle beams travel in opposite directions, close to the speed of light before they collide.[159] Independent researchers claim that CERN is impacting the earth's magnetosphere. The magnetosphere, protecting against the radiation effects of the Sun, is vital to life on Earth. Fluctuating the sun's activities, including sunspots, solar flares, and coronal mass ejections cause distortions in the magnetosphere. Researchers are discovering correlations between the firing of CERN and changes in the magnetosphere. [160]

Beyond particles and magnetic resonance, researchers speculate that CERN operations may focus on hyperdimensionality and

---

159 CERN is currently in a Long Shutdown in preparation for the next run in 2021 and also to prepare for High-Luminosity LHC project in 2025. https://www.universetoday.com/140769/the-large-hadron-collider-has-been-shut-down-and-will-stay-down-for-two-years-while-they-perform-major-upgrades/.

160 While CERN is in a temporary shutdown, currently there are 30,000 operational particle accelerators around the world, which are sharing data. Dr. Joseph Farrell in his book *The Third Wave* (2015) examines the work of CERN, specifically detecting strangelets—strange quark-gluon condensate, or plasma, that would eventually suck all matter into contact with it, converting it all to a hyper-dense lump of matter with the mass of a star, but compacted into a small volume of space, less that the size of a planet Earth. These strangelets function as a black hole sucking matter and creating. This information is verified by Eric Penrose, who examined CERNs safety page. https://www.heavyionalert.org/docs/CERNContradictions.pdf.

torsion, leading to experiments proving parallel universes. CERN physicist Mir Faizal recounts the possibilities.

We predict that gravity can leak into extra dimensions, and if it does, then miniature black holes are produced at the LHC. Normally, when people consider the multiverse, they think about the many-worlds interpretation of quantum physics, where every possibility is actualized. This can not be tested so it's a philosophy and not science. This is often not what we mean by parallel universes. What we mean is real universes in extra dimensions. As gravity can effuse of our universe into the additional dimensions, such a model may be tested by the detection of mini black holes at the LHC.[161]

An often overlooked but essential aspect of CERN is data collection. It generates millions of bits of data per second per day, which "dwarfs all other database management problems, save perhaps those of NSA planetary spying program."[162] This data collection is rooted in CERN's role in the creation of the internet. [163] Tim Berners-Lee, a British scientist, invented the world wide web while working at CERN. The introduction of quantum computing and AI boosts CERNs experimentation and data collection. CERN and IBM collaborate on data collection.

In 2009 a California researcher called public attention to the Naval Research Lab's Charged Aerosol Release Experiment (CARE), which created clouds in near-earth orbit, such that rocket

---

161 Pionic,"LHC Could Reveal Possible Parallel Universe", *Medium*, March, 2017. *https://medium.com/r3fl3ct1ons/lhc-could-reveal-possible-parallel-universe-c1a18b794390*

162 Joseph Farrell, *The Third Way: Nazi International, European Union and Corporate Fascism (Adventures Unlimited, 2015)*, p. 264.

163 According to Farrell, CERNs experiments generate data, analyzes the data, and its programming selects and stores the data.

exhaust particles triggered artificial dust clouds. These dust clouds are released 55 miles above the earth and gradually settle to a lower altitude.

Following HAARP's 20 years of weather modification, in 2010, the US House of Representatives published its first congressional report on geoengineering. By then, the geoengineering infrastructure was in place, and citizens ignored its presence.

Planetary Space Fence Completion

Layer 5
According to Elena Freeland, the Space Fence is a second-generation Space Surveillance System. A 2009 collision between US and Russian communications satellites called for an upgraded radar system. This defense demand led to building a US Air Force Satellite radar array structure, a 7,000 square foot installation in the Marshall Islands, Kwajalein Atoll in the Pacific. The facility locates, identifies, and tracks objects, even small objects hundreds of miles above the Earth. Reports indicate that the Space Fence shut down in 2013 due to budget cuts and re-engineering needs, but space surveillance intensifies.

In 2019, Planet Labs launched 300 small satellites into space, that combined can photograph the entire landmass of the Earth every day —1.2 million images every 24 hours. Engineered and built-in downtown San Francisco, the small satellites, called doves and are stored in nests, launch in flocks.

The same year, 2019, Trump announced the Space Force's formation as the sixth branch of the armed forces with the 2020 National Defense Authorization Act. Remember the 1996 Pentagon paper, "Weather as a Force Multiplier?" With the Space Force, Trump proclaimed full spectrum dominance of space, land, sea, and air. Gen. Mark Milley, Chairman of the Joint Chiefs of Staff, affirmed the President's authorization, "In military operations, space is not just a place from which we support combat operations in other domains, but a warfighting domain in and of itself." If you own space, you own the planet—so they assume. Tech will take us there.

A year later, in 2020, The U.S. Space Force publicized its improved Kwajalein Atoll radar system designed to track objects in space that are as small as 4 inches. NASA estimates that half-million objects with a diameter between 0.4 and four inches are circling the Earth at a speed of 22,000 miles an hour. So, the risk of even these small objects colliding with spacecraft or satellites is catastrophic. In 2021 the Pentagon plans to build a second radar site in Western Australia. [164]

According to Elena Freeland, the Space Fence is a vast environmental infrastructure built around and within human society to control weather, near-earth space, and encompass organic life. And, we would add full control of human consciousness.

Section 3

Common Ground

Readers must note the glaring difference when comparing the scientifically sophisticated and comprehensive Space Fence infrastructure to Exoconscious Humans' cosmic consciousness and abilities like OBE and teleportation. While the government, military, corporations, and universities organized, collaborated, and built a coordinated structure, Exoconscious Humans remain disorganized and unstructured. Is our future, as Exoconscious Humans, to remain disenfranchised, ignored, and continue to react to our environment controlled by others?

Ufology spent decades seeking insider information, receiving FOIA requests of blacked-out documents, and supporting

---

164 Kyle Mizokami, "The U.S. Space Force Is Ready To Turn on Its All-Seeing 'Space Fence'," *Popular Mechanics*, February 7, 2020, https://www.popularmechanics.com/military/weapons/a30798053/us-space-force-space-fence/.

government whistleblower information. This work was essential in pulling back the veil of secrecy of information that citizens should demand and an industrious, heroic few pursued to the benefit of all. Unfortunately, most of these diligent activities also heightened our awareness of how humans are disposable, nonessential, and disenfranchised. Aware of being treated in this manner, humans exhibit a reactive response. But, there is another option.

Practical Exoconscious Antidotes

Question: Is an overwhelmed, perhaps angry, or defeated response our only option when confronted with the behemoth Transhuman Space Fence? Once reactive, we move into trauma responses, which limit our ability for critical thinking. The sympathetic nervous system that automatically, often unconsciously, moves us toward survival takes control of our decisions and reactions. We see transhumanism or the Space Fence as threatening our lives. We are under attack.

Though survival may require trauma responses in dire circumstances to keep us alive, it also leaves us open to manipulating our primal fears in situations that may not warrant it. Our trauma responses develop during our early childhood and, as such, are often unconscious and unexamined. Interestingly, our trauma responses are our "familiar"; they make us feel good when we experience them. Our early imprinted nervous system loves to recreate our first childhood trauma reactions. We like to react and light up our imprinted nervous system. Feel the "old" feelings. Until it no longer works because our relationships crumble or our health suffers, our life goes in the wrong direction. Then we look for a solution.

Creating a mature, balanced, and grounded Exoconscious Human life, we openly and honestly examine our trauma response and hold ourselves accountable. We admit that we no longer need to recreate situations to satisfy our nervous system. We become conscious of our reactions and hold ourselves responsible for choosing healthy responses. Antidotes to our natural trauma reactions work. We can change our trauma reactions and therefore rewire our nervous system

Here are some options for dealing with the overwhelming presence of transhumanism and the Space Fence. Which is your trauma reaction? Which antidote works for you?

Flight: In a flight trauma response, we ignore the Space Fence and pretend it doesn't exist. We live in another dimension of consciousness, separate and safe, while reality unfolds. This escape reality may be through drugs, anxiety, or even endless meditation. These behaviors are flight responses. Persons who exhibit a flight response feel safe when disconnected, living in another reality. An extreme fight response leads to dissociation, which is the separation of commonly related mental processes. The **antidote** to flight is to ground in facts and reality, mindful of the potentials within yourself and other humans.

Freeze The freeze trauma response of overwhelm is a surrender to helplessness. This behavior is a freeze of all reactions. A typical freeze expression is "I feel stuck." Often it is similar to bending into a fetal position, protecting yourself from the world. A freeze response also triggers feelings of being isolated, invisible—a victim. Persons who exhibit a freeze response feel safe being a victim and separate. While the freeze response may be complicated, the **antidote** is to get moving—read books and articles, have conversations with others, and talk through your feelings. Recognize and enhance your strength and power to cope.

Fight: In a fight response, you increase your level of resentment and anger to become fierce and fight the invasion of transhumanism. This behavior is an aggressive, sometimes violent fight response. The person with a primary fight response perceives their environment as a series of threats that they need to combat either through direct aggression or covertly with passive aggression. Fighters are people who feel safe being an aggressive bully. They see fighting as the only solution to the continual threats that define their life. The **antidote** is peace. Find peace in calming yourself with facts and opportunities. Focus on life situations that are peaceful and supportive. Choose to make every response a calm response.

Fawn: The Fawn trauma response takes the high moral ground and judges others for the evil of erecting a Space Fence and rolling out transhumanism while holding yourself as an essential helper, a savior for others. This behavior is a fawn response. It is the least recognized trauma response since being a helper is culturally acceptable. This fawn response is used by people who feel safe caring for others, to the detriment of themselves. "I do and do for others." The **antidote** for this response is to focus first on yourself. Gather your strength and find a peaceful outcome first within yourself. Shift your attention away from others to yourself.

Using antidotes and making conscious decisions to move out of unconscious trauma reactions commences individual moral autonomy.

CHAPTER 6

EXOCONSCIOUS MORAL
AUTONOMY PREFERRED
TRANSHUMAN MORPHOLOGICAL
FREEDOM PREFERRED

Section 1

Moral Autonomy

November of 1954, the 25-year-old, newly installed pastor of Dexter Avenue Baptist Church, stood before a congregation of doctors, lawyers, teachers, and business owners. The Reverend Martin Luther King, Jr. preached a fiery sermon calling his community to become "transformed non-conformists." He urged them to release their mindless conformity to the world and instead, use their mind—their moral conscience, their awareness of God's power within—to transform the world.

We are called to be people of conviction, not conformity; of moral nobility, not social respectability. We are commanded to live differently and according to a higher loyalty.

Little did the faithful parishioners, perched on wooden pews scarred by 70 years of hands grasping for strength, know that within one short year, a swell of events would turn tumultuous, and they would bend into the depths of transformation. Walk, linked arm, and arm into the uncertain and unknown.

Within one year, Rosa Parks refused to vacate her seat on the bus and make room for white passengers. Outraged women would gather to mimeograph thousands of leaflets to organize a one-day boycotting of city buses. Community religious leaders would form the Montgomery Improvement Association.

Their new association would choose the young pastor King to lead them. He was ready—recently completing his doctoral dissertation at Boston University, consolidating his theological belief that God was a living force who was responsive to our heart's deepest yearning. Individual hearts. Autonomous hearts. Moral hearts.

According to King, "transformed non-conformists" are created through encounters with the other within themselves, their spiritual self, a living God. Their inner transformation would lead to social change through acts of goodwill and love for one's neighbor.

King urged his community to adopt American philosophy, quoting from Ralph Waldo Emerson and Henry Wadsworth Longfellow—proponents of individualism and moral autonomy.

He demanded a non-violent community rooted in love. Dramatically, he laid down a gauntlet of non-violence and love as he stood on the porch stairs of his home, embers still burning from a firebomb thrown while his wife and child were at home. The destructive firebomb represented an outside force, heteronomy, which King confronted with moral autonomy.

Brazilian scholar Rodolfo De Oliveira[165] defines heteronomy as actions influenced by forces outside the individual. Philosopher Jean-Jacques Rousseau describes heteronomy as the condition of being ruled, governed, or under another's sway. It is the counter/opposite of autonomy, which is the capacity to make an informed, uncoerced decision.

---

165 https://www.academyfraternitatem.com/.

In his writing, De Oliveira defines moral autonomy as based on spiritual awakening and individuation:

Autonomous individuals are in harmony with the natural moral law within their hearts and mind, which we can describe as a divine spark of love, the root of our moral life.

Moral autonomy is about establishing a profound connection with our true nature (which is why it is also commonly referred to as "awakening") and thus becoming vehicles of expression of singular forms of intelligence and organization. We recognize that we are parts of a system. It is a state of redemptory sovereignty. As in a holographic system, the parts reflect the whole, and the whole is its parts.

It should be self-evident that as a certain critical mass of humanity attains this consciousness state of moral autonomy, that earth will be a different planet.

King referred to God or the divine as "other" when defining "transformed non-conformists." De Oliveira and exoconsciousness refer to "other" by several terms: the field of consciousness, God-source, spirituality, and the ET, multidimensionals. According to De Oliveira, humanity's crossing into moral autonomy is also humanity's ticket to the advent of exoconsciousness, where we co-create with other intelligent beings throughout the cosmos as part of a more extensive, more complex autonomous system.

King's moral compass was aimed at a relationship with God, grounding human freedom from racism and social/economic inequality, achieved through acts of nonviolence rooted in love. While these high moral achievements of King's era continue to call us today, our exoconscious community grapples with different ethical challenges related to freedom in this transhuman era.

With Consciousness Liberty for All

Like King's legacy, human freedom is a moral pillar of exoconsciousness. Both King and exoconsciousness include 1) moral autonomy, 2) liberty, and 3) spiritual commitment to non-violence. Similar to King's challenge of racism and hate, today, Exoconscious Humans confront a new form of enslavement: Transhumans' captivity of the human mind, human consciousness through ever-encroaching AI. King called for a transformation in how we relate to the suffering caused by other humans. Exoconscious Humans call for a change in how we relate to the suffering caused by transhumanism and technocracy. Establishing moral autonomy is essential in the encounter with an invasive AI, machine culture.

Instead of firebombs exploding a front porch or crosses burned in yards, invasive machine intelligence moves silently through wireless platforms, hidden computer algorithms, and covert codes that capture private identity data, minds, emotions, and human consciousness.

In the twenty-first century, slavery adopts a new meaning as humans increasingly enslave themselves to machines and AI space infrastructures. Tragically, mainstream religious and moral leaders seem to be either blind or illiterate when confronted by this emerging form of slavery.

Human-sourced slavery continues to spread throughout the planet in the form of racism and child, sexual, and worker trafficking. This enslavement is by no means minimized. The contagion of slavery remains an epidemic. Amid this epidemic, religious voices lack a vision, plan, or enthusiasm. The progress of ridding the planet of human slavery is a patchwork of conflicting statistics and claims of conspiracy, counter-intel, and lawsuits to divert creating solutions. The mainstream media offers back-patting positive stories and briefly covers then submerges horror stories as elite networks and organizations embroil in scandals like Weinstein, Epstein, and the Wuhan affiliated scientists.

Overwhelmed by the extent of human to human slavery, it is no surprise that religion and moral teachings deny or minimize Transhuman enslavement of human consciousness. To date, we possess no historical/spiritual text or logical, theological, or scientific argument that frames the challenge of human slavery by AI and synthetic biology.

However, we have an abundance of historical texts to guide us in addressing human to human slavery. Philosophically we have Rousseau and Kant and spiritual/religious writing of the Torah, Jesus, Buddha, Mohammad, and King to lean on for human to human slavery. Moral citizens have repeatedly written the abolition of slavery into our genetic blueprint. We know slavery is wrong, unethical.

Unfortunately, we have no moral blueprint for identifying and abolishing the AI machine enslavement of humans. The emerging reality of our human bondage by machines is murky and censored. We have no text, no leader, no moral genetic code to reference. Our culture compass is worthless.

Where do we turn for guidance on the Transhuman AI machine-based capture of human consciousness?

Exoconscious Moral Compass:
Liberty and Individualism

At its foundation, our Exoconscious compass points out that humans must claim their right to freedom of thought, creativity, will, enterprise, and autonomous morality. Exoconscious Humans are the vanguard voicing the right to free and unrestricted access to the field of consciousness—freedom of thought. Humans move dimensionally, explore this field in our dreams, and consciously and unconsciously in our everyday lives.

Exoconsciousness is grounded in humans and their consciousness. Human consciousness is our primary resource. Not oil, or gold, or machines—but human minds. Not extraterrestrial mind or multidimensional expression—but human minds. Our focus always returns to humans and the fundamental right to freedom of mind and thought.

Exoconsciousness is grounded in individual experience. ET, multidimensional contact, communication, and co-creation is primarily a personal experience. It may evolve as a group experience, but the intense journey of awakening to the multidimensionality of our mind and body, along with the presence of beings such as ETs, is, first and foremost, an individual experience.

Thus, the development of exoconsciousness requires a cultural context for 1) liberty and 2) individualism.

The Institute for Exoconsciousness is an international community, so this examination of moral autonomy spans global cultures to access how they integrate liberty and individualism. Our community respects that cultures worldwide have different historical perspectives, values, and expressions of freedom and individualism.

The individual's rights correspond to an Exoconscious Human's quest for moral autonomy to freely co-create with ETs and multidimensionals. A community of Exoconscious healers, inventors, scientists, educators, and artists are the architects and builders of an Exoconscious Civilization. To accomplish this, innovative Exoconscious Humans require liberty. Primarily, they need mental freedom to pursue the outer reaches of the multidimensional field of consciousness to creatively access and use information and energy available in the field of consciousness.

Over 300 years ago, cultural ideas of liberty and individualism developed in Britain, France, Germany, and eventually throughout Western Europe. Liberty and individualism flourished among the colonist of what became the United States.

During this era of enlightenment, liberty was a big deal. The cry for freedom seeded the success of the American Revolution and the creation of a new country. However, it was not unique to America. Their leaders studied the work of French, British and German ideals. But unlike those countries, US citizens carried less anger toward monarchies or elite institutions due to geographical distance. Thousands of miles from Europe, they expressed limited distress at their enslavement by unelected governments. No cry of "off with their heads"—Americans, instead, demanded liberty. Pure and simple.

From its roots in the revolution, the American concept of liberty required individualism and moral autonomy. Protestants who rebelled against their homeland's reliance on church and clerical authority intensely valued the individual—conscience, soul, mind, and direct relationship with God. Liberty ran through the new country's spiritual veins.

Governments, monarchies, hierarchies, corporations, popes, and priests were to be continually balanced by individual needs— autonomous moral individuals. And so, America became an engine of spiritual energy, but not a collective. They were a political and social experiment of individuals—most of whom had experienced rebellion against their family, homeland, church, and crown—to take up residence where their moral conscience gave them the right to be free to judge themselves and their progress. The individual was the standard.

While Western European philosophy influenced the colonists, according to Patrick Kiger, some historians argued that we ought to give the Iroquois credit for inspiring the birth of American democracy. These historians suggested that the U.S. Constitution and a system of self-government based upon the Iroquois Great Law.[166] The Native American leader, Canastego, expressed frustration at the colonists' quarreling with one another: "We heartily recommend Union and a good agreement between you, our brethren," he admonished the colonists. He advised that they follow the example of the Iroquois who had established a well-organized system of self-government, codified in the Great Law of Peace, with both a central council and checks and balances that protected individual freedoms."

As referenced, the exoconscious community is international. How does the spirit of liberty and individualism express in other countries with a different history and culture? A consulting and training group, Hofstede Insights, provides an online evaluation of individualism from statistics gathered across global cultures.[167]

---

166 https://history.howstuffworks.com/history-vs-myth/iroquois-great-law-peace-source-us-constitution.htm.

167 https://www.hofstede-insights.com/country-comparison/.

Examining various countries, Hofstede Insights highlights differences in the degree of individualism expressed by countries. Often, the cultural context of collectivism defines individuality. For example, in Russia, the Enlightenment ideal of liberty and individualism is tempered by a greater emphasis on collectivism, the importance of state, and broader government culture.

China has a similar emphasis on collectivism rather than individualism, but its culture has a distinct definition of "self" or individual. The Chinese "self" is not hindered by a gross split between mind and body or between nature and experience. The Chinese self is organic. It develops as a person relates to the environment. In this way, the Chinese have holistically integrated concepts of self and person, compared to dualistic Western traditions. [168]

The continent of Africa has 54 separate countries, which vary in collectivism and individuality. Nigeria, Ethiopia, Egypt, and South Africa have the largest populations. According to Hofstede-Insights, South Africa, with a score of 65, is an Individualist society. This score indicates a high preference for a loosely-knit social framework in which individuals expect to take care of themselves and their immediate families only. Collectivistic nations include Nigeria, with a score of 30, Ethiopia, with a score of 20, and Egypt, with a score of 25. This designation manifests in a close long-term commitment to the member 'group': a family, extended family, or extended relationships. However, according to Ibrahim Anoba, African culture retains a robust individualistic tradition. The African individual is as important as life itself, and respect for his dignity, a virtue. The only difference was that they saw individual prosperity as more realistic when embedded in each African community's well-being.[169]

In India, where Hinduism is predominant, their culture affirms that humans possess a self, Atman, one with the body. Like China,

168 https://www.iep.utm.edu/ind-chin/ Individualism in Classical Chinese Thought.
169 https://www.studentsforliberty.org/2017/05/22/ibrahim-anoba-libertarian-thought-individualism-african-morality/.

their language of self is more organic. Yet, Buddhist countries have a doctrine of Anatman, which negates the self. According to Anatman doctrine, humans possess no permanent, underlying substance that can be called the soul. Instead, the individual is composed of five factors that are continually changing.

According to Stefan Pacovski, a fundamental difference between Hinduism and Buddhism concerns the self (or soul) of living beings. Hinduism affirms that living beings possess self, namely Atman. Atman is not physical and is distinct from the body. In contrast, Buddhism negates the self and strictly upholds the belief of Anatman.[170]

According to Dutch researcher Geert Hofstede, the verdict on India is mixed. It ranks lower in individualism than most former English colonies like the US, Canada, or Australia. Still, individualism is higher than many of the Asian countries that are adjacent to it. Here is Hofstede's analysis:

India, with an average score of 48, is a society with both collectivistic and individualistic traits. The collectivist side means a high preference for belonging to a broader social framework in which individuals act by following the greater good of one's defined in-group(s). In such situations, various concepts such as the opinion of one's family, extended family, neighbors, workgroup, and other social networks influence the individual. For a collectivist, to be rejected by one's peers or to be thought lowly by one's extended and immediate in-groups leaves individuals rudderless and with a sense of intense emptiness.[171]

Notably, the Indian concept of individual liberty rests on a clear-eyed knowledge of human depravity and virtue as a given. Individual liberty, yes, but within the context of vulnerability and

---

170 https://www.academia.edu/10671835/Comparing_the_Hindu_theory_of_atman_with_the_Buddhist_theory_of_no-self._Which_is_more_plausible.

171 https://www.hofstede-insights.com/country-comparison/india/.

tendency to corruption, as well as virtue, intelligence, and imagination. Balance, not perfection, is the Indian reality.

Mohammed Borhandden Musah cites that Islam views individualism (accountability) and collectivism (innovation) as foundational concepts. In Islamic culture, individualism is a fundamental building block that constitutes principles of responsibility in human activities. Collectivism is a creative element that flourishes from principles of accountability and stipulates social activities.[172]

The planet's diversity of philosophy, religion, and cultural opinions on liberty and individualism is a fact. However, the Exoconscious community's respect for human dignity remains a unifying fact. The Exoconscious Human perspective, in which humans are one race of beings, is a sane, healthy path forward for humanity, Earth, and our entry into the populated conscious cosmos of beings. Emphasizing humans joining a conscious universe of beings provides a means to maintain the human's independence and sanctity—anchoring humans to Earth and simultaneously opening innate abilities to relate to ETs and multidimensional beings throughout the cosmos as we gradually move respectfully into space.

Exoconscious Humans affirm that independent, sovereign citizens will determine our galactic future. Awareness of our seeded ET and multidimensional nature and connection strengthens human identity. Consequently, Exoconscious Humans regard themselves as independent yet related to a greater universe of beings.

Consciousness is our most precious resource—to be nurtured, expanded, and loved beyond current human imagination. Consciousness is a shared cosmic field. Humans are but one participant among many races and beings in this multi-dimensional field.

Human consciousness advances through the development of numerous psychic abilities. Humans are a race of doers. We create,

---

172 Https://Www.Academia.Edu/5490549/THE_CULTURE_OF_INDIVIDUALISM_AND_COLLECTIVISM_IN_BALANCING_ACCOUNTABILITY_AND_INNOVATION_IN_EDUCATION_AN_ISLAMIC_PERSPECTIVE.

craft, and use our minds, bodies, and spirits to reach beyond our current state to develop advanced abilities. Furthermore, humans should not be subservient to technology by becoming a hybrid human-cyborg. Humans are neither machine nor a cog in a Transhuman wheel.

If technology should artificially dominate, it will limit human consciousness, conscripting human abilities to narrowly defined channels of knowledge, beliefs, and skills. With AI domination, the capturing of humans is complete.

And yet, the fact remains that we participate in in the field of consciousness as somewhat fragile, incredibly complex, and vulnerable human beings. The entire human body and its energetic, nervous system participate in consciousness. The physical body acts as an instrument of consciousness. It is not data-driven and deterministic like a computer. Instead, human participation in the field of consciousness is unexplored and limited only by our lack of knowledge and exploration.

As humans push into space, consciousness may act as the propellant—the force and fuel. Becoming Exoconscious Humans, awake and utilizing our cosmic consciousness via our ET, multidimensional contact, should be a priority for those responsible for earth and space ventures.

However, the reality of our Earth space-based economy and exploration remains mired in secrecy. There is no morally autonomous individuality in a secret government operation or culture. This hidden space system and its overarching planetary surveillance represent an example of transhuman morality.

Section 2

Morphological Freedom

My husband, a former commercial and corporate pilot, often imagines driving fun transport vehicles. He wanted to buy a van so he can transport all the members of our family. His preference is to buy a van with a drop-down television screen to show movies. The family voted down his idea.

" Not DVD movies! We want individual seats with charging outlets so that we can use our tablet and watch the shows we like."

When I heard my family's response, I noted the comprehensiveness of customized viewing adopted by people of all ages. Toddlers to seniors prefer their personalized library of favorites. Shared displays are a thing of the past—except for arranged family entertainment.

Customization of favorites and feeds makes us feel autonomous—unique, and individual. Using our handheld screens, we are customized, independent individuals. Our habits, preferences, behaviors, movements, and personality create and register our exclusive data, becoming our go-to identifying algorithm. This automated, self-contained feed even knows how to manage our emotions—trigger us, calm us, and involve us, and yes, also dismiss us. And yet, we believe we can't possibly be Pavlovian conditioned dogs who have created our stimulus that someone else manages, monitors and measures. But we are. We are the perfect compliant consumer—shopping away on Disney, Expedia, Amazon, or purchasing products featured in our favorite Netflix or Hollywood films. We excitedly dedicate time to binge-watching weekends where we splurge on the same food as the actors.

We are perfectly engineered consumers. We consume what we want. Or so we believe. We rarely consider being steered to see what institutions, government, entertainment, and billionaire corporations want us to see and consume. Here's a disturbing fact: if we find it on Google, then the information is meant to be found. And we are intended to see it because it fits the technocratic narrative. Nothing online is synchronistic.[173] Nothing online is original or

---

173 Was Carl Jung's work on synchronicity and collective unconscious popularized because it fit the emerging engineered consumer reality of seemingly magic information appearing in our artificial online reality? In 1948, Jung was part of the National Association of Mental Health

organic. It is all formula, to appear as manufactured magic. Leaving us wondering how our feed knew what food we want to eat, places we want to travel, or products we need to buy right now. Magic!

Our every click feeds our dragon. But, as our customized data grows, our choices diminish. Any desire for products and services outside of the "net" is immediately lassoed and led back to safe, homogenized options. Silently, we sell ourselves to the corporation with the most massive marketing budget. We don't stand with our hands tied behind our back on a slave traders platform sold to the highest bidder—against our will. We are complicit slaves. Eagerly complicit. We simply click a popup and follow artificial images to obediently sell ourselves and pay for the privilege on a credit card that we believe grants us magical points to buy even more stuff.

Is this autonomy? Is this freedom? Does our moral choice enslave or free us?

As a new phase in human development, transhumanism develops a new language for their brand of morality and freedom. Examining it will deepen our understanding of ourselves and our customized reality.

Transhuman Morphological Freedom of Rights

Morphological freedom refers to a person's civil right to either maintain or modify their body on their terms. It holds a powerful allure.

I recall my excitement of going to the bookstore in the 70s and buying my copy of *Our Bodies Ourselves*, returning home, and reading it cover to cover. It filled my mind with an inspiring array of women's health information. Ourselves' history began in 1969 at Emmanuel College, founded by the Sisters of Notre Dame de Namur as the first Catholic college for women in New England. At this small college in Boston, 12 women met informally to share

---

(NIMH), which joined with Tavistock Institute and United Nations to coordinate worldwide psychological operations. Jim Keith, *Mass Control: Engineering Human Consciousness* (Adventures Unlimited Press, 2003).

information and discuss their health with a group of doctors. A year later, their first textbook, hand-stapled on newsprint, sold for 75cents. Today the updated book has sold millions of copies and garnered numerous honors.

We yearn for information about our bodies. Our body represents our autonomous self.

Maybe it's the Arizona sun and year-round sleeveless fashion, but moving from Washington, DC to Phoenix in 2016, I was intrigued by how many people displayed elaborate tattoos. While I assumed that tattoos were more popular with young people in their teens and 20s, tattoos are most popular in the 30 to 50 age group. Sleeves, neck, back, and face tattoos adorn a large segment of this population.

Scarification is scratching, branding, and cutting designs into the skin. Scarification, found in tribal initiation rites, represents cutting gone mainstream. It is riskier than tattooing and escapes second thoughts—it's permanent. Ear lob shaping, multiple piercings, and plastic surgery to sculpt bodies and faces escalate scarification.

We aspire to embellish our bodies. Embellishment increases our perceived autonomy.

In 2018, 80 employees of Three Square Market company in Wisconsin injected rice sized chips in their hands. The employees used the chips for security, computer access, and even to buy a Dr. Pepper in a vending machine. The RFID chips were inserted between the thumb and forefinger, so a mere wave of the hand opened doors and debit cards. Sweden began a program to implant its citizens for identification purposes as well as travel and banking. Germany, India, and many other countries followed.

We want the ease of one-touch ID. We want the effortlessness of quantum dot RFID permission. Information, embellishment, ease—it's all about our body—the focus of morphological freedom in Transhumanism.

Transhumanism's success moving mainstream depends on humans claiming morphological freedom to change their bodies with anthro-technological devices.[174] Coined by transhumanist Max Moore in his 1993 paper[175], morphological freedom means extending a human's right to their body. It encompasses not only self-ownership but also the right to modify one's body according to individual desires. Philosophical arguments claim that the right to own and change one's body relates to humans' survivability and further relates to the human right to happiness. Morphological freedom equals sustainability and meaning. Anders Sandberg argues that humans would die out as a race, the purpose of life wither, and human potential weaken without the right to own and modify their body. [176]

> Morphological freedom can, of course, be viewed as a subset of the right to one's body. But it goes beyond the idea of merely passively maintaining the body as it is and exploiting its inherent potential. Instead, it affirms that we can extend or change our potential through various means. It is strongly linked to self-ownership and self-direction.

Assuming Darwinism, transhuman arguments imply that humans are doomed to decline without acceptance of anthro-technological implants. Your anthro-technological options are signup for success or signoff for failure. Their arguments ignore untapped innate conscious abilities of psychic intelligence or spiritual transcendence to open human potential. Instead, implants are the solution to human survival. Yet, in many instances, their prediction of

---

174 Anthro-technological devices are customized through personal data collection to fit your needs. F. Jotterand, (2010). "Human Dignity and Transhumanism: Do Anthro-Technological Devices Have Moral Status?," *The American Journal of Bioethics*, 10(7), 45–52. doi:10.1080/15265161003728795 sci-hub.tw/10.1080/15265161003728795.

175 Max More (1993) "Technological Self-Transformation: Expanding Personal Entropy," *Extropy* #10, 4:2.

176 Anders Sandberg (2001) "Morphological Freedom—Why we Not just Want it, but Need it," TransVision Conference Berlin.

signup or signoff is accurate. Employees who refuse implants may be ignored or sidelined for privileges the implanted receive.

In countries like India, moving to a cashless society (probably to shut down untaxed black markets), microchipping is mandatory. In this scenario, the bank has the freedom to shut off your access to your money. In a cashless society, all transactions are digital (stored on a cloud that may or may not be private and protected—as a satellite). Financial transactions are monitored and controlled by the click of a button.[177] Though Transhumanists argue that others cannot force you to change your body, social and economic pressures will prevail and deprive humans of freedom to choose.

With the spread of anthro-technological devices into human bodies, those who refuse to comply lose out not only socially and economically—they lose out functionally. Medical and pharmaceutical corporations are on the cusp of literally changing how humans function with innovative intelligence, sexual and genetic changes, DNA repair, and vaccinations. The COVID vaccine RFID, quantum dots technology, and digital certificates for passports and citizen documents represent morphological freedom.

In all of these instances, morphological freedom is a misnomer. There is no freedom. The system has built-in consent. Whether you want to be transhuman or not, you will be living among them—either cooperatively or estranged. As devices proliferate, freedoms diminish.

Section 3

Common Ground
Is Morality Hardwired into Brain?

Neuroscience explores the biological mechanisms—the disease and dysfunction and the activity and abilities of the human brain. This

---

177 Tim Hinchliffe (2016) "India's ban on paper money, cashless societies and the loss of freedom," https://sociable.co/technology/cashless-societies/.

science is useful to both Exoconscious Humans and Transhumans in discussing human morality.

According to Canadian philosopher Patricia Churchland, author of *Conscience: The Origins of Moral Intuition,* the foundation for human morality is sourced in our species survival instincts that developed biological faculties, rather than sourced in philosophical or religious ideas. Morality functions in the human brain developed through instincts. For example, altruism, concern for others' wellbeing, evolved as food-sharing between parents and infants. Furthermore, altruism formed to promote the survival of the species because it was easier for females to procreate if protected.

Instincts geared to survival created moral networks. In the brain, the hormone oxytocin increases social attachment. Called the love hormone, oxytocin increases as a mother holds her infant and gazes lovingly into their eyes. The infant then forms a close, secure attachment to the mother and the father and extended family. This attachment, in turn, creates a feeling of being safe and protected in the world. Human-to-human transference of the love hormone leads to the healthy development of a child.

According to Churchland, the chemical release of dopamine and serotonin teaches morality. In the parent-child relationship, dopamine releases when behavior is approved and serotonin releases during disapproval. A brain chemical release occurs as a child learns a moral code of right from wrong.

Transhumans, basing their morality and consciousness theories in the brain, have evidence of brain biological functions' importance. Exoconscious Humans, referring to the field of consciousness and relationship, also cite the importance of the brain and chemical-based mother-child relationships that are not possible between a machine and a human.

Moral Reason

Reason has a position of prominence in moral philosophy and theology. It is how individuals determine the difference between what is right and wrong using information and logic. Ethics in the Western tradition began with ancient Greek philosophy (Socrates, Plato, Aristotle) and threads through philosophy, especially Kantian ethics. An early originator of Western ethics was Judaism, the oral and written Torah of ethical behavior, adopted by writers of the New Testament and Christian communities. The need for reason-based ethics is vital in any innovation, especially AI.

DARPA, a research arm of the Department of Defense, plays a significant role in the development of AI, deep learning. In an attempt to explain the reasoning behind the conclusions and decisions made by AI, deep learning, and neural networks, DARPA launched the Explainable Artificial Intelligence (XAI), an initiative launched in 2016.

David Gunning, program manager of XAI, supervises the program and has become the public spokesperson as DARPA attempts to explain how a machine reasons. Gunning's work tills a common ground for Transhumans and Exoconscious Humans as they meet the challenges of moral reason in dialogues about the future of human consciousness.

As Gunning describes it, the problem with deep learning is that it is a black box. By that, he means that it is challenging to investigate the reasoning behind the decisions that deep learning makes. He attributes this to the opacity of AI algorithms, especially where mistakes can have severe impacts.

One of the XAI research areas is autonomous systems (self-driving cars, aircraft, ships, and submarines). In accidents, victims and specialists like insurers and attorneys will want to know how AI came to a decision. As Gunning describes it, they are "trying to explain the decision points and its decision logic as it is executing a mission."[178]

XAI consists of 11 teams working on similar projects to create explainability methods and AI models. They modify the AI learning

---

178 Ben Dickson, "Inside DARPA's effort to create explainable artificial intelligence," *TechTalks*, January 10, 2019.

process, producing a more explainable model, for example, pulling out information used for explanation. Next, they focus on clients, end-users, making it understandable for them. This method includes a description of the human-to-computer interface or using cognitive psychology to explain the process.

Furthermore, Gunning highlights the limits of deep learning and neural networks by referring to NYU professor and cognitive scientist, Gary Marcus who cites his agreement with Yoshua Bengio, who wrote in Technology Review,

> I think we need to consider the hard challenges of AI and not be satisfied with short-term, incremental advances. I'm not saying I want to forget deep learning. On the contrary, I want to build on it. But we need to be able to extend it to do things like reasoning, learning causality, and exploring the world to learn and acquire information.[179]

Paralleling Gunning's work, Marcus and Bengio promote the need for AI, deep learning to reason, making logical inferences, determine causality, and integrate abstract knowledge.

The scientific confusion experienced during COVID-19 exposed the limits of AI and deep learning when confronted with a mountain of disparate medical data to fashion feasible predictions. The World Health Organization (WHO), UK's Imperial College, Center for Disease Control (CDC), and professors at esteemed US universities disputed one another's findings. They developed proprietary systems and talked over one another when citizens asked for a voice of reason amid confusing information.

Conflicting information and guidance in treating health issues like epidemics and chronic disease opens a window of opportunity

---

179 Gary Marcus, "The deepest problem with deep learning," *Medium* December 1, 2018, https://medium.com/@GaryMarcus/the-deepest-problem-with-deep-learning-91c5991f5695.

to consider alternatives like frequency and consciousness-based healing. Refinement and expansion of these innovations are the building blocks of an Exoconscious Civilization. The source of this innovative path starts at an exotic location— the headwaters of the Amazon.

CHAPTER 7

EXOCONSCIOUS HUMAN
CIVILIZATION IS PREFERRED
SURVEILLANCE EMPIRE IS PREFERRED

Section 1

Seeding an Exoconscious Civilization

A young man with long dark hair pulled back in a tie stood to speak from the middle of the aisle of a conference in Brazil. He conversed in perfect English, having come from Belem, a city at the headwaters of the Amazon, and educated at a university in Florida. Lucas asked me a question. It was a simple but profound question that seeded many of the ideas of this book.

"How will you know if exoconsciousness is successful?"

Though I offered a partial response to Lucas, the truth was, not only did I not know the answer, but the possibility of success had not occurred to me. At the time, success and failure were not in my thoughts. Exoconsciousness was new and forming so quickly that, honestly, I was more focused on getting the concept into the international vernacular and providing a language structure for experiencers to discuss its details. I had not yet considered the ramifications of success or failure. What IF exoconsciousness succeeded? Lucas' question aroused me.

What if exoconsciousness spread through human awareness? What if we used it in everyday conversation? What would that mean for experiencers, for culture, for all sectors of our society? What would success look like?

In that moment, provoked by Lucas' question, exoconsciousness shifted into a new phase, from an idea to material reality. Contemplating success had many implications— intentions, relationships, projects, and an overarching emphasis on how an exoconscious life could be lived individually and in community.

Immediately, I began to list possibilities for success: acceptance of psychic intelligence, co-creation with ETs, multidimensionals, opportunities for free enterprise, freewill, peaceful prosperity, a fair and just economy, and health. All necessary for what I defined as a good life. And while this list warmed my heart, I knew that it was far too vague and idealized.

We needed to define successful exoconsciousness in practical reality. Not leave it in some idealized past or utopian future perspective. Instead, view human nature and behavior as given through verifiable facts. Social engineers validate this and use it to steer us into the preferred behaviors they wish to emphasize. Human nature and action, for the most part, remain constant. People act altruistically and selfishly, exhibit evil and goodness, trust their creativity, ignore their inner knowledge, and live both aware and asleep. How can exoconsciousness succeed in this reality?

As I shared in the book's introduction, Kyle Munkittrick's outline for the conditions for transhumanism's attainment provided a starting point for focusing on current reality. Rapidly unfolding transhumanism and technocracy are culturally dominant with little public analysis and factual discussion. Transhuman perspectives and lifestyles are culturally dominant. This dominance intensifies by the google search engine's overarching role, social, and journalistic media using AI. The infrastructure of space, social, and biological engineering strengthens transhumanism and technocracy. I thought long and hard about how exoconsciousness related to these immense movements that are now a mainstream reality.

Fortunately, at a saturation point, vision clears. Writing this book, I progressed through numerous emotional states of digesting transhumanism and technocracy. I felt denial, anger, resentment, futility, depression, confusion, vulnerability, invisibility, and fear. It took time to write this book because I needed to absorb, assimilate, and expand the ideas to create a healthy integration of what I learned.

Often I caught myself thinking about the unthinkable and digesting toxic information resulting in heartburn. I saw psychopathological intentions and manipulations. I moved through the darkness, shuffling, one step at a time.

Then came the most intense phase: confronting uncomfortable and complex questions about my human nature—not the "collective human nature." Was my exploration of transhumanism and technocracy more about me—my SELF—than I dared admit? What in me was capable of the toxic and dysfunctional applications I witnessed in transhumanism?

I recalled the 12 Steps of Alcoholics Anonymous, the 3rd step: Made a searching and fearless moral inventory of ourselves. This phase of inner work began. I forced myself to face how I cooperated with reality shaped by transhumanism and technocracy. Once I dug in, I uncovered loads of examples of my complicit ideas and behaviors. No wonder AA calls for being fearless. Our own "stuff" is the vilest.

Fear forced me to clarify what I assumed about the reality of my physical health—my innate ability to heal, my human mortality. Where did I stand on synthetic biology drugs and vaccines, GMOs, and socially engineered computer-modeled worldviews? Where did I stand on transhumanism replacing humans as parents, friends, and professionals? I challenged my views of online teaching vs. classroom teachers, social collective vs. family, online acquaintances vs. friends, and hybrid AI-humans across the full spectrum of businesses and employees—social workers, attorneys, military, journalists, police, social and service workers, health care practitioners, all professions. Was the well-intentioned green economy to save the Earth or open a path for Transhuman global cryptocurrency positioning humans as a commodity to be monitored and monetized? Were we further along than I imagined?

Exoconsciousness demands fearless individual moral examination. We examined this in the chapter on ethics with the discussion of the moral autonomy of Exoconscious Humans. The first requirement of exoconsciousness is an intimate examination, the fearless debris collection of our dark underbelly.

Throughout history, when confronted by unthinkable darkness, poetry finds words.

> And did those feet in ancient time,
> Walk upon England's mountains green?
> And was the holy lamb of god
> On England's pleasant pastures seen?

> And did the countenance divine,
> Shine forth upon our clouded hills?
> And was Jerusalem builded here
> Among these dark satanic mills?

The poet, William Blake, composed through feelings aroused by England's industrial age of black soot skies, grinding repetitious assembly lines, and cities crammed with impoverished people seeking work. He yearned for his Jerusalem of green and pleasant land, his utopia. Yet, looking back, through the industrial revolution, humans prevailed through this toxic sludge. History confirms that many factories closed or scrubbed their soot, workers trained for new careers, and England's pleasant green land remains. Nature remains.

Seeding Exoconscious Civilization

Significantly, a community of morally autonomous individuals who have ongoing, healthy contact, communication, and co-creation with ETs seed an Exoconscious Civilization. Humans remain. The characteristics and motivations of independent individuals with discerning ethics are ancient and reliable.

Exoconscious Humans replace the Transhuman view of humans as a Resource with a view of humans as sovereign. This sovereignty means that individuals hold themselves accountable and responsible for their beliefs and actions. It also means that sovereign individuals live within countries, states, communities and participate and respect their laws and regulations. It is a balanced view that empowers both the individual and communities.

Exoconscious Humans are not involved in replacing government, monetary, educational, judicial, corporate, or military systems; instead, they promote the necessity of being an informed citizen, eager to engage in a full spectrum of conversations. Exoconscious are apolitical, free of political ideology.

These sovereign individuals acknowledge the usefulness of AI in a computerized society but assert the need for vigorous oversight, mindful of human biological, psychological, and spiritual needs.

From Device to Psychic Intelligence: Exoconscious Humans focus on advancing and utilizing innate psychic intelligence. Their goal is to foster advanced consciousness to solve problems and create new products valued within one or more cultural settings. To that end, they are continually developing new ideas, inventions, and goods to be used by others.

The aim of developing and advancing psychic intelligence is to integrate Exoconscious Humans into all sectors. Exoconscious Humans work and contribute to every sector of society—health, justice, media, science/technology, spirituality, arts, economics, education, environment, and governance.

Claiming innate human psychic intelligence is a first step in becoming an Exoconscious Human. This step involves opening conscious awareness of their ability to continuously contact, communicate, and co-create with ETs and multidimensionals.

From Weapon to Collaborator: While groups within the military, government, universities, banking, and corporations seeded Transhumanism, moral individuals who practice respectful collaboration and strive to be in harmony with the natural Earth world of humans and multidimensions seed an Exoconscious Civilization. Exoconsciousness enhances harmony and balance of nature, not controlling or manipulating its essence.

Collaboration demands a high threshold of self-awareness, transparency, and education. It rejects control, compartmentalization, and secrecy and requires a multidisciplinary, generalist breadth of knowledge. This knowledge relates across a broad spectrum of subjects, synthesizing and viewing patterns and relationships. Transparency of subjective emotions, perceptions as well as information is essential for discussion and eventual agreement.

From Personal to Public Community

Eventually, Lucas' question metamorphosed into a vision of a community of Exoconscious Humans creating a civilization. An idea emerged of working together to create a reality founded in respect for all humans, acceptance of psychic intelligence, co-creation with ETs, multidimensionals, free enterprise opportunities, freewill, peaceful prosperity, a fair and just economy, health, and happiness.

Ancient, Not New

Self-refinement and analysis eventually led to a reaffirmation of what it means to be a healthy human. Like a pleasant green land, Exoconscious Humans thrive despite transhumanism and technocracy. We apply our cosmic consciousness—an ancient force driven forward by ancient feet.

But, again, to be clear, Exoconscious Humans are neither a NEW Human nor, as Stanford Research Institute posited—a "changed image of man to fit a new future." A discussion of New Humans or a New Age often translates into transhumanism and technocracy. Humans, as synthetic biology connected to a Space-Earth infrastructure in a technocratic economy. Humans as one of many economic resources to be metered, monitored, and monetized. Oneness in all.

Ideas to enslave humans or create "new humans" are not original. Cute marketing phrases cannot hide the truth. It is vital to briefly examine the history and some of the leading players and infrastructure of the New Human, or New Age movement, as it will reveal their transhuman, technocratic connections.

Section 2

Surveillance Empire is preferred
Seeding the Silicon Valley

In 1968 the US Office of Education commissioned Stanford Research Institute (SRI) to peer into the future and design possible scenarios. The result was a book called *Changing Images of Man*, edited by O.W. Markley and Willis Harman (cofounder of Institute for Noetic Sciences with Dr. Edgar Mitchell).[180] *Changing Images of Man* was later popularized by New Age proponent Marilyn Ferguson's book, *The Aquarian Conspiracy: Personal and Social Transformation in Our Time.*

SRI's vision was a "blueprint for a vast social engineering project undertaken by the very highest levels of the military/industrial complex."[181] SRI's vision was not new but had seeded the establishment of Silicon Valley since the 1930s.

Individuals may seed transhuman movements, but large organizations and infrastructures often promote and finance those individuals. Columbia University birthed and boosted technocracy. Military, government, universities, and corporations birthed and

---

180 You can download a copy of 1982 Changing Images of Man reprint at https://archive.org/stream/ChangingImagesOfMan/ChangingImagesOfMan-OCR_djvu.txt.

181 "10,000 Heroes - SRI and the Manufacturing of the New Age: Part One," March 2007, http://web.archive.org/web/20070324152205/http://dreamsend.wordpress.com/2007/03/19/10000-heroes-sri-and-the-manufacturing-of-the-new-age-part-one/#more-90.

promoted Silicon Valley transhumanism. That is transhumanism's bloodline—their family of origin.

Memes like New Age and New Humans are simply the public faces of a well established economic and cultural infrastructure. No magic. No mental gymnastics. No metaphysics. Just boots on the ground. Command, communication, control, and computerize—as we explored through synthetic biology and the Space-Earth Fence.

Differentiating Exoconscious Humans from the New Human and New Age of transhumanism expose separate root systems. The military pushed deeper into Silicon Valley in the early 30s when the Navy purchased Moffett Field as a hub for the aerospace industry to port the USS Macon. Moffett Field housed Ames Research Center (NASA), which in 1949 became the world's most massive wind tunnel, used for research and development.

Corporate roots also grew in the 30s with the founding of Hewlett Packard in Palo Alto, which was initially tasked with manufacturing oscilloscopes to display and analyze electronic signals. In the early 1940s, William Shockley invented the computer processor, semiconductor. His corporation was subsequently split by the "traitorous eight" who formed new computer-based corporations.

University-corporate root lines merged in earnest in the 1940s when Frederick Terman, dean of Stanford's School of Engineering, created the visionary tradition of encouraging faculty to launch businesses. Voila. A Terman designed win-win for university and industry that would spawn generations of Silicon profit. Startups, founded by Stanford faculty, became the university's benefactors as budgets soared. The university provided resources and stability. Professors depended on their university salaries while launching financially vulnerable startups. They also benefitted from a trained community of academic peers to discuss and expand ideas, a pool of potential professorial partners, university labs to test applications, and an eager free student workforce.

The university component's power and influence were heightened in 1969 when Stanford Research Institute founded ARPANET that became the internet of today, casting a global, cosmic net.

Corporate financing began in earnest in the early 1970s when Eugene Kleiner of Kleiner Perkins—a venture capital firm specializing in investing in incubation, early stage, and growth companies, took advantage of a once in a lifetime development opportunity. California proposed Interstate 280 between San Francisco and San Jose along the Santa Clara Valley. Kleiner wisely selected the halfway point, Sand Hill Road, for his firm's headquarters. Smack dab in a vortex of Silicon Valley.

Like the university, banks bought into the startup solution to boost their bottom line. Glass-Steagall, which set limitations on bank investment in risky securities, was overturned in 1999 with the Gramm-Leach-Bliley Act. This act opened the deposit drawers of banks to participate in commercial and investment. Bank money moved into hedge funds, startup ventures until Congress implemented the Volcker Rule, restoring a modified Glass-Steagall.

Not to be left out of the money loop, Stanford (Stanford Management, currently an endowment of 7,000 individual funds) and other heavily endowed universities quickly moved into risky investments, but potentially high yield investments: equities, hedge funds, and private equity. All in the name of university endowments. This closed-loop of characters—all university, finance-banking, startups-corporations—benefited from government and military contracts.

The US military, Department of Defense, was the primary Daddy Warbucks who created the sensation of Silicon Valley. Without the military/government, the Valley would have waned into minor significance.

According to Leslie Berlin, historian for the Silicon Valley Archives at Stanford, "All of modern high tech has the US Department of Defense to thank at its core, because this is where the money came from to be able to develop a lot of what is driving the technology that we're using today."[182]

---

182 April Dembosky, "Silicon Valley rooted in backing from US Military," *Financial Times*, June 2013, https://www.ft.com/content/8c0152d2-d0f2-11e2-be7b-00144feab7de.

While we like to hero-worship Steve Jobs and Bill Gates, the source of their inventions belonged to DARPA. [183] The CIA's non-profit, In-Q-Tel invented technologies that underlie Google, Yahoo, Facebook, and most data collecting corporations. In 2013 In-Q-Tell backed 59 IT companies involved in image and data analysis. Today, the number of IT companies they back, though difficult to find, must be significantly higher.

Despite Silicon Valley's media image as the home of geeky, quirky, creative, and rebellious geniuses, it is a closed family system. It is top-down, hierarchical, controlled, and not cool. This tech family identification emerges through the list of comfortably remunerated board members from the military, government, banking, investment, university, and intelligence that direct Silicon Valley firms. Silicon Valley family rule is a golden age where organizational bloodline, the family of origin, knew no bounds, as long as they followed strict adherence to CEO, executive allegiance.

But, even with this available history, not all family members revealed themselves. One curious group kept a low, if not a hidden profile.

Metaphysicians of the Valley

To reveal this group, we go back to Willis Harman, SRI, and the New Human, New Age visionaries of the Valley, who were keenly aware of the potentials of both Inner and Outer Space. They saw not only how the lines blurred between as above, so below, but they also capitalized (literally) on the potentials of technology mixed with metaphysics. Capturing consciousness was primary.

In the late 1940s, a small metaphysical community migrated from upstate New York to northern California. They transported religious and metaphysical knowledge and methods of creating new humans who could produce innovations.

---

183 "10 Brilliant DARPA inventions," *Transmissions Media*, https://transmissionsmedia.com/10-brilliant-darpa-inventions/.

Irish immigrants John and Agnes Varian joined Dr. William Dower's Temple of the People in Syracuse, New York. From Syracuse, they transported their Blavatsky, Besant metaphysical teachings to Halcyon, California, and established a community and healing practice specializing in treating addiction.

Russell and Sigurd Varian, the sons of John and Agnes, grew up in the Halcyon community and were inspired by their parents' teachings and scientific research. Eventually, Stanford recognized the young men's talent, and they joined early Silicon Valley entrepreneurs advancing their invention of the klystron—the chief component of radar, telecommunications, and microwave technologies.

During the early years of the 50s, the brothers established their company, Varian Associates, as a co-operative with employee-owned stock. They supported progressive social politics and lived in a cooperative. But eventually, the financial lure of military contracts and the Cold War led them to develop products for atomic bombs.[184]

Varian was the first Silicon Valley business to go public, and they became the first tenant in the Stanford Research Park, infused with ongoing military contracts. Government contracts continued to provide corporate funds for over forty years, through the 1990s.

Like the Varian brothers, Willis Harman and the New Age movement recognized that implementing their vision needed a mental reset to accomplish the future envisioned by the military. The mass culture's world view needed tweaking to accommodate new technology. Religion was a primary target in the *Changing Images of Man* agenda. It had to go. Out with religion, in with spirituality via promotion of drugs, meditation, and channeling. Recalling information about MK-ULTRA's use of drugs for mind control and the CIA's role in introducing LSD to the culture, San Francisco became another test market, a spirituality petri dish.

---

184 Christina Robertson and Jennifer Westerman, *Working on Earth: Class and Environmental Justice* (Las Vegas: University of Nevada Press, 2015).

But interestingly, much of the channeling movement, for example, *Course on Miracles*, was also carried out via the hidden hand of intelligence oversight, if not direct involvement. CIA operative, William Thetford, collaborated with medium Helen Schucman by typing, editing, promoting her *Course on Miracles*. Thetford and Schucman's academic home, Columbia University, was a breeding ground of technocracy, cybernetic social engineering, and intelligence operations. 2020 Presidential candidate Marianne Williamson, who launched her career publishing books based on *Course on Miracles*, further mainstreamed the CIA operation into the Oprah fanbase and political party discussions.

Historically, Stanford University, Silicon Valley's proud parent, promoted cybernetics and closed-loop mind control. In 2006, Stanford University artist, Robert Horn, unveiled a massive interactive mural visualizing the History of Ideas of Cybernetics and General Systems to celebrate the 50th anniversary of the International Society for the Systems at Sonoma State.[185] It is living art, as cybernetics is an ongoing process, with the art continually updated. If you believe cybernetics is a forgotten science—think again. Better yet, think outside a closed loop.

Transhuman Technocracy Formula

The military, government, universities, banking, and corporations parented and promoted Silicon Valley. Their family of origin also included a dominant lineage of Technocrats.

Technocracy is not a political system; it is an economic system open for all politicians and parties to participate. Genius. To review, according to Patrick Wood, it is an economic system of total control over resources, production, and consumption. Pricing based on service, manufacturing, and distribution energy replaces human-driven commercial systems such as supply and demand and free enterprise. Energy is the primary currency—digital, of course.

---

185 https://web.stanford.edu/~rhorn/a/recent/CyberneticsMural.pdf.

This energy is calculated by instantaneous measuring, monitoring, taxing, and auditing of every human possession, production, consumption via the IoT, internet of things. National and international spending priorities include expanded IoT, social engineering, and geospatial intelligence.

For Transhuman technocracy to succeed, humans gradually had to adopt a new identity (including ID 2020). Transhuman identity for technocracy cultivates three dominant human identities: Humans as Resource, Humans as Device, and Humans as Weapon. Do you see the military, transhuman, technology, and technocratic overlay throughout our global culture?

Humans as Resource incorporates humans as a factor in technocracy's economic system of total control over resources. Through massive data mining, humans became an essential financial component, surveillance programs carried out by the military, government, universities, banking, and corporations. These surveillance tools include Google, Genome, Facebook, all social media, Sentient World Simulation, and Clearview. Our trail and movements instantly marked and monetized. Humans become akin to Rockefeller oil—full of myth and confusion.

In 1892, Rockefeller sent representatives to a science conference in Geneva to boost oil prices based on scarcity, where participants discussed and identified an organic substance. They concluded that organic substances were hydrogen, oxygen, and carbon. Thus, Rockefeller's representatives cited that oil formed from living matter since its composition was hydrogen, oxygen, and carbon. The term fossil fuel was born. And the myth remains alive today through iterations like "peak oil."[186] Implying the deadline when we run out of dinosaur remains.

Spinning the myth and confusion of humans as a commodity began in earnest during COVID-19. Andrew Cuomo, Governor of New York, announced an alliance between his state and former

---

186 Colonel Fletcher Prouty explains history of how oil was fasely classified a "fossil fuel" in 1892, https://youtu.be/vdSjyvIHVLw.

Google CEO Eric Schmidt to set up a blue-ribbon billionaire commission to reimagine the state's post-COVID-reality. The solution involved permanently integrating technology into every aspect of civic life. Of course, the commission also included Bill Gates, who would re-vision an educational and medical system. Others would develop a technological prison and law enforcement system.

Suddenly, a host of hands-on professionals became obsolete: teachers, social workers, police, clergy, artists, therapists, nurses, doctors. Helping professions replaced by technology.

Anuja Sonalker, CEO of Steer Tech, a Maryland technology company, summed up the new human myth and confusion: " Humans are biohazards, machines are not."[187] In a COVID political reality, humans are too dirty to touch other humans. Suddenly humans are a virus-ridden species, a cockroach not to be touched and eventually exterminated.

Will we be aware when humans, a commodity resource to be mined and processed, are labeled as either scarce or peaked? What will be our byproducts (sludge) as a recyclable resource? What will be the technocratic, transhuman myths and confusion that define us?

As a resource, will future humans be traded on the commodity market in Chicago and New York? Are we identified as hard commodities such as oil and other natural resources? Or are we soft commodities such as livestock and agriculture? Or are we a new category?

Humans as Device incorporates humans as another technological device on the IoT. Psychologist Erich Fromm coined the term "gadget man" in his book *On Being Human*. He warned about creating conditions for *homo consumens* or *homo technicus* or gadget

---

187 Naomi Klein, "Screen New Deal, Under Cover of mass death, Andrew Cuomo Calls in the billionaires to build a high-tech dystopia,"May 8, 2020, https://theintercept.com/2020/05/08/andrew-cuomo-eric-schmidt-coronavirus-tech-shock-doctrine/.

man. Humans, as devices, are similar to an incarnated gadget. Fromm also speculated that humans love mechanical gadgets more than living beings. Perhaps more accurate speculation would be that it is easier for humans to form a relationship with mechanical gadgets than living beings. Synthetics and metals may be a more desirable, less challenging attachment than other humans. As devices on the IoT, humans experience not only isolation; they also experience activation as a device and alienation as another accessory.

Are humans aware of their activation as a device on the IoT, for example, through 5G or 6G activating the synthetic nanotechnology biology in their body? Will humans know when they are triggered as a device—turned off and on?

Humans as Weapon casts human identity into the role of weaponry—like a knife, saber, gun, missile—used against themselves and others. Steered through the IoT, humans may attack as a kind of hive mind against a determined target like a swarm surrounding an enemy. Does this targeting now occur politically through social media? Might social media be more interested in running experiments to test how humans can target as a hive than they are with advocating for one side of politics or the other? Since social media technology is military sourced, it is a logical assumption. Indeed, the military has sights on hive attack—super-soldiers equipped with neural-internet connections marshal their forces in unison to accomplish a military objective. Stormtroopers built to swarm on command.

Are humans aware of being mobilized for swarm activities to carry out objectives orchestrated through IoT? Are humans prepared to forfeit their autonomous free will to participate in these swarm IoT activities?

You may ask, how is this possible? Won't human refuse, push back? That depends on the extent of their synthetic biology's connection to IoT or Internet of Biology. That depends on how far AI and biotech compromise human critical thinking. That depends on the suppression of human consciousness.

Dissociation, Dilution, and Denial

Psychologically, human behavior cooperates and even welcomes their identity on IoT. Three powerful influences determine this cooperation: Dissociation, Dilution, and Denial.

Dissociation As dissociated, humans lack secure, healthy attachments and security. They quickly fall prey to fantasy play, cultural memes, and hallucinogenic drugs. Over time, they prefer a dissociated reality found online through entertainment, social media, and drugs, which encourages them to adopt a new identity quickly.

Dilution Through dilution of knowledge and information, humans perceive both history and tradition as flawed and antiquated. New ideas are effortlessly found by scanning AI created news headlines, watching short videos, listening to an audiobook, or watching documentaries filled with memetics. New ideas are entertaining, immediate, and reactive. By comparison, an in-depth study of ideas and history accessible in primary sources found in libraries and thoughtful discussions is time-consuming, demanding critical thinking and intellectual discipline to restrain jumping to false conclusions.

Denial exposes an inability to tap into one's inner knowing to define reality. This inner knowing includes psychic intelligence, especially intuition, to navigate life and read the environment. Instead of consciousness, the first navigational beacons for self and environment are Google maps, engineered entertainment, and social media discussions and rewards through comments and likes. CERN and other extensive behavioral data-gathering tools are psychic barometers. Algorithms create all-knowing, synchronistic online events.

Beyond dissociation, dilution and denial lie integration, strength, and responsibility, values of an Exoconscious Human, embodied in the Institute for Exoconsciousness (I-EXO).

Chapter 8

Conclusion

The Institute for Exoconsciousness: I-EXO.com

What IF exoconsciousness is Successful? How would life change? What is I-EXO's vision of the future?

I-EXO predicts that the presence of ETs and multidimensionals will continue to emerge on our planet. With this, communication and co-creation among humans and ETs, multidimensionals will influence one another's realities and open vistas of possibilities.

More than a future prediction, exoconsciousness is a present reality that unfolded gradually. In 2016 an international mastermind of experiencers gathered monthly to discuss how to implement exoconsciousness. Two years later, a website (I-EXO. com), formal 501c3 status, and a working Board of Advisors was in place.

I-EXO is the first nonprofit startup whose mission is to develop exoconsciousness to elevate, advance, and protect natural human consciousness. Human consciousness is an invaluable resource. It allows us to reach our highest evolution as a species. The driving force behind I-EXO is to safeguard this asset. This safeguarding can only be accomplished by first understanding the critical importance of preserving our human consciousness's role in our evolution to the next level of its expected growth.

I-EXO is the first organization to support human innovation and creativity by working with natural human and off-world intelligence. We aspire to the achievement of this lofty purpose. The Institute has two goals to support this mission.

Seeding co-created inventions and innovations

Through its Entrepreneurial Division, I-EXO mentors and funds various creative inventions, designs, devices, and innovations to benefit humankind and planetary well-being. These invention categories include healing, agriculture, energy, technology, economics, education, communication, and spirituality.

Educating a generation of co-creators

The role of the I-EXO's Educational Division is to educate and network inventors, creators, and thinkers. The Educational Division, I-EXO Academy, offers training, conferences, social platforms, and learning centers to encourage exoconscious development.

Foundational Principles

Three foundational principles necessary for the Institute's success include:

Trust: Transparency assumes trust. For Exoconscious Humans, trust is consistent with healthy behavior over time. Trust is a trial and error process with a built-in gauge of moral awareness, a willingness to make a searching and fearless moral inventory of ourselves. Not others—ourselves.

Trust prioritizes conscious awareness and core knowledge. This knowledge includes the practice of learning to translate and utilize psychic intelligence—a trial and error process of refinement.

Trust as consistency highlights a commitment to shift psychic intelligence into the material world. This shift emphasizes the importance of authenticating psychic intelligence before sharing. The social media world overflows with an ever-changing array of psychic predictions and promotions regarding the past, present, and future. This wave of predictions will continue, but Exoconscious

Humans hold back, submitting themselves to a high standard until the time is right.

Authentication is the standard. Authentication asks: does it work? Has the information been carefully vetted to provide evidence? Has the idea been sufficiently implemented to prove authentication? Philosophers, religious, paranormal, and spiritual practitioners have long sought to integrate metaphysics and the physical world—psychic ideas and the material world. Another standard of authentication is whether the innovations and ideas are grounded in goodness or fear, life or destruction, nature, or artificial reality. We continue in the tradition in a careful, deliberate, and disciplined manner.

Freedom of Will and Enterprise are foundational as Exoconscious Humans create an infrastructure to integrate the psychic and the material. I-EXO is a trustworthy, transparent organization dedicated to bringing practical products seeded through psychic intelligence and exoconscious connections into the mainstream. I-EXO authenticates the intent and accomplishment of these products, including ethical standards of application. Ethics and human freedom are lynchpins: free will spirit embodied in exploration and creativity and free enterprise to produce products beneficial for all.

Listed below are some possible examples of I-EXO innovations conducted with co-creation:

Biology: Work enhancing the body's natural health and lifespan through hands-on, collaborative, or remote types of energy healing modalities.

Agriculture: Utilizing nature's energies for robust seed growth, plant production, and agricultural practices.

Technology: Development of protection systems to safeguard human freedom of thought, creativity, will, and enterprise.

Communication/Community: Forming a holistic mind, body, and spirit connection to the cosmos to reestablish self-aware, secure, and multi-dimensionally balanced perceptions and communications.

Economy: Establishing systems that allow free enterprise, trade, and flexibility in work-based upon individual choices free of artificial manipulation.

Education: Advancing exoconscious learning styles based upon natural human capacities, including psychic exploration and the full range of consciousness experience.

Spirituality: Fostering exoconscious humans in collaboration with consciousness scientists to bring about a deeper understanding of the nature of immortality, soul, and spirit.

More information is available at I-EXO.com. We invite your support and participation.

Appendix I

Exoconscious Human

Bill of Rights

Preamble

We, Exoconscious Humans, confirm the Extraterrestrial Presence on Earth. This confirmation results from accumulated information from seven decades of Ufology research on craft sightings, landings, and contactees' experiences. This information gleaned from a historical, eyewitness, scientific sources, and independent study. Extraterrestrial research is on-going but now re-contextualized with confirmation of an extraterrestrial and multidimensional presence.

We confirm the Field of Cosmic Consciousness in which humans and extraterrestrials share information and energy. We define humans who experience this shared cosmic consciousness as Exoconscious. These humans are aware of, working with, and living through the extraterrestrial origins, dimensions, and abilities of their human consciousness. Exoconsciousness is an innate ability to contact, communicate, and co-create with extraterrestrials.

We declare that Exoconscious Humans have the following rights and freedoms by confirmation of the Extraterrestrial Presence and the shared human-extraterrestrial field of Cosmic Consciousness, which is Exoconsciousness.

Exoconscious Human Bill of Rights

Exoconscious Humans have a right to express and manifest their relationship with extraterrestrials without fear of rebuke, judgment, harm, or retribution from other humans, governments, and organizations.

Exoconscious Humans have a right to live in multidimensional consciousness, free of the confines and control of limited brain-centered mind theories and artificial mind-control technologies.

Exoconscious Humans have a right to stand independently in the wisdom of their personal extraterrestrial experience—free of isolation, denial, and diagnosis by experts and institutions void of exoconscious experience.

Exoconscious Humans have a right to create a new language that expresses extraterrestrial contact.

Exoconscious Humans have a right to shift or create new timelines, free of ancient prophecies, stories, sources, and control systems.

Exoconscious Humans have a right to be trustworthy, healthy, and creative—free of violence, trauma, and fear that once defined extraterrestrial contact.

Exoconscious Humans have a right to access all Earth and Cosmic knowledge to explore their extraterrestrial origins and connections.

Exoconscious Humans have the right to nourish, perpetuate, and develop a culture of human consciousness based on connecting, communicating, and peer-to-peer co-creation with extraterrestrials

Exoconscious Humans have the right to share their ET contact and communication experiences openly and honestly, as a primary Ufology source.

Exoconscious Humans have the right to freedom from algorithmic, game-theory based AI manipulation and communication. We have the right to ignore and dismiss all AI communication. We have the right to refuse participation in an artificial reality.

Exoconscious Humans have a right to information regarding their taxation and financial reporting standards. We have a right to request and be promptly provided information on all government programs funded by our taxes and provided oversight through government accounting practices and reporting standards. We have a right to free research to obtain this information.

Exoconscious Humans have a right to receive support, respect, and compassion from other ET experiencers. We have a right to join the emerging community of citizens who live the paranormal as normal—exoconscious, near-death experiencers, psychics, mediums, and spiritual healers.

Exoconscious Humans have a right to use and advance all of their psychic abilities in a spirit of love, kindness, and peace.

Exoconscious Humans have a right to live holistic, healthy, and integrated lives, sharing the field of cosmic consciousness with extraterrestrials and multidimensionals.

Rebecca Hardcastle Wright, Ph.D., 2009, Phoenix, Arizona Revised 2014 Laramie, Wyoming

BIBLIOGRAPHY

"10 Brilliant DARPA inventions." *Transmissions Media*. https://transmissionsmedia.com/10-brilliant-darpa-inventions/.

"10,000 Heroes-SRI and the Manufacturing of the New Age: Part One". March 2007. http://web.archive.org/web/20070324152205/http://dreamsend.wordpress.com/2007/03/19/10000-heroes-sri-and-the-manufacturing-of-the-new-age-part-one/#more-90.

5G Appeal. https://www.jrseco.com/wp-content/uploads/2017-09-13-Scientist-Appeal-5G-Moratorium.pdf.

Amen, Daniel. "The Neuroscience of Psychic Experience." https://www.doctoroz.com/article/neuroscience-psychic-experience.

Aubeck, Chris. http://ufoupdateslist.com/2003/may/m30-027.shtml.

Brain States Technology. https://brainstatetech.com/.

Brookings Institution. https://ntrs.nasa.gov/archive/nasa/casi.ntrs.nasa.gov/19640053196.pdf.

Budello, Luca. "The Power of Place: Geospatial is Transforming our World". *Geospatial World*, October 2020. https://www.geospatialworld.net/blogs/geospatial-is-transforming-our-world/

Campbell, Colin. "Researchers Criticize CBS film 'First Steps'". *New York Times*, March 21, 1985. https://www.nytimes.com/1985/03/21/arts/researchers-criticize-cbs-film-first-steps.html.

Cannon, Dolores. "The Three Waves of Volunteers and the New Earth: Three Generations of New Souls", https://dolorescannon.com/waves-volunteers-earth-generations-souls/.

Chalmers, David. "Toward a Scientific Basis of Consciousness." http://consc.net/papers/facing.pdf.

Changing Images of Man reprint. https://archive.org/stream/ChangingImagesOfMan/ChangingImagesOfMan-OCR_djvu.txt.

Chaturvedi, Dr. Alok, Tony Cerri. "Sentient World Simulation (SWS): A Continuously Running Model of the Real World." https://krannert.purdue.edu/academics/mis/workshop/AC2_100606.pdf.

Clynes, M. & Kline N., 1960, "Cyborgs and Space", Astronautics. http://www.guicolandia.net/files/expansao/Cyborgs_Space.pdf.

Coleman, John. "Tavistock: The Best Kept Secret in America." July 2001. https://www.educate-yourself.org/nwo/nwotavistockbest-keptsecret.shtmle.

Crowe, Jack. "AOC's Chief of Staff Admits the Green New Deal Is Not about Climate Change." https://www.nationalreview.com/news/aocs-chief-of-staff-admits-the-green-new-deal-is-not-about-climate-change/.

Crowley, Tony. Lo-tech Navigator. Sea Farer Books, 2004.

David, River. "Forget 5G for a moment. Instead imagine 6G". Wall Street Journal. April 12, 2020. https://www.wsj.com/articles/forget-5g-for-a-moment-instead-imagine-6g-11586743200.

Dembosky, April. Silicon Valley rooted in backing from US military." Financial Times, June 2013. https://www.ft.com/content/8c0152d2-d0f2-11e2-be7b-00144feab7de.

DeRose, Chris."Genecoin: DNA For the Blockchain." Bitcoin Magazine, November 2014. https://bitcoinmagazine.com/articles/genecoin-dna-for-the-blockchain-1415660431.

DeWitt, Bruce, Neill Graham. The Many-Worlds Interpretation of Quantum Mechanics. Princeton Series in Physics, 1973.

Dickson, Ben. "Inside DARPA's effort to create explainable artificial intelligence." TechTalks, January 10, 2019.

DiSalvo, David. "Study finds the unexpected in Brains of Spirit Mediums." Psychology Today, December 2012. https://www.

psychologytoday.com/us/blog/neuronarrative/201212/
study-finds-the-unexpected-in-the-brains-spirit-mediums-0.

Doffman, Zak. "COVID-19's New Reality—These Smartphone
APPS Track infected People Nearby." *Forbes*, April 7, 2020.
https://www.forbes.com/sites/zakdoffman/2020/04/07/covid-
19s-new-normal-yes-your-phone-will-track-infected-people-
nearby/#d85a52e7f0db.

Don, Norman, Gilda Moura. "Topographic Brain Mapping of
UFO Experiencers." *Journal of Scientific Exploration*, Vol 11, No.
4, pp 435-453, 1997. https://pdfs.semanticscholar.org/a171/
f52e058266cbe69cbc3a9efec7c7f464c4f8.pdf.

Durden, Tyler. "Your every move will be watched: Post COVID offices
to resemble China's social credit system." May 2020, https://
www.zerohedge.com/health/your-every-move-will-be-watched-
post-covid-offices-will-resemble-chinas-social-credit-system

Dyson, Freeman. *Disturbing the Universe*. New York: Basic Books,
1981.

Engelking, Carl. "Reprogrammed Bacteria Build Self-Healing
'Living Materials'." *Discover*, March 24, 2014. https://www.
discovermagazine.com/technology/reprogrammed-bacteria-
build-self-healing-living-materials.

Epstein, Jeremy. "Companies of the Future, No Boss, Managed
by Blockchain." *Never Stop Marketing* https://venturebeat.
com/2017/04/23/companies-of-the-future-no-ceo-no-boss-
managed-by-blockchain/.

Estulin, Daniel. *Tavistock Institute: Social Engineering the Masses*. Trine
Day, 2015.

Farr, Christina. "How a handful of Apple and Google employees
came together to help health officials trace Coronavirus."
CNBC, April 4, 2020. https://www.cnbc.com/2020/04/28/
apple-iphone-contact-tracing-how-it-came-together.html.

Farrell, Joseph. *The Third Way: Nazi International, European Union
and Corporate Fascism* (Adventures Unlimited, 2015).

Fenwick P, Galliano S, Coate MA, Rippere V, Brown D. "'Psychic
Sensitivity', Mystical Experience, Head Injury and Brain

Pathology." *British Journal of Medical Psychology*, March 1985. https://www.ncbi.nlm.nih.gov/pubmed/3986152.

Fernandes and D'Armada. *Celestial Secrets: The Hidden History of the Fatima Incident.* Anomalist Books, 2007.

Festinger, Leon Festinger, *A Theory of Cognitive Dissonance.* Stanford University Press, 1962.

Florida Atlantic University, "Depression study examines levels of 'love' hormone and its impacts on mother-baby emotional bonding" Science News, March 2016. https://www.sciencedaily.com/releases/2016/03/160322100712.htm.

Freeland, Elana. *Under an Ionized Sky: From Chemtrails to Space Fence Lockdown.* Port Townsend, Washington: Feral House, 2018.

Friedman, Matthew J. "PTSD History and Overview." Last updated on February 23, 2016. https://www.ptsd.va.gov/professional/ptsd-overview/ptsd-overview.asp.

Gardner, Howard E. *Frames of Mind: The Theory of Multiple Intelligences.* New York: Basic Books, 1983.

Gazit, Mark. "The Fourth Generation of AI is here and it's called Artificial Intuition" *The Next Web*, September 2020. https://thenextweb.com/neural/2020/09/03/the-fourth-generation-of-ai-is-here-and-its-called-artificial-intuition/.

Gyarmathy, Kaylie. "Comprehensive Guide to IoT Statistics You Need to Know in 2020". https://www.vxchnge.com/blog/iot-statistics.

Hardcastle Wright, Rebecca. "An Exoconscious Human Reality." *Journal of Abduction Encounter Research*, November 2017. http://www.jar-magazine.com/in-depth/76-exoconscious-human-reality.

Hardcastle Wright, Rebecca. "An Exoconscious Proposal: The Common Ground of Consciousness Science and Psychic Intelligence." https://goo.gl/MqBIMn (2015).

Hardcastle Wright, Rebecca. "An Exoconscious Reality." *Medium.* https://medium.com/@Exoconscious/an-exoconscious-human-reality-f278a78cc4c4.

Hardcastle Wright, Rebecca. "Edgar Mitchell Wikileaks Email to John Podesta is Authentic." *Exoconsciousness Blog,*

October 19, 2016. https://rebeccahardcastlewright.com/edgar-mitchell-wikileak-email-to-john-podesta-is-accurate/.

Hardcastle Wright, Rebecca. "Exoconsciousness: Beyond the Brain A Second Chance." *Exopolitics Journal,* January 2006. https://exopoliticsjournal.com/Journal-vol-1-2.htm.

Hardcastle, Rebecca. *Exoconsciousness: Your 21st Century Mind.* Authorhouse, 2008.

Hausdorf, Hartwig. *The Chinese Roswell: Ufo Encounters in the Far East from Ancient Times to the Present.* New Paradigm Books, 1998.

Hernandez, Rey, Joh Klimo, Rudy Schild. *Beyond UFOs: The Science of Consciousness and Contact with Non Human Intelligence.* Volume 1, FREE, 2018.

Hinchliffe, Tim. "India's ban on paper money, cashless societies and the loss of freedom." https://sociable.co/technology/cashless-societies/.

Horgan, John. "A Dig Through Old Files Reminds Me Why I'm So Critical of Science." *Scientific American,* November 2, 2013. https://blogs.scientificamerican.com/cross-check/a-dig-through-old-files-reminds-me-why-ie28099m-so-critical-of-science/.

http://avalonlibrary.net/Dragonfly_Drones_CARET_document_archive/MUFON%20Special%20Investigation%20Drones%20and%20the%20CARET%20Documents.pdf.

http://spiritwaywellness.com.

http://www.asc-cybernetics.org/foundations/history/MacyPeople.htm.

http://www.chemtrailplanet.com/PDF/DrColetestimony-Checmtral%20biochemwarfaretesting.pdf.

http://www.stopsprayingcalifornia.com/What-are-they-Spraying.html.

https://blombladivinden.wordpress.com/2012/03/05/can-a-satellite-read-your-thoughts-physics-revealed/.

https://celestrak.com/columns/v04n01/.

https://emerj.com/ai-case-studies/news-organization-leverages-ai-generate-automated-narratives-big-data/.

https://en.wikipedia.org/wiki/Augmented_reality.

https://en.wikipedia.org/wiki/Decade_of_the_Brain.

https://en.wikipedia.org/wiki/The_Leonardo_da_Vinci_Society_
for_the_Study_of_Thinking.

https://forbiddenknowledgetv.net/history-is-made-two-google-
engineers-join-forces-to-expose-tech-tyranny/?utm_
source=newsletter&utm_medium=email&utm_campaign=Two
+Google+Engineers+Expose+Tech+Tyranny.

https://history.howstuffworks.com/history-vs-myth/iroquois-
great-law-peace-source-us-constitution.htm.

https://id2020.org/.

https://pdfs.semanticscholar.org/380d/9d470d607f51975fe0cae7
6a136dec0bbef3.pdf?_ga=2.83234704.704052089.1579217693-
1443367240.1579217693.

https://qz.com/1205017/saudi-arabias-robot-citizen-is-eroding-
human-rights/.

https://science.howstuffworks.com/question529.htm.

https://web.stanford.edu/~rhorn/a/recent/CyberneticsMural.pdf.

https://www.academia.edu/10671835/Comparing_the_Hindu_
theory_of_atman_with_the_Buddhist_theory_of_no-self._
Which_is_more_plausible.

https://www.academia.edu/5490549/The_Culture_Of_
Individualism_And_Collectivism_In_Balancing_
Accountability_And_Innovation_In_Education_An_Islamic_
Perspective.

https://www.academyfraternitatem.com/.

https://www.armstrongeconomics.com/international-news/dis-
ease/nurse-speaks-out-that-people-are-being-murdered-in-hos-
pitals/.

https://www.cnbc.com/2019/06/01/how-much-do-uber-drivers-
really-make-three-drivers-share-the-math.html.

https://www.earthfiles.com/?s=issac+caret&cat=0.

https://www.etymonline.com/word/matrix.

https://www.forbes.com/sites/gregautry/2019/05/21/
space-launch-overheating/#57bd05217732.

https://www.genome.gov/human-genome-project.

https://www.geospatialworld.net/blogs/do-you-know-how-many-satellites-earth/.

https://www.heavyionalert.org/docs/CERNContradictions.pdf.

https://www.hofstede-insights.com/country-comparison/.

https://www.hofstede-insights.com/country-comparison/india/.

https://www.iep.utm.edu/ind-chin/ Individualism in Classical Chinese Thought.

https://www.mirror.co.uk/tech/watch-sophia-sexy-robot-claim-7606152.

https://www.optometrystudents.com/vision-therapy-neuroplasticity-optometry-student-perspective/.

https://www.pbssocal.org/programs/amanpour-co/clearview-ai-ceo-defends-facial-recognition-software-nuyagm/.

https://www.smartrac-group.com/about.

https://www.statnews.com/2020/03/17/a-fiasco-in-the-making-as-the-coronavirus-pandemic-takes-hold-we-are-making-decisions-without-reliable-data/.

https://www.studentsforliberty.org/2017/05/22/ibrahim-anoba-libertarian-thought-individualism-african-morality/.

https://www.universetoday.com/140769/the-large-hadron-collider-has-been-shut-down-and-will-stay-down-for-two-years-while-they-perform-major-upgrades/.

https://www.wanttoknow.info/bluebird10pg.

https://www.weforum.org/about/world-economic-forum

https://www.youtube.com/channel/UCsT4PTgK2D-wgCzrB_t6ZSw.

Huxley, Julian. *Transhumanism: In New Bottles for New Wine*. London: Chatto & Windus, 1957.

"Inside DARPA, The Pentagon Agency Whose Technology Has 'Changed the World'." *NPR*, March 2017. https://www.npr.org/2017/03/28/521779864/inside-darpa-the-pentagon-agency-whose-technology-has-changed-the-world.

James Mitchell Crow, "Life 2.0: inside the synthetic biology revolution, Cosmos: The Science of Everything." *Cosmos*,

April 17, 2018, https://cosmosmagazine.com/biology/life-2-0-inside-the-synthetic-biology-revolution

John Mack Institute. "Human Transformation and Alien Encounters." http://johnemackinstitute.org/category/human-transformation-and-alien-encounters/.

Johns Hopkins University, "Researchers get humans to think like computers." *Science Daily*, March 22, 2019. https://www.science-daily.com/releases/2019/03/190322090239.htm.

Jotterand, F. "Human Dignity and Transhumanism: Do Anthro-Technological Devices Have Moral Status?" *The American Journal of Bioethics*, doi:10.1080/15265161003728795 sci-hub.tw/10.1080/15265161003728795.

Justice, Blair. *Who Gets Sick: Thinking and Health*. Peak Press, 1987.

Keith, Jim. *Mass Control: Engineering Human Consciousness*. Adventures Unlimited Press, 2003.

Kelleher, Colm. "Retrotransposons as Engines of Human Bodily Transformation." https://wmthost.com/ndeinfo/ndeinfo/Human%20Bodily%20Transformation.pdf.

Klein, Naomi. "Screen New Deal, Under Cover of mass death, Andrew Cuomo Calls in the Billionaires to build a High-tech Dystopia." *The Intercept*, May 8, 2020, https://theintercept.com/2020/05/08/andrew-cuomo-eric-schmidt-coronavirus-tech-shock-doctrine/.

Lipton, Bruce. *The Biology of Belief: Unleashing the Power of Consciousness, Matter, & Miracles*. Hay House, 2008.

Lowe, Larry. "Dr. Edgar Mitchell, The Unexpected Benefit of Apollo 14." *Journal of Anomalous Science*, 2012. https://www.paradigmresearchgroup.org/graphics/Unexpected%20Benefit%20of%20Apollo%2014.pdf.

Mack, John. "Interview with John Mack Psychiatrist, Harvard University.", *Nova Online*, 1996. http://www.pbs.org/wgbh/nova/aliens/johnmack.html.

Mack, John. *Passport to the Cosmos: Human Transformations and Alien Encounters*. Three Rivers Press, 2000.

Mahany, Barbara and Jack Houston. "Mom, 2 Kids Reunited." *Chicago Tribune*, May 1, 1985, https://www.chicagotribune.com/news/ct-xpm-1985-05-01-8501260604-story.html.

Manobianco, John. Global Environmental Mems Sensors (Gems): A Revolutionary Observing System for the 21st Century, https://people.eecs.berkeley.edu/~pister/publications/2004/Manobianco%20GEMS.pdf.

Marcus, Gary. "The deepest problem with deep learning." *Medium*. December 1, 2018. https://medium.com/@GaryMarcus/the-deepest-problem-with-deep-learning-91c5991f5695.

Marr, Bernard. "Smart Dust Is Coming. Are You Ready?" *Forbes*, September 16, 2018. https://www.forbes.com/sites/bernardmarr/2018/09/16/smart-dust-is-coming-are-you-ready/#1fd7a90f5e41.

Michael, Donald M. "Proposed Studies on the Implications of Peaceful Space Activities." The Brookings Institution 1960. http://www.nicap.org/papers/brookings.pdf.

Mitchell, Edgar. "Nature's Mind: The Quantum Hologram." http://www.experiencer.org/natures-mind-the-quantum-hologram-by-edgar-mitchell-sc-d/.

Mitchell, William. *Me++: The Cyborg Self and the Networked City*. Cambridge: MIT Press, 2004.

Mizokami, Kyle. "The U.S. Space Force Is Ready to Turn on Its All-Seeing 'Space Fence'." *Popular Mechanics*, February 7, 2020. https://www.popularmechanics.com/military/weapons/a30798053/us-space-force-space-fence/.

More, Max. "Technological Self-Transformation: Expanding Personal Entropy." *Extropy* #10, 4:2

Morton, Timothy. *Hyperobjects: Philosophy and Ecology after the End of the World*. Posthumanities, 2013.

Muehsam, Chevalier, Barsotti, and Gurfein. "An Overview of Biofield Devices." https://www.ncbi.nlm.nih.gov/pmc/articles/PMC4654784/.

Munkittrick, Kyle. "When will We be Transhuman: Seven Conditions for attaining Transhumanism." *Discover Magazine*.

https://www.discovermagazine.com/mind/when-will-we-be-transhuman-seven- conditions-for-attaining-transhumanism.

Murray, Alan and David Meyer, "Why Accenture thinks the 'Henry Ford moment of the digital era' is coming", *Fortune Magazine*, September 2020. https://fortune.com/2020/09/17/accenture-julie-sweet-digital-transformation-ceo-daily/.

Nowak, Claire. "Why do we use Emojis anyway? A Fascinating History of Emotions." *Reader's Digest*, https://www.rd.com/culture/history-of-emoji/.

Paddison, Sara. *The Hidden Power of the Heart: Achieving Balance and Fulfillment in a Stressful World.* Planetary Publications, 1993.

Pangaro, Paul. "What is Cybernetics?" https://youtu.be/Oad8Ro8j_fE.

Peters, Ronald. "Epigenetics: The Science of Gene Regulation." https://youtu.be/Es9F_9fcyVc.

Peters, Ronald. "The Natural Therapeutic Experience: Living from your Heart," https://www.healmindbody.com/the-natural-therapeutic-experience/.

Pionic."LHC Could Reveal Possible Parallel Universe." *Medium,* March 2017. https://medium.com/r3fl3ct1ons/lhc-could-reveal-possible-parallel-universe-c1a18b794390.

Poponin, Vladimir. "The DNA phantom effect Direct Measurement of a New Field in the Vacuum Substructure." *Worlds Within Worlds*

Potin, Mark Williams. "The Total Information Awareness Project Lives On." *MIT Technology Review*, April 2006. https://www.technologyreview.com/2006/04/26/229286/the-total-information-awareness-project-lives-on/.

"Program for Extraordinary Experience Research." http://johnemackinstitute.org/2003/01/program-for-extraordinary-experience-research-peer/.

Prosser, Michael B. *Memetics—A Growth Industry in US Military Operations*, Academic Year 2005-2006. https://apps.dtic.mil/dtic/tr/fulltext/u2/a507172.pdf.

Prouty, Colonel Fletcher. https://youtu.be/vdSjyvIHVLw.

"Quantum-dot tattoos hold vaccination record.". https://bioengineering.rice.edu/news/quantum-dot-tattoos-hold-vaccination-record.

Rappoport, Jon. "Altering Human Genetics Through Vaccination." https://childrenshealthdefense.org/news/altering-human-genetics-through-vaccination/.

Reedy, Christianna. "Kurzweil Claims That the Singularity Will Happen by 2045 Get ready for humanity 2.0. Futurism." https://futurism.com/kurzweil-claims-that-the-singularity-will-happen-by-2045.

Ring, Kenneth. *The Omega Project: Near-Death Experiences, Ufo Encounters, and Mind at Large.* New York: William Morrow, 1992.

Robertson, Christina, Jennifer Westerman. *Working on Earth: Class and Environmental Justice.* University of Nevada Press, 2015.

Rodwell, Mary. *The New Human: Awakening to our Cosmic Heritage.* New Mind Publishers, 2016.

Rosin, Carol. "Opening Interview with Carol Rosin about the Late Wernher von Braun, " Ventura California, 2004. https://www.bibliotecapleyades.net/exopolitica/esp_exopolitics_zcb.htm.

Sandberg, Anders. "Morphological Freedom—Why we Not just Want it but Need it." *TransVision Conference Berlin.*

Sanders, Charles L. "Speculations about Bystander and Biophotons, Dose-Response." December 2014. https://www.ncbi.nlm.nih.gov/pmc/articles/PMC4267444/.

Sauder, Richard. *Kundalini Tales.* Adventures Unlimited, 1998.

Saunders, David. "The History of Brainwashing is a Red Flag for Techno-Therapy." *Aeon.* https://aeon.co/ideas/the-history-of-brainwashing-is-a-red-flag-for-techno-therapy.

Scaer, Dr. Robert. "Dr. Robert Scaer on Trauma." *Thriving Now,* February 2010. http://www.thrivingnow.com/scaer-trauma/.

Scardino, Albert. "Experts Question Data about Missing Children." *New York Times,* August 18, 1985. https://www.nytimes.com/1985/08/18/us/experts-question-data-about-missing-children.html.

Sheetz, Michael, Magdalena Petrova, "Why in the next decade companies will launch thousands more satellites than in all of history." *CNBC*, December 2019. https://www.cnbc.com/2019/12/14/spacex-oneweb-and-amazon-to-launch-thousands-more-satellites-in-2020s.html.

Sheldrake, Rupert. "Morphic Fields and Family Constellations." https://youtu.be/JydjryhEl5o.

Sheldrake, Rupert. "Morphic Resonance and Morphic Fields - an Introduction". https://www.sheldrake.org/research/morphic-resonance/introduction.

Sherman, Jeremy E. "Robo-Envy and Why People flock to authoritarian leaders." *Psychology Today*, May 21, 2019. https://www.psychologytoday.com/us/blog/ambigamy/201905/robo-envy-and-why-people-flock-authoritarian-leaders.

Simon, Matt. "Meet Xenobot, an Eerie New Kind of Programmable Organism." *Wired*, January 13, 2020. https://www.wired.com/story/xenobot/.

Simon, Vivienne, "Passport to the Cosmos: An Interview with John Mack, MD". http://johnmackinstitute.org/2000/04/passport-to-the-cosmos-an-interview-with-john-mack-m-d/.

Skymind AI Wiki, https://skymind.com/wiki/.

"Summary of the Dr. Edgar Mitchell FREE Experiencer Research Study." http://www.experiencer.org/initial-research- data-summary/ (December 1, 2016).

"The Next Generation Vaccines Will Permanently Alter Your DNA with Synthetic Genes." *Need to Know News*, October 2019. https://needtoknow.news/2019/10/the-next-generation-vaccines-will-permanently-alter-your-dna-with-synthetic-genes/.

The Phoenix Lights. http://www.thephoenixlights.net/Bio.htm

"The very French history of the word 'surveillance'", *BBC NEWS*, July 2015, https://www.bbc.com/news/blogs-magazine-monitor-33464368.

Tiller, William. "How the Power of Intention Alters Matter with Dr. William A. Tiller: Scientific proof that human intention raises local symmetry in the substratum of space." *The Spirit of MAAT*, Vol 2, No 8 http://www.spiritofmaat.com/archive/mar2/tiller.htm.

Trauma Prevention. https://traumaprevention.com/.

Tuszynski, Karkeshian Jumar and Barclay, Simon. "Are there optical communication channels in the brain?" *Front Bioscience*, March 2018. https://www.ncbi.nlm.nih.gov/pubmed/29293442.

Ulam, Stanislaw. "Tribute to John von Neumann." *Bulletin of the American Mathematical Society: 5*, 64, #3, part 2, May 1958.

Vasquez, Aldo. "Did You See Strange Lights in the Sky Last Night? Here's Why." http://www.abc15.com/news/state/did-you-see-strange-lights-in-the-sky-last-night-here-s-why.

Vimal, Ram Lakhan Pandey. "Meanings attributed to the term 'consciousness': an overview." *Journal of Consciousness Studies: Special Issue on Defining Consciousness*, 16 (5), 9-27. https://goo.gl/4TVSym.

Wanshel, Elyse. "10 Reasons why you shouldn't give your child a smartphone or tablet," https://www.littlethings.com/reasons-not-to-give-children-technology/.

Webb, Whitney. "Google & Oracle to Monitor Americans Who Get Warp Speed's Covid-19 Vaccine For Up To Two Years." *The Last American Vagabond*. October 2020. https://www.thelastamericanvagabond.com/google-oracle-monitor-americans-who-get-warp-speeds-covid-19-vaccine-for-two-years/.

Witcher, T.R. Witcher. "Is teleportation possible?" *Las Vegas Weekly*, 2005.

WO2020060606 - CRYPTOCURRENCY SYSTEM USING BODY ACTIVITY DATA, https://patentscope.wipo.int/search/en/detail.jsf?docId=WO2020060606

Wood, Patrick. *Technocracy Rising: The Trojan Horse of Global Transformation*. Coherent Publishing, 2014.

Wright, Turner. "Blockchain 'Immunity Passport' could get you Back to Work." *Cointelegraph*. https://cointelegraph.com/news/controversial-blockchain-immunity-passport-could-get-you-back-to-work.

READING GROUP GUIDE

1. Before reading this book, how much did you know about psychic intelligence, consciousness, and Exoconsciousness? Do you define consciousness as a body-brain function or as participation in a field beyond the body?

2. Before reading this book, how much did you know about transhumanism, artificial intelligence (AI), and synthetic biology? Do you perceive transhumanism as beneficial or do you have reservations? How does the role and identity of humans change in an AI dominant culture?

3. Do humans risk the gradual deterioration and disappearance of natural carbon-based consciousness in a dominant AI Transhuman culture? What are the implications of this loss? Will human free will survive?

4. What is your preference for humans to evolve: a natural consciousness-based culture or an AI, Transhuman culture?

5. Did you identify with the author's feeling of overwhelm when writing about encountering traumatizing research and her need to take time to calm down and integrate the information? How do you manage your emotions when you are overwhelmed by information? How do you integrate challenging ideas?

6. Can you imagine your future in 2030? What will be the impact of AI on your personal life, work, education, religion, culture, and community? How do you feel about these changes?

7. In a transhuman culture are you prepared to grant robots citizenship and all the extended rights that humans share? Are you being socially, biologically, and technically engineered to become a machine and identify with robots? If so, how will your freedom of thought and movement be impacted? How will your soul and spirit be impacted?

8. Is psychic intelligence crucial to navigate technology changes in our culture? Have you explored and experienced your psychic intelligence? Do you trust it? Is it reliable?

9. Have you experienced intuitive knowing, telepathic communication, out of body experiences, precognition, ESP, or visitations? Have you experienced creativity or ideas you felt were sourced outside yourself, perhaps from the field of consciousness?

10. Have you felt a cosmic consciousness that links you beyond Earth to the stars, the universe? Do you feel the cosmos is alive and intelligent or dark and lifeless? Have you used cosmic consciousness to contact and connect with extraterrestrials and multidimensionals?

11. Do you regard yourself as a free sovereign moral human? How do you balance what is good for the individual with what is good for the community? Would your definition of what is good extend to cosmic communities beyond Earth? Are these extraterrestrial communities a threat or an opportunity for humans to advance in self-understanding?

12. Before reading this book, how much did you know about technocracy? Can you identify economic technocratic changes in your personal life and your community? How do you feel about being

steered, monetized, and metered in an AI, synthetic biology economic system? How would you adapt to a planetary digital economy?

13. As the US Space Force military branch expands, how does Earth-Space technology impact you, your nation, and the planet? How do you manage the invisible surveillance engineered into this military infrastructure? Does 24-7 surveillance violate your human rights, or do you welcome it for protection?

14. What are your thoughts about humans connected to the Internet of Things and the Internet of Biology where your body, behavior, and thoughts are monitored? How do you protect your mind, body, and spirit with these nanotechnology AI systems? How do you maintain health and a calm feeling of security? Are you physically affected by 5G or do you regard your cell phone and computer as indispensable?

15. As mainstream media and the international press cover the military's response to Unidentified Aerial Phenomena (UAP, UFO), what will be the result of official government disclosure of an extraterrestrial presence? What if we discover we are not alone and have never been alone? What if humans acknowledge shared ownership of Earth? How will religion respond? How will nation-states respond?

ABOUT THE AUTHOR

Rebecca Hardcastle Wright, PhD, is the founder of the Institute for Exoconsciousness (I-EXO). She is a leading researcher into the future significance of ET and multidimensional experiencers. She was a member of Apollo 14 Astronaut, Dr. Edgar Mitchell's Quantrek international science team, which integrated zero-point energy, consciousness, and the ET Presence. Her experience with Quantrek guided her to establish I-EXO with a commitment to mainstreaming inventions and innovations co-created by humans and ETs, multidimensionals. As a therapist, life-long contactee, and Exoconscious Coach, she assists experiencers in integrating and applying their contact experience. She is the author of *Exoconsciousness: Your 21st Century Mind* and *How Exoconscious Humans Guide our Space-Faring Future,* available in Portuguese as *Fronteira Final.* She contributed to *Beyond UFOs: The Science of Consciousness and Contact with Non Human Intelligence, Vol 1.*

Rebecca's website is exoconsciousness.com

Made in the USA
Coppell, TX
20 March 2023

14452388R00163